M000211820

PRISON TIME:

LOCKED UP IN ARIZONA

SHAUN ATTWOOD

First published in Great Britain by Random House in 2014

Second edition published by Gadfly Press in 2019

Copyright © Shaun Attwood 2019

The right of Shaun Attwood to be identified as the author of this work
has been asserted by him in accordance with the Copyright, Designs and
Patents Act 1988. All rights reserved

This book is a work of non-fiction based on research by the author

A catalogue record of this book is available from the British Library

Typeset and cover design by Jane Dixon-Smith

ACKNOWLEDGEMENTS

A big thank you to Mark Swift (Editor at Reedsy),
Jane Dixon-Smith (cover design and typesetting)

For the prisoners whose stories made this book possible:
Two Tonys, Shannon, T-Bone, Iron Man, Weird Al,
Long Island, She-Ra, Gina, Mochalicious, Midnight,
Max, Magpie, George, Bud, Ken, Booga, Cannonball,
Hammer, Blackheart and Jim Hogg

SPELLING DIFFERENCES: UK V USA

This book was written in British English, hence USA readers may notice some spelling differences with American English: e.g. color = colour, meter = metre and = jewelry = jewellery

SHAUN'S BOOKS

English Shaun Trilogy
Party Time
Hard Time
Prison Time

War on Drugs Series
Pablo Escobar: Beyond Narcos
American Made: Who Killed Barry Seal?
Pablo Escobar or George HW Bush
The Cali Cartel: Beyond Narcos
We Are Being Lied To: The War on Drugs (Expected 2019)
The War Against Weed (Expected 2019)

Un-Making a Murderer:
The Framing of Steven Avery and Brendan Dassey
The Mafia Philosopher: Two Tonys
Life Lessons

Pablo Escobar's Story (4-Book Series)
T-Bone (Expected 2022)

SOCIAL-MEDIA LINKS

Email: attwood.shaun@hotmail.co.uk
Blog: Jon's Jail Journal
Website: shaunattwood.com
Twitter: @shaunattwood
YouTube: Shaun Attwood
LinkedIn: Shaun Attwood
Goodreads: Shaun Attwood
Facebook: Shaun Attwood, Jon's Jail Journal,
T-Bone Appreciation Society

Shaun welcomes feedback on any of his books.
Thank you for the Amazon and Goodreads reviews!

CONTENTS

AUTHOR'S NOTE

Prison Time is a complete story, but also the third book in the English Shaun Trilogy. Chronologically, the trilogy starts with *Party Time*, the story of everything that led to a SWAT team smashing down my door – my English upbringing, my move to Arizona as a penniless graduate, my rise as a stockbroker and millionaire day trader, and how I formed an organisation that threw raves and imported Ecstasy. The second book, *Hard Time*, is about how I survived twenty-six months in the jail with the highest death rate in America, run by the infamous Sheriff Joe Arpaio, where gang members and even guards were murdering inmates. *Prison Time* starts half a year after I received a nine-and-a-half-year sentence for drug offences. It begins at Buckeye prison, forty-three miles west of Phoenix, where each housing unit is named after a guard the prisoners had murdered.

During my incarceration, the brutality continued, but I also gained an insight into the less aggressive sides to my fellow inmates, whose intimate relationships were far more complex than I had imagined. Transgender inmates find it offensive when referred to as "he" or "him," so throughout *Prison Time* I've used *she* and *her* italicised for my trans friends.

DEFINITIONS

ADOC – Arizona Department of Corrections

Aryan Brotherhood – white supremacist prison gang

celly – cellmate

cheeto – transsexual

chomo – child molester

dog – mate

DOC – Department of Corrections

DW – Deputy Warden

dope – crystal meth or heroin

feds – federal law-enforcement officers

fish – new prisoner/guard

headcount – an inventory taken by counting prisoners

hole – a prison within the prison used for punishment

homey – a fellow gang member or close friend

lockdown – a prison within the prison used for punishment or a security measure that requires all of the prisoners to be locked in their cells

L&R – love and respect

meds – medication

meth – crystal meth, a strong form of speed

shank – homemade knife

supermax – supermaximum-security prison

trustie – a prisoner trusted to work

UA – urine drug test

whack – murder

CHAPTER 1

Nov 18, 2004

"I've got a padlock in a sock. I can smash your brains in while you're asleep. I can kill you whenever I want." My new cellmate gazes with no trace of human feeling in his eyes. Muscular and pot-bellied, he's caked in prison ink, including six snakes on his skull, slithering side by side. The top of his right ear is missing in a semi-circle.

The waves of fear are overwhelming. After being in transportation all day, I can feel my bladder hurting. "I'm not looking to cause any trouble. I'm the quietest cellmate you'll ever have. All I do is read and write."

Scowling, he shakes his head. "Why've they put a fish in with me?" He swaggers close enough to waft his cigarette breath. "Us convicts don't get along with fresh fish."

"Should I ask to move then?" I say, hoping he'll agree if he hates new prisoners.

"No! They'll think I threatened you!"

In the eight by twelve feet slab of space, I swerve around him and place my property box on the top bunk.

He pushes me aside and grabs the box. "You just put that on my artwork! I ought to fucking smash you, fish!"

"Sorry, I didn't see it."

"You need to be more aware of your fucking surroundings! What you in for anyway, fish?"

I explain my charges, Ecstasy dealing and how I spent twenty-six months fighting my case.

"How come the cops were so hard-core after you?" he asks, squinting.

"It was a big case, a multi-million-dollar investigation. They raided over a hundred people, and didn't find any drugs. They were pretty pissed off. I'd stopped dealing by the time they caught up with me, but I'd done plenty over the years, so I accept my punishment."

"Throwing raves," he says, staring at the ceiling as if remembering something. "Were you partying with underage girls?" he asks, his voice slow, coaxing.

Being called a sex offender is the worst insult in prison. Into my third year of incarceration, I'm conditioned to react. "What you trying to say?" I yell angrily, brow clenched.

"Were you fucking underage girls?" Flexing his body, he shakes both fists as if about to launch punches.

"Hey, I'm no child molester and I'd prefer you didn't say shit like that!"

"My buddy next door is doing twenty-five to life for murdering a chomo. How do I know Ecstasy dealing ain't your cover story?" He inhales loudly, nostrils flaring.

"You want to see my fucking paperwork?"

A stocky prisoner walks in. Short hair. Dark eyes. Powerful neck. On one arm: a tattoo of a man in handcuffs above the word **OMERTA** – the Mafia code of silence towards law enforcement. "What the fuck's going on in here, Bud?" asks Junior Bull – the son of "Sammy the Bull" Gravano, a Mafia mass murderer who was my biggest competitor in the Ecstasy market.

Relieved to see a familiar face, I say, "How're you doing?"

Shaking my hand, he says in a New York Italian accent, "I'm doing all right. I read that shit in the newspaper about you starting a blog in Sheriff Joe Arpaio's jail."

"The blog's been bringing media heat on the conditions." While in the Maricopa County jail, I documented the human rights violations on sweat-soaked scraps of paper, using a tiny pencil sharpened on the door. Hidden in legal paperwork and old letters, my writing was smuggled out of Visitation by my aunt – right under the noses of armed guards – and posted to

2

the Internet as a blog, Jon's Jail Journal. In recent months, it had drawn international media attention.

"You know him?" Bud asks.

"Yeah, from Towers jail. He's a good dude. He's in for dealing Ecstasy like me."

"It's a good job you said that 'cause I was about to smash his ass," Bud says.

"It's a good job Wild Man ain't here 'cause you'd a got your ass thrown off the balcony," Junior Bull says.

I laugh. The presence of my best friend, Wild Man, was partly the reason I never took a beating at the county jail, but with Wild Man in a different prison, I feel vulnerable. When Bud casts a death stare, my smile fades.

"What the fuck you guys on about?" Bud asks.

"Let's go talk downstairs." Junior Bull leads Bud out.

I rush to a stainless-steel sink/toilet bolted to a cement-block wall by the front of the cell, unbutton my orange jumpsuit and crane my neck to watch the upper-tier walkway in case Bud returns. I bask in relief as my bladder deflates. After flushing, I take stock of my new home, grateful for the slight improvement in the conditions versus what I'd grown accustomed to in Sheriff Joe Arpaio's jail. No cockroaches. No bloodstains. A working swamp cooler. Something I've never seen in a cell before: shelves. The steel table bolted to the wall is slightly larger, too. *But how will I concentrate on writing with Bud around?* There's a mixture of smells in the room. Cleaning chemicals. Aftershave. Tobacco. A vinegar-like odour. The slit of a window at the back overlooks gravel in a no-man's-land before the next building with gleaming curls of razor wire around its roof.

From the doorway upstairs, I'm facing two storeys of cells overlooking a day room with shower cubicles at the end of both tiers. At two white plastic circular tables, prisoners are playing dominoes, cards, chess and Scrabble, some concentrating, others yelling obscenities, contributing to a brain-scraping din that I hope to block out by purchasing a Walkman. In a raised box-shaped plexiglas control tower, two guards are monitoring the prisoners.

Bud returns. My pulse jumps. Not wanting to feel like I'm stuck in a kennel with a rabid dog, I grab a notepad and pen and head for the day room. Focussed on my body language, not wanting to signal any weakness, I'm striding along the upper tier, head and chest elevated, when two hands appear from a doorway. Grabbed, I drop the pad. The pen clinks against grid-metal and tumbles to the day room as I'm pulled into a cell reeking of backside sweat and masturbation, a cheese-tinted funk.

"I'm Booga. Let's fuck," says a squat man in urine-stained boxers, with **WHITE TRASH** tattooed on his torso below a mobile home, and an arm sleeved with the Virgin Mary. Shocked, I brace to flee or fight to preserve my anal virginity. I can't believe my eyes when he drops his boxers and waggles his penis. Dancing to music playing through a speaker he has rigged up, Booga smiles in a sexy way. "Come on," he says in a husky voice. "Drop your pants. Let's fuck." He pulls pornography faces. I question his sanity. He moves closer. "If I let you fart in my mouth, can I fart in yours?"

"You can fuck off," I say, springing towards the doorway.

He grabs me. We scuffle. Every time I make progress towards the doorway, he clings to my clothes and I'm dragged back in. When I feel his penis rub against my leg, my adrenaline kicks in so forcefully I experience a burst of strength and wriggle free. I bolt out as fast as my shower sandals will allow, and snatch my pad. Looking over my shoulder, I see him stood calmly in the doorway, smiling. He points my way. "You have to walk past my door every day. We're gonna get together. I'll lick your ass, and you can fart in my mouth." He blows a kiss and disappears.

I rush downstairs. With my back to a wall, I pause to steady my thoughts and breathing. In survival mode, I think, *What's going to come at me next?* In the hope of reducing my tension, I borrow a pen to do what helps to retain my sanity: writing. With the details fresh in my mind, I document my journey to the prison for my blog readers, keeping an eye out in case anyone else wants to test the new prisoner. The more I write, the more I fill with a sense of purpose. Jon's Jail Journal is a connection to the outside world that I cherish.

Someone yells, "One time!" The din lowers. A door rumbles open. A guard does a security walk, his every move scrutinised by dozens of scornful eyes staring from cells. When he exits, the din resumes and the prisoners return to injecting drugs to escape from reality, including the length of their sentences. This continues all day with "Two times!" signifying two approaching guards, and "Three times!" three and so on. Every now and then an announcement by a guard over the speakers briefly lowers the din.

Before lockdown, I join the line for a shower, holding bars of soap in a towel that I aim to swing at the head of the next person to try me. With boisterous inmates a few feet away, yelling at the men in the showers to "Stop jerking off," and "Hurry the fuck up," I get in a cubicle that reeks of bleach and mildew. With every nerve strained, I undress and rinse fast.

At night, despite the desert heat, I cocoon myself in a blanket from head to toe and turn towards the wall, making my face more difficult to strike. I leave a hole for air, but the warm cement block inches from my mouth returns each exhalation to my face as if it's breathing on me, creating a feeling of suffocation. For hours, my heart drums so hard against the thin mattress, I feel as if I'm moving even though I'm still. I try to sleep, but my eyes keep springing open and my head turns towards the cell as I try to penetrate the darkness, searching for Bud swinging a padlock in a sock at my head.

CHAPTER 2

With Bud and his coterie of clones constantly in the cell, cracking jokes about raping me and boasting about former rapes, smoking, gambling, tattooing, injecting heroin and crystal meth, I spend as much time in the day room as possible. After getting grabbed a few more times by Booga, I learn to creep or dash past his cell. He seems to genuinely believe that we're destined to have sex.

During the second day, I take breaks from writing to challenge the chess and Scrabble champions, holding my own with the former, but getting smashed by the latter who own Scrabble dictionaries, and have memorised every two-letter word. I contest the word "ai," delighted to have trumped my opponent, but he snatches up a dictionary and, with an expanding smile, reveals that ai is a three-toed sloth from South America.

As going on the toilet requires returning to the cell and asking Bud and company to leave, I fight the urge until I'm on the verge of an accident. When I enter the cell, my request for privacy is met with mockery and threats. When the subject turns to "tapping my ass," I decide to outdo them in shock value. In prison, acting crazy can sometimes be a useful strategy. The last thing they expect me to do is moon them. I doubt they'll try to knock me down to rape me. If that happens, I'll go one step further: I'll smear their faces with my own crap. I'm neither big enough nor possess the skills to fight them, but I will go to any length to avoid getting raped. I doubt it'll come to that. I hope to take them by surprise.

Dropping my jumpsuit and boxers, I say, "Who'd want to rape this pale hairy English arse?"

"Goddam, England!"

"Is that a nest of tarantulas?"

"He's got some crazy-ass werewolf shit going on down there."

"Put that away, England!"

Smiling, cackling, they shake their heads, eyes wide, incredulous, on faces pale in all of the wrong places. I'm finally speaking their language. Bud hides his tattoo gun: a piece of guitar string inside the outer casing of a pen with a needle on one end and the motor from a Walkman on the other. I'm left alone in the smoky cell.

On the toilet, I'm far from wiping when my name is called by a guard downstairs with my deck shoes, followed by a chorus of inmates yelling, "Hurry the fuck up!" With everyone wearing sneakers, I'm suffering a handicap in sandals if I have to fight. Clenching my behind to retract what hasn't fully emerged, I grab toilet roll and speed clean. I rush out, but forget to exercise caution passing Booga's cell. He leaps out. Jumping away, I hit the railing. *Clang.* I bat him off and dash away to laughter below. By the time I get downstairs, the guard with my shoes is leaving.

"I'm Attwood!" I yell, catching up with her. She turns and squints with disdain. "Can I have my deck shoes, please?"

"What deck shoes? You took too long." She exits the building.

Perhaps feeling sorry for me, more prisoners introduce themselves. Reading newspaper articles about my blogging against the much-hated Sheriff Joe Arpaio has earned their respect. They donate old T-shirts, trousers, deck shoes and a sweatshirt as I only have what I'm wearing.

Three times a day, guards escort 100 of us out of the building, yelling military style for us to stay in a straight line. We filter into the chow hall, a massive warehouse with tables and chairs bolted to the floor, ringing with an aggressive deafening noise that's a multiple of the din in the day room. Compressed between a wall and a wrought-iron fence, I'm nudged along by the flow of prisoners until I arrive at a narrow slot in the wall. A tray of kid's-meal-size chow emerges as if by magic. I barely have time to see the hands of the kitchen worker holding it from the other side.

The anonymity is an attempt to stop "homey hook-ups" – extra portions of food given to friends by kitchen workers – but it prevents nothing. Our carefully crafted starvation is the foundation of a black market. Stolen food was taped underneath tables before we arrived. Kitchen workers wiping tables and mopping are passing items like cheese wrapped in plastic to prisoners.

The convict code requires that we sit with members of our own race, so I join some of the less intimidating whites. The chow teases my hunger. It's sufficient to finish if swallowed with minimal chewing in the fifteen minutes permitted to eat. I discover a caterpillar wriggling on a salad leaf. The prisoners laugh. An almost seven-foot Lakota Indian reaches over from the next table, takes the insect and eats it.

Special diets that have no medical basis must be approved by the chaplain, so, to get vegetarian food, I registered as Hindu upon arrival – a trick I learnt at the jail to avoid the mystery-meat slop called "red death." With freedom of religion guaranteed under the Constitution, prisoners have won certain rights over the years, and prisons fear losing money in costly lawsuits for violating them. The Jewish diet is considered the best, so there are Mexican Mafia Jews, Italian Mafia Jews such as Junior Bull and Aryan Brotherhood Jews whose neo-Nazi tattoos include **88** – a code for HH: Heil Hitler!

I'm eating toast when a sumo-sized prisoner with bulging eyes growls like a wounded bear, marches to a slot in the wall for tray disposal and stands guarding it.

"Fuck, Slingblade's on the hunt for leftovers," says a prisoner at my table.

"What's the deal with him?" I ask, worried about getting by him.

"Slingblade's a Vietnam vet who had a flashback and murdered his father-in-law. If he grabs your tray, just let him have it."

With a nimble sidestep, Slingblade blocks a young Mexican American, locks his eyes on the tray, and emits a guttural, "You gonna leave that?" Before a response is issued, Slingblade snatches the tray. Without looking back, the inmate rushes for the door.

Slingblade sits, devours half-eaten spaghetti, stands and licks his lips. He roams the room, giggling, and grabs more trays. When his head convulses, he stops eating. The sack of skin below his chin quivers. His right arm shakes as if strumming a banjo. He stands and guards the slot again.

My body tenses as I approach him. "You want this?" I ask, holding my tray at arm's length as if feeding a dangerous animal. He burps vaporised tomato sauce and ground beef onto my face. I jump as a shovel of a hand swoops on a glazed cake. I put my tray in the slot and exit. Outside, guards are selecting prisoners at random, patting them down, confiscating food hidden in socks, armpits and underwear.

I'm allowed to fill out a commissary form once a week. Those of us lucky enough to have money in our inmate accounts deposited by family and friends or accrued from prison work with wages ranging from ten to fifty cents per hour can spend it. That's how I get stamps, envelopes, pens and paper. In the hope of better managing my hunger, I order two jars of peanut butter, crackers and squeeze cheese. Most of the items on the form are overpriced sweets that with cigarettes and coffee – the mainstays of prisoners – provide massive profits to Keefe, the largest vendor of products to prisoners in the US.

I'm thrilled to learn that I'm allowed one hour each week in the library. Prior to my arrest, I never read fiction. Upon being told that reading would improve my writing, I set a goal of reading 1,000 books before my release. Having never set foot in a prison library, I arrive excitedly in a tiny room with limited books tended by a placid librarian. The company of fellow readers generates a feeling of safety. Most of them grab paperbacks by John Grisham and Stephen King and disappear. Wanting to prolong my time in this sanctuary, I browse each aisle to see how the books are categorised, relishing the musty odour. I crouch down to scan the dusty classics section and gravitate towards *Great Russian Short Stories* – due to my newfound passion for Chekhov and Tolstoy

– and *The Norton Anthology of World Masterpieces* with Voltaire's *Candide*. Returning to my cell with five books, I worry about Bud derailing my reading programme.

Besides books, the two things I live for are mail call and visits. Because of my blog, I receive letters from kind strangers around the world. Their outpouring of support has helped restore the trust I lost in humanity after experiencing the conditions in Sheriff Joe Arpaio's jail. In medium security, I'm allowed a weekend visit from 7:30 AM until 3 PM. My parents are flying over in just six weeks for Christmas 2004. Each day, my excitement to see them grows. Writing letters home, I feel less isolated and I'm distracted from the feelings of abandonment I've struggled with since the split from my fiancée, Claudia, after almost two years in the county jail.

I'm allowed outside twice each day for two-hour recreation sessions in the mirage-inducing heat of the Sonoran Desert. The earliest at 6:30 AM, the latest at 4:30 PM. The rec area is a large field edged by a running track, enclosed by chain-link fence, razor wire and security floodlights on tall poles. There are two basketball courts, a volleyball court, work-out stations, six picnic tables, eight reverse-charge phones, one urinal and a drinking fountain. Guards with rifles patrol the top of the gun tower overlooking the area. My first time out, having been confined to medium-, maximum- and supermaximum-security cells for over two years, I'm overwhelmed by the amount of space. It feels as if the world is opening back up in all directions. Surrounded by battleship-grey prison buildings scattered across a desert landscape as barren as the moon, and a sky clear except for funnels of steam rising from the Palo Verde Nuclear Generating Station, I call Barry, Claudia's father, who insists we speak every week and accepts expensive reverse-charge calls even though Claudia and I split up months ago.

"How's it going, Barry?"

"Same old same old. But I've got good news. Claudia wants you to call her."

"What?" I say, overjoyed.

"She wants to come and see you, buddy."

Deliriously happy, I walk around the track, daydreaming about reuniting with Claudia. Eventually, I find a space on the field away from people to do yoga – which I started at the jail, where it contributed to saving my sanity. Seeing the grass is rife with ants and the odd tiny transparent scorpion and giant orange centipede, I put down a towel. I don't want to project any signs of sexual availability, so poses such as cat and dog that involve bending over with my behind sticking up are out of the question. Apprehensive about being watched, I start with ten advanced sun salutations, which include jumping my legs back into a push-up position, and kicking them up for handstands, almost like a gymnast. I heat up fast. Stiff and awkward muscles rejoice at being stretched and loosen up. After arm-balancing postures such as crow and crane with my body raised off the ground and my knees resting on the back of my upper arms, I move onto inversions.

Eyes closed, focussed on breathing, stilling my mind into meditation mode, I hear, "Stop doing headstands!" from a megaphone. I think I'm imagining things until it's repeated.

"Better drop that, homey, before they shoot your ass!" a prisoner yells.

I lower my feet and stand up, dizzy, blood draining from my head. The prisoners have stopped parading their physiques, dozens of topless tattooed men in knee-length orange shorts, Walkmans clipped to their hips, staring at me through thick dark sunglasses. I blush.

"Headstands are not allowed!" a guard yells from the gun tower, another guard next to her toting a rifle. "Stop doing them or else I'll throw you off the field!"

"Are you gonna ban push-ups next?" an inmate yells.

Others join in, protesting. *So much for not attracting attention to myself.* Shook up, I walk the track, quickly joined by inmates offering advice.

"You need to put a grievance form in on that guard!"

"That's bullshit! Have a guard tell the Deputy Warden!"

I don't want to cause any fuss, but an incensed prisoner fetches a guard and explains what happened. The guard – wanting to prevent the outrage from escalating – radios the Deputy Warden, who gives him permission to allow headstands. With the inmates urging me to resume headstands, I have no choice but to disregard my fear of the guards in the tower. I lay my towel down and stand on my head, bracing to hear a gunshot.

Heading back to the building, the inmates reveal why the guards are on edge. The longest hostage crisis in US prison history recently happened here. During a botched escape attempt, two prisoners serving life seized control of the gun tower for fifteen days and held a male and female guard hostage, repeatedly raping the female.

CHAPTER 3

"Bud's one of the biggest psychos on the yard," Junior Bull says. "He's a serial home invader torturer. He was breaking into drug dealers' houses, tying them up with Duct tape and taking hammers to their kneecaps. He has hepatitis C, so don't share anything like his shaver with him." Hepatitis C is the deadliest and hardest to treat form of the disease. Bud has been offering me his shaver.

One night after lockdown, when the lights are dimmed, I climb off the bunk to use the toilet. Aware of Bud on his bunk a few feet behind, watching my every move, I'm concentrating on trying to pee, aiming my penis at the centre of the bowl because Bud freaks if I accidentally hit the rim, when a flashlight shines on my crotch. I look up. I'm almost face to face with a big female guard outside of the cell, her brow wrinkling angrily.

"I'm gonna write you up for indecent exposure!" she yells, maintaining the light on my penis. Bud laughs.

I'm under instructions from my lawyer to avoid serious disciplinary tickets as the prison can deny my half-time release, which would add over two years to what I must serve. In a panic, I yank up my trousers. "How was I supposed to know you were there?"

"You could hear me walking the run."

"I didn't hear anything. I waited for lights out to take a pee."

"Stupid fucking fish," Bud mumbles, revelling in my misfortune.

"You weren't peeing. There was no pee coming out. You were masturbating."

"I was about to pee!" I yell, shocked. "If I was masturbating, it would have been hard."

"His dick's as small as mine. I'm surprised you could even see it." Bud laughs.

"Would you like me to search this cell?" she snarls at Bud.

Bud turns serious. "He just got here. The fish is clueless. I would have smashed his ass if he was jerking off."

"You're just backing your celly up," she says.

"You know how I feel about sex offenders," Bud says in a grave tone.

Exhaling loudly, she eyes Bud. "OK. I'm gonna give him a pass 'cause he's a fish." She turns to me. "If that ever happens again to me or any other female staff, you'll be going straight to the hole!"

As soon as she walks away, Bud leaps up and launches into a lecture about the need to be aware of guards walking the run. "If this cell ever gets searched 'cause of you, I'm gonna fuck you up with my padlock."

It dawns that he only rescued me to prevent his drug and tattoo paraphernalia from being discovered. He probably knew she was walking the run and let me get caught for his own amusement. To get his mind off violence, I climb up to my bunk and say, "Hey, Bud, I heard your arrest made headline news."

"You wanna hear the whole story?" Bud puffs out his chest.

"Yes, I love a good story."

Bud mentions breaking into a house. He held three occupants at gunpoint and split a man's nose and head open with a hammer, knocking the man out. He attached the man's arms to a shower with Duct tape. When the man's eyes opened, Bud "played tic-tac-toe [noughts-and-crosses] on his chest" with a six-inch knife until the victim gave up a safe combination. Bud stuffed a duffel bag with $10,000 cash and crystal meth worth $50,000. He was about to leave, but more roommates arrived, spotted blood, fled and called the cops.

Bud hopped a fence and landed in a back yard. A lady cradling a poodle opened a French window. Pointing a .357 Magnum at her face, he yelled, "Freeze, police! In the house now!" In the living room, he came across a scantily clad, dishevelled young couple who'd ventured downstairs to investigate the commotion. "Freeze, motherfuckers! On the ground!" Bud yelled. Keeping an eye on a German Shepherd, he locked the windows and doors, and switched the lights off. "I've done killed nine people tonight. Let's not make that twelve."

They watched Bud on the news. The police knocked on the door, shone flashlights in the back yard and left. After a few hours of drinking beer and smoking weed with hostages keen to get inebriated to steady their nerves, Bud left in their truck.

Two days later, acting on a tip-off, Bud's house was surrounded by a SWAT team, a helicopter, an armoured vehicle and news crews. He barricaded himself in the garage. A negotiator threw him a black box containing a phone that he grabbed with a rake.

"Hello."

"Today's a good day to die," Bud said. "What do you think?"

"I'm here to help get you out. Have you got any hostages?"

"Yeah," he lied, worried about them storming in.

"We're not coming in. Is there anything you need?"

"A pizza."

"What else?"

"A helicopter."

"You've been watching too many movies." The negotiator laughed.

A girlfriend who saw the stand-off on the news arrived. "Hi, honey. Are you gonna give up and come out?"

"I've got dope and smokes. I'm OK."

"You're big-time surrounded. Look down the street."

Bud noticed an armoured vehicle with a battering ram ready to knock down the garage door.

"They're coming, honey. They promised that no shots will be fired and I'll get to talk to you if you come out right now."

With his hands in the air, Bud emerged …

Bud finishes his story excited, content. He gets on his bunk, puts on a set of headphones and watches a tiny TV, both made from clear plastic so no contraband can be concealed inside. Feeling the beginning of a bond with him, I sleep better.

In the morning, I wake up to Bud stood, holding a chest hair.

"I woke up with one of your fucking pubes in my mouth!" he yells, setting the tone for the day. Other than headcounts, I spend the day out of the cell.

After lockdown, I ask Bud for another story. He says that in a fourteen-man cell at Alhambra, a processing unit for new prisoners, a sex offender arrived. Presiding over a kangaroo court, Bud ordained the man be tortured. "Read this," he says, waving legal paperwork.

The paperwork states that after tying up the sex offender "they stuffed strips of cloth in his mouth prior to the stabbings to see how the muffle worked." His boxer shorts were pulled down and he was mocked for having "a little one." According to the sex offender's testimony, "At that point was where I got stabbed in the stomach several times." Bud stabbed him eleven times and put the shank to the face of a witness who said, "He put it to the corner of my eye like he was gonna shove it in there, and he says, 'You say anything, and I'm gonna take this and shove it in your eye, and pop your eye out. Then we're gonna eat it.'" For stabbing the sex offender, Bud got thirty months added to fifteen years.

"A small price to pay," Bud says proudly.

"How about I post this story to my blog and we ask the public what they think of your convict justice on the child molester?" I ask. *With sex offenders despised, he'll probably be hero worshipped. Plus getting him an audience might change his attitude towards me.*

"I've never been on the Internet." Bud eyes me suspiciously. "How does a blog work?"

"I write your story down and mail it to my parents in England. They type it up, post it to the Internet at my blog, Jon's Jail Journal. People read it and post comments. After a week or so of it gathering comments, my parents print the story and the comments and mail it to me."

"Fuck it!" Bud says, smiling. "Give it a try. Hey, check this out." Bud waves me to the door.

I spot two guards escorting Booga from the building, the back of his thighs and boxers coated in blood. "What the hell!"

"Booga's always at Medical, complaining he's bleeding from the rectum," Bud says. "What does he expect if he keeps sticking things in his asshole?"

A few weeks later, I receive an envelope from my parents. I tear it open, praying for comments supportive of Bud, dreading having to deal with him if they're not. My relief increases as I read each comment. Bud's eyes light up as they settle on:

"What he done to the child molester was certainly called for."

"Bud is the kind of criminal I could get behind."

"Way to go, Bud! Judge and jury all in one! Fervent admirer."

While Bud runs around the day room flaunting the comments, one in particular sticks in my mind: "I would be scared shitless of this guy if I were you."

CHAPTER 4

Jail etiquette demands that cellmates take turns cleaning the room, but no matter how much effort I put into scrubbing the toilet and mopping, Bud finds fault and gets angry. He has a certain way of doing things and any other way irritates him. Junior Bull suggests I hire his cleaner, George – stout, soft-spoken, silver-haired, in his early 50s – who charges $2 a week in commissary to do the cell and extra to wash and fold laundry – a service in high demand from prisoners due for visits from wives and girlfriends. Bud allows me to hire George.

While cleaning, George puts on an English accent, addresses me as "governor" and sings "Rule Britannia." He begs me to read a few pages of *Harry Potter* aloud. George is also a masseur. After I agree to a massage, Junior Bull says not to lie down, but to sit on a stool to prevent George's hands from wandering in-between my legs. As expected, George says to relax on his bunk, but I refuse to leave the stool. He puts lotion on my back. I enjoy the sensation of his hands kneading the stress from my muscles. Every time a knot in my back pops, I groan.

When the massage is over, George rests on the bottom bunk. In a high-pitched female-impersonator voice, he says, "Shaun's too shy to get oral sex. Shaun's too inhibited to get his willy played with by another man. Oh no! What if the Queen of England were to find out that a man had been fiddling with Shaun's Prince William!"

Taken aback, but no stranger to sexual attention from prisoners, I say, "Inhibited? Shy? I'm too heterosexual? Is that what you mean?"

"You're homophobic."

"I used to party at gay bars all the time!"

"Then you're confused. There's nobody that's 100-per cent heterosexual or homosexual. Humans are curious about sex. If you took away people's inhibitions, there'd be a lot of bisexuals. Look at the sixties, free love." George smiles as if reminiscing. "One minute you're going down on a vagina, and the next minute there's a penis in your face, and you're just going to town on it."

I laugh. "Jesus, George!" I say, shaking my head. "I've never been in a situation like that!"

"It's an orgy. You're just rolling around from person to person without a care in the world. Surely you've been near a penis at some point in your life?"

"Nope."

"Not even peeing contests or circle jerks?"

"I helped put a fire out by peeing on it with a bunch of lads."

"See, you have had a penis near you!" he yells, pointing at me. "Don't you think that if it didn't have social stigma you would do anything that feels good?"

"Such as letting you suck my dick? Is that where this is heading?"

"I say if it feels good, let it happen."

"No chance! You're a fiend."

"Let me ask you this then: if you stick your dick into a glory hole—"

"A what?"

"A hole through which fellatio is performed anonymously. And you didn't know if it was a man or a woman sucking it, what difference would receiving the pleasure make?" he asks, tilting his head, cocking his brows suggestively.

"I wouldn't know."

"But you agree that they'd both feel good, right?"

"That's called a tie down. You're asking me a question to solicit a yes answer?"

"You know they'd both feel good," he says slowly, smiling slyly.

"No, I don't!"

"You need to toss out your preconceived notions of right and wrong. Lose your inhibitions."

"It seems you're beating me with semantics."

"Yay! I won. Now you have to drop your knickers and close your eyes."

"Bugger off, George! At least you have choices in here. Us heteros don't."

George waves a hand dismissively. "Think about my question again. If you put your penis in a glory hole, and you didn't know if it was a male or a female giving you satisfaction, wouldn't it be equally pleasurable?"

"I'll write about this and see what my blog readers think. Then I'll find out if you're a madman or not." I stand.

"I'll leave it at that for now, governor, shall I?" Looking me up and down, George slides his tongue across thin yellowy crooked teeth like flaked almonds and licks his top lip.

"Most definitely." I depart fast.

CHAPTER 5

Returning from a shower, I try to enter my cell, but get pushed out by Bud's neighbour, a muscular Aryan Brother with a shaved head serving twenty-five to life for murdering a child molester. "You can't go in your cell right now 'cause the fellas are shooting up," he says in a deep dangerous voice.

"What am I supposed to do?" I ask, frustrated.

"Come back in ten minutes."

Passing Booga's cell, I hear him yell, "Hey, England, are you uncut?"

"Uncut?" I ask, rushing away.

He appears in his doorway. "Uncircumcised. It's hard to find. I saw it in European porn. I just love to see it. It drives me wild!" Watching him out of the corner of my eye, I can't help but smile at his insanity. "I can tell you are! C'mon, show me your foreskin."

Ignoring him, I go downstairs and watch Scrabble. Fifteen minutes later, I return to the cell, relieved only Bud is there. Climbing up to my bunk, I prick my foot. "Shit, Bud, I got a needle stuck in my foot!" I say, worried about catching hepatitis C, wondering whether he left it out on purpose. I remove the needle, relieved no blood is seeping out.

"What have I told you?" he yells, taking the needle. "You need to be more aware of your fucking surroundings!" I ignore him.

His associate, Ken, swaggers in, a beast of a biker with a black ponytail, an imposing handlebar moustache and Harley-Davidson wings tattooed on his forehead. On his tree trunk of a neck is a patch resembling plastic where a rival took a blowtorch to him. "What's up, dude!" he says, smiling, and wrenches my ankle. My shoulders slam against the mattress. He drags my body halfway off the bunk. Just when I'm about to fall, I grab the metal and hold on with all of my strength. "Give me your Walkman or else I'm gonna fuck you up!" he yells, letting go of me.

"Fuck you! I use it!" I leap down, grab my writing supplies and leave for the day room until lockdown.

At night, I read *Don Quixote* on my bunk. Absorbed by the story, I laugh aloud at the antics of the protagonist. Bud springs off the bottom bunk and yells in my face, "What the fuck's so funny up there?" High on heroin, the sudden movement makes him ill. He belches sickly air, grabs his stomach, rushes to the toilet and vomits.

"This book's pretty funny," I say, wincing at the stench of partially digested meat and refried beans.

With vomit and drool streaking down his face, Bud manages to stand. "There's something about you I can't figure out. Something you're hiding. When I figure out what it is, I'm gonna smash you, fish."

"I don't know what you're talking about," I say, my pulse climbing. "I've showed you my charges. Junior Bull even vouched for me."

He produces a sock and extracts a padlock. "See this. I can kill you at any time," he says, stroking the metal.

Spotting a pen on my bunk within reaching distance, I consider sticking it in his eyeball. Considering myself a peaceful person, I'm surprised by my momentary glee. *Don't be stupid. It could add years to your sentence.*

He asks about imaginary sex offences into the small hours, so high he keeps saying the same questions. Repeating my answers, I feel as if I'm trying to reason with a drunk. After a few hours' sleep, I wake up for breakfast with blurry vision. In the day room, I write to a friend:

My cellmate gave me the third-degree interrogation last night, for, lo and behold, being quiet! Yes, as I am quiet in here, it has aroused his suspicion that I'm hiding something! Despite my case being in the news, and people knowing about me from the blog, somehow I'm hiding something. There are some in here who will just not let people do their own time. Why should I have to explain myself to anyone? On top of all that it is documented that he has attacked and threatened inmates and guards. It's exhausting answering his ridiculous questions, including – get this – he started insisting that I'd said there were fifteen-year-old girls partying with me at the raves! So his mind is developing this plot that I fiddled with fifteen-year-olds. That's not a good sign! Plus, I have to put up with his smoking, yet there's a dozen things he's found fault with me for. They range from not folding my laundry properly to lint falling off my upper bunk onto his bunk. I have no control over gravity! I've had approximately a dozen cellmates before him, and never had any problems with any of them. When the guards put me in this cell, they laughed, and said, "Your new celly is a bit of a joker!" I wondered what they meant, and I now find the joke is on me. How did I get so unlucky? I'm more nervous as well because my mum and dad will be here soon.

You asked how I felt when I was transported to Buckeye. It was entertaining – the drive. I felt like a young lad on a day out. But I was sad and shook up by the time I got here. I was sad when I saw free people driving by the prison bus, and I was even more sad when I saw places I used to live, and my stockbrokerage office – the 13th floor of the high-rise at 3101 N. Central Avenue – where I was the top producer two years in a row, making a sweet six-figure salary, and winning awards. How stupid I was to throw away my life.

I manage to stay strong most of the time in here, so you're glimpsing a moment of weakness reading this letter.

At recreation, I wait until no one's near a phone, and call my aunt Ann. "I need your help getting my cell changed," I say in a low voice, hoping no one overhears.

"Why? What's happened?" Ann asks, alarmed.

"It's my cellmate." I crane my neck to see if anyone's

approaching. "He's out of control and paranoid on heroin and meth. He keeps threatening to kill me in my sleep with a padlock in a sock. He's so off his head, I can't reason with him. Can you have my dad call the British Embassy, and ask them to call the prison and request I get moved? I've been through a lot of stuff, and I've never asked them to get involved, so they should know it's serious. But they can't tell the prison that I'm being threatened because I'd be viewed as a snitch, and everyone will want to kill me." I return to the building, apprehensively, dreading what might happen next. I go downstairs and try to write, but can't concentrate. Expecting a backlash from Bud, I hope it'll be worth it to escape from him.

A few hours later, I'm extracted by a guard, eyed suspiciously as I leave for the office of the Deputy Warden (DW) – a woman in a navy-blue business suit stood next to a broad-shouldered female lieutenant in uniform, both scowling.

"Why is the British Embassy calling to get you moved?" she asks sharply.

"I'm not getting along with my cellmate," I say.

"Has he threatened you?"

"No. We're just incompatible."

"Are you aware of the procedure for inmates who want to move cells?"

"No. I've only been here a few weeks," I lie, aware the procedure, if approved at all, can take weeks and sometimes months.

"I'm not going to authorise a move if he's not threatened you, and you've gone outside our internal procedures."

"Then send me to lockdown." To stop my hands trembling, I claw my thighs. "I refuse to go back to that cell."

"You'd rather go to lockdown and lose your commissary?"

"I've spent most of the last year locked-down. It doesn't bother me."

"Do you have mental-health issues?"

"Diagnosed bipolar."

"Are you on meds?"

"No."

"You need to see the psychiatrist." She turns to my escorting officer. "Lock the building down, and move him, but keep him in the same building." Addressing me, she says, "Don't ever go outside our internal procedures again. If you request any more moves, you will be sent to lockdown."

"OK. Thank you." I'm escorted to the foot of the control tower in my building.

An announcement: "Lockdown! Everybody, lockdown!"

The inmates trudge to their cells, cursing the lockdown. When I'm escorted into the day room, the inmates flock to their cells, some shaking their heads as if they want to hurt me. George waves goodbye. I follow the guard upstairs.

He opens my door. "Grab your property, and take it to cell 2."

"What's going on?" Bud snarls, hands on hips.

"They're moving me downstairs."

The prisoners watch as I move boxes of books, letters, blog printouts and commissary to cell 2, next door to Slingblade in cell 3. Relieved that I won't have to pass Booga's door anymore, I spot him smiling and blowing kisses, his boxers round his ankles, one hand cradling his scrotum, the other jerking his penis. When everything's moved, the guard locks my door. I breathe easy for a few seconds before imagining what's going through Bud's mind. Ten minutes later, our doors open. Not wanting to appear weak by staying in my cell, I stride out to deal with Bud head on.

"You motherfucker!" Bud yells, flying down the stairs.

I turn towards him, expecting to be attacked, ready to strike his chin in the hope of knocking him out. Prisoners mob around, all eyes glued to us.

"What the fuck have you done?" he yells, fists balled, his pale face red with rage. He rushes at me. "If you said anything about me, I'm gonna smash you right now, fish!"

Raw nervous energy crackles through me, exploding into battle mode. "If I said anything about you, you wouldn't be here," I say, holding his gaze.

"Smash him, Bud!"

"Fuck him up!"

His associates circling magnify my sense of danger.

"We're gonna bend you over in the shower, England."

"We're gonna take that English ass."

"What did you tell them about me?" Bud yells, spit flying.

"That we're incompatible. That's all."

"Then how come they moved you so fast?"

"The British Embassy put a call in."

"The British Embassy! You're so full of shit! Who the fuck do you think you are? James fucking Bond? I've got a guard checking out exactly what happened! When I find out what you said about me, I'm gonna fucking kill you! And if you survive, and they send me to lockdown, I'll have someone else kill you! Do you understand me, motherfucker?"

"If you snitched Bud out, you're a dead man, England."

"I understand that, but I didn't."

"I'm gonna find out!" He storms off.

Relieved we didn't fight, I return to cell 2. Anticipating violence, I wait. Bud's associates cluster outside my door, rearing to attack when the order comes.

George arrives, excited. "Well done, governor! That was the fastest move in the history of DOC. Did you call in a favour from Queen Elizabeth?" He grins.

"Not quite. The British Embassy." I recount the story, aware he'll spread the word, and that he may even be on a fact-finding mission for Bud.

Every time a prisoner stops by, I brace to fight, but I breathe easier as each offers congratulations for escaping from Bud. Just before lockdown, an object flies into the cell and hits my leg, stinging my thigh. I spot a battery on the floor, and rush to the door, but see no one.

CHAPTER 6

At Visitation, I hug my parents, both in good shape from hiking and ballroom dancing, but the brightness in their eyes dimmed by the stress of my incarceration and fatigue from a twelve-hour flight.

"The orange suits you," Mum says.

"You look like a giant baby," Dad says. "In an orange Babygro."

We laugh and sit at a circular plastic table in a room that's empty because there are no other special visits – weekday ones approved for out-of-state visitors. Dad puts down a bag containing $20 in coins. I eye a row of bean burritos – the vending-machine food is considered luxurious in comparison to chow – and reach for the coins.

"No touching the quarters, Attwood, otherwise your visit will be ended!" yells a guard in a beige uniform sat at a desk.

I yank my hand back as if from fire. "How am I supposed to get food?"

"Your visitors have to do it. You're not allowed beyond the yellow line," he says, pointing at a line painted on the floor several feet away from the walls all the way around the room.

My mum gets a bean burrito and heats it in a microwave.

Aware that my parents are worried about the situation with Bud, I say, "I feel much safer now that I'm out of Bud's cell."

"Thank God." Mum shifts in her seat.

"When Ann rang us," Dad says, "she said your life was in danger. It took ages to get through to the Embassy."

"We decided that a mother's pleading might work best, so I spoke to the consul," Mum says. "Initially they were unsympathetic. I told the consul that you were being threatened by your cellmate. She said prisoners never like their cellmates and are always asking to be moved, and they can't get involved in petty squabbles between prisoners. Frustrated and angry, I asked to speak to her superior and, when she came on, I got the same story. I told them that in the two years you'd been incarcerated, you'd never once complained about anything or caused any trouble, and that if you said your life was in danger, it was in danger, and that I wasn't going off the phone until they assured me that they would get you moved. The terror in my voice must have alarmed her as she told me she would do whatever she could."

"Neither of us could sleep after that, so we lay awake for the rest of the night waiting for the alarm to ring at 5 AM, so we could get to the airport," Dad says.

"It was the worst night of my life." Mum's expression darkens. "Not knowing if they'd moved you, or if you'd been murdered by your cellmate. We're just relieved that the Embassy got you moved."

Unsettled by their pain, I change the subject. "So, what do you think of the state prison versus Arpaio's jail?"

"It's much cleaner," Mum says. "The guards are more polite."

"A prisoner on an old yellow bus drove us here. He was chatting and joking with everyone." As the euphoria of the visit wears off, they look exhausted.

"Did it take you long to get here?" I ask.

"No," Dad says. "Just over an hour. It's a picturesque setting for a prison. The sky was blood red before the sun rose over the mountains. Along the highway are instructions to keep headlights on day and night. The length of the road and its straightness makes distant cars look invisible."

"And it was spooky," Mum says, "when we passed the road sign **STATE PRISON – DO NOT STOP FOR HITCHHIKERS**. We knew we were getting close to your home. There were a lot of ID checks and searches. We had to leave our belongings in the car. We were only allowed one ring, one watch and the car key. Our belts and jackets were X-rayed, and we had to walk through a scanner."

"We went through a fenced passage," Dad says, "and a guard with a dog yelled, 'Backs to the fence and hands by your sides!' We had to line up while an Alsatian jumped up and down behind us. Then, we went through another scanner. My belt buckle and shoes set off the alarm. A guard ran a wand over me, and there were two more electronic doors to get to here."

"Bloody hell! I had no idea you had to go through all that. So how long did it actually take you to get in?"

"Another hour," Dad says.

"It'll be worse on the weekend when the regular visitors are here," I say.

"Have you heard from Claudia?" Mum asks.

"Her dad said she wants to visit, so I mailed her the paperwork." We all smile.

"If she's going to visit, she must still be interested," Mum says. I beam.

An alarm sounds, followed by an announcement: "Lockdown. Lockdown …" The Visitation guard scrambles for his radio. Guards run outside. The atmosphere charges up with danger. My parents shuffle in their seats.

"What's going on?" I ask the guard.

He leaps off his seat. "The whole complex is locking down," he says, swivelling his head, watching guards run outside. "They're sending backup and a SWAT team to Buckley Unit. No one's allowed to leave Visitation."

Better not tell them someone's been stabbed, murdered or a riot's in progress. "You're officially imprisoned in prison," I say to my parents. We watch SWAT members in body armour march by with guns. The crisp *bop-bop-bop* of firing makes Mum jump.

"What if the prison gets overrun while we're stuck in here?" Mum asks, shaking.

"It's a different yard. They're all self-contained. It could happen there, but not here," I say, unsure of the truth.

For an hour, my parents sit uneasy, wide-eyed, their heads twitching and ears pricking at every sound, until the lockdown ends, and the guard says, "I'm pleased to inform you, you won't be spending the night in prison."

Returning to my cell, I enter the day room. Hearing a scream, I look up and see the big biker Ken dangling a young person by the neck from the upper tier, his victim hanging onto the railing. While Ken chokes him, his legs pendulum above the prisoners' heads. Ken releases his neck, and he falls against the railing with a clang, but hangs on, coughing, gasping. Ken walks away, cackling. Straining to pull himself up, he clambers onto the upper tier.

Nearly every day for the next two weeks, I spend the permitted morning hours at Visitation, chatting with my parents, gorging myself on burritos. We could be in any café, in any country, smiling, talking, exchanging views on crime and justice, life and death, sorrow and joy.

Eager to make the most of the final visit, and sad my parents are leaving, I rush down a corridor crowded with prisoners returning from breakfast, paying little attention to the surroundings.

"England!" a voice yells.

Trying to see who shouted, I scan the prisoners streaming ahead. *That's odd. Shouting my name and disappearing. Maybe he'll shout again.*

Bam! A punch from behind almost knocks me off my feet. I spring into a defensive mode, spinning around, raising my arms. With so many prisoners scattering away, I can't see the assailant. By the time I sense a figure approaching from the side – *bam!* – I'm struck in the torso. Breath is forced from me, scraping my windpipe. It's Ken. I twist in time to prevent a kick from striking my crotch. It hits my leg. *Fight back, fight back* … With adrenaline flooding my system, I kick and swing, but his body absorbs my blows like a bag of cement. His punches spin me around. A kidney punch knocks me down. Ken raises a leg as if to stomp on my head.

"One time!" yells a prisoner, warning of a guard.

"You need to give me your fucking Walkman!" Ken disappears.

I scramble to my feet and dash towards Visitation, rattled,

hoping to conceal my injuries from my parents. Catching my breath, I check in with the guard. With pain intensifying in my back and ribs, I sit down, sensing Mum's concern.

"What happened?" she asks.

"Oh, nothing. I'm fine," I say, forcing a half-smile. For the rest of the visit, I put on a brave face, hoping they don't return to England as worried as they came. When it's time to leave, Mum clings to me as if she never wants to let go. She trudges away, wiping tears. Heading back to my cell, I feel sick for putting my parents through so much. I brace for things to escalate with Ken.

CHAPTER 7

A psychiatrist puts me on lithium (a mood stabiliser), Prozac (an antidepressant), and the waiting list for psychotherapy. Reluctantly, I swallow pills designed to smooth out emotional highs and lows. Nervous of the side effects, I jot down how I feel at hourly increments.

1 hour: I can feel my heart pounding. My anxiety has increased – I am trembling and uneasy. My mind is clouded. Breathing feels difficult – slow and heavy. I feel dizzy. There is a strange taste in my mouth. My eyes are heavy.

2 hours: I have urinated twice – long, clear jets. My eyes are aching and squinting, the book I am reading is going in and out of focus. I have a headache. My heartbeat feels odd and the left side of my chest feels tight.

3 hours: I have urinated two more times – more clear pee. I threw up a small amount of vomit – it looked as if blood was in it, but it may have been the tomatoes I ate at lunchtime. My hands are trembling. My head is pulsating. My skin feels strange to touch. I am experiencing sudden flatulence. I have completely lost my appetite. I am feeling occasional stabbing pains in the right side of my brain.

The pills sap my creativity and induce a stupor. Being more motivated to stare at a wall than pick up a pen is scary. A week later, when the nurse appears with a pill tray strapped over her shoulders like an usherette with ice cream, I wait until she dispenses a collection of pills in assorted shapes, colours and sizes to my neighbour, Slingblade, and I tell her, "I'd like to stop the meds because of the side effects."

"Once you've started the meds, you can't stop them. You have to request to see the psychiatrist, and it's up to him to stop them. In the meantime, you can sign a refusal every day, and I won't give them to you."

Off the medication, I increase yoga to reduce my anxiety. New to psychotherapy, I read about it, finding the cognitive approach helpful. It states that our negative interpretations of events – not the events themselves – are what cause us problems. A chain of negative thoughts can be broken by replacing them with positive ones. In short, changing our reactions to situations. Relaxation through humour, conversation, yoga, meditation and listening to music are recommended.

Since my arrest, I've been unable to listen to rave music. Hearing it at Sheriff Joe Arpaio's jail in 2002 manifested sadness. Too many memories were released. I curled up on my side in the foetal position and pined for freedom. In jail, I discovered Vivaldi. I've continued to listen to classical on National Public Radio (NPR), which helps block out the din and improves my reading concentration. Every so often, NPR plays music that energises my soul. To absorb its magic, I have to stop what I'm doing.

I'm lying on my bunk, eyes closed, smiling, listening to a Beethoven piano concerto, when I hear my name yelled. Opening my eyes, I spot Bud's murderer associate in the doorway. Fear and Beethoven's rapid piano notes raise the hair on my forearms. Having been on guard since the attack by Ken, I curse my lapse into Beethoven. I jump up, scanning the space behind him to see if Bud and Ken are approaching.

Bemused, he stares at my panicked expression. "You feeling all right, England?"

"Yes. I was just listening to Beethoven."

"Don't fucking go anywhere! I'll be right back." He disappears.

What's going on? Another set-up? Unable to read the situation, I wait, breathing and sweating hard, my heart palpitating.

A few minutes later, he returns and throws objects that I catch. "I've got a fucking anger problem, so my doctor tells me that when I feel like hitting someone, I've got to listen to these." There are two tapes: Mozart for Meditation and Bach's Greatest Hits Volume 2. After he leaves, I play Bach, touched by his gesture, wondering whether – without the tapes – he'll smash someone.

In a tiny windowless office, I arrive to see Dr Austin, a middle-aged bespectacled psychotherapist with friendly blue eyes and short brown hair. His tanned face is clean-shaved, his jaw square. He's wearing a sky-blue shirt, jeans and smart tan brogue shoes. Having heard that some medical staff only resort to prison work after getting barred from public practice, I'm wary, but his sincere demeanour and soft soothing voice put me at ease. Over a beaten-up graffiti-etched wooden desk, we discuss my background and medical history.

"What's your definition of success?" he asks enthusiastically.

"It was material success, but now I know that being mentally successful is what matters."

"Can you describe the cycles of success and failure in your life?"

"I had two big runs. One when I was a stockbroker, and one when I traded stocks online. Both times, I thought I had it made. I thought I'd found the right woman. I had plenty of money, cars and gadgets. Then I self-destructed. I partied more, and lost nearly everything – my wife, my house, my wealth. The peaks were so high that I felt on top of the world, and the troughs were so low, I contemplated suicide."

"You seem to thrive during the building up part – when you have a challenge. But when you achieve your goals, you look around, and ask yourself, *What do I do now?* It's almost as if you have no purpose when your goals are achieved, so, you knock down everything that you've built, and start all over. It seems as if you allow no happy medium between work and play. You work tirelessly to build, which seems to be your main drive. Then, when you're successful, you switch to the partying and raving, which brings you down. You said that for the most part you lived reclusively, but on the weekends you'd go raving and be the life and soul of the party. When did you start living reclusively? At what age did you withdraw from your friends?"

"As I became an older teen, I studied more and hung out less with my friends."

"Why did you stop hanging out with them?"

"I was into studying, whereas most of my friends frowned on higher education. They celebrated when they finished high school. They wanted to go out all of the time or they were with their girlfriends."

"Is it possible that your American raver friends were substitutes for those you separated from in England? As if when you went raving you were going back to your original friends?"

There's no way that I can tell him I used to hear wolves inside of me howling to come out and party. He'll think I'm crazy. "I don't know."

"Perhaps you should organise your time better. What if you researched stocks until 3 PM, and allocated time for social relationships? Wouldn't you achieve a balance, instead of letting stress build up in your system, and losing control of your life?"

"Yes, I need to do that."

After the session, I return to my cell feeling unburdened, glad I've got someone to talk to, hoping for progress with Dr Austin even though I know applying his advice won't be easy.

CHAPTER 8

In Visitation, Claudia is attracting stares from inmates and guards. In jeans, sandals and a pink T-shirt, she walks forward, smiling, even more beautiful than I remembered, her blonde hair cascading, her long supple limbs displaying pale delicate skin, her big Norwegian eyes glowing with a warmth that permeates my body. Hugging, I relish her familiar perfume. "Thanks so much for coming." Suddenly, I feel self-conscious in my orange trousers and T-shirt. "I thought I'd never see you again," I say, my heart weighed down by the guilt of everything I've put her through.

Although she came to my sentencing hearing eight months ago, I haven't seen her since, but I've thought about her every day. Our relationship was frozen in time at the moment the SWAT team smashed down our door. The night before, we'd discussed marriage, made love for the last time, and I'd held her in my arms as she fell asleep.

"I still care so much about you, Shaun."

I want to believe she means more than just friendship. We sit at a table. I take her hands in mine. The twenty-six months I was un-sentenced and facing a maximum of 200 years was torture for us, made worse when our visits were stopped by my prosecutor's trickery. I don't want to put Claudia through any more pain after all she's done, and yet I can't help but hope. "I've only got three years left, and I've got these long weekend Visitation hours now. We get to hug and kiss, and we can even walk hand-in-hand in Lovers' Lane."

"Lovers' Lane!" she shrieks.

"Yes, the outdoor area," I say, pointing at prisoners walking in circles around picnic tables, holding their partners' hands.

She laughs. Gazing at her hands, she turns quiet and nervous.

She raises her eyes. "When you're finally deported, can you come back to Arizona?"

"Er, not exactly. I can sneak back in through Mexico, but if I'm caught, I'd end up having to serve another five to ten years, and I'd get deported again. It's in my plea bargain that I'm banned from America."

Her face stiffens. "For how long?"

"Life." Her eyes bulge.

She's worried about not seeing her family if she comes to the UK. "I'm afraid there's no way around it. The prosecutor insisted on putting that in my plea bargain." Seeing tears, I hope to calm her. "Maybe down the road if I make a lot of money, I can pay an attorney to fight it."

She nods. I change the subject. We talk about her job and family. It's incredible to be chatting to her so easily after so long. When it's time for her to leave, I'm almost scared to ask if she'll keep visiting. "Yes, I will," she says.

Warmth runs through me again. With my spirits raised, I return to my cell. Seeing her has reminded me of everything I lost, and how I didn't appreciate the good things in life. Now I'm daring to hope that she is back and I can make it up to her somehow.

CHAPTER 9

A young prisoner, tall, muscular, pale, head shaved, swaggers into cell 2 and throws his mattress on the concrete. "I'm your new celly, Long Island," he says with a New York accent.

Appraising his gang-style tattoos, his wild eyes with dark patches underneath, I think, *Here we go again. The end of peace and quiet in this cell.* "I'm England. Pleased to meet you." I grip his hand, staring firmly.

"England!" His eyebrows leap. "Hold on a minute. Do you know a dude called English Shaun?"

"That's me," I say, surprised.

His face lights up. "I've just come from supermax. My neighbour was Gangsta Dan. He said you and him worked together on the streets."

"Kind of," I say, reluctant to disclose my relationship with Gangsta Dan, a loose cannon in the rave scene who preyed on Ecstasy dealers.

"He said if I run into you, to give you his address, his love and respect, and to look out for you because you and him were crime partners, and you're a good dude. I can't believe you're the first person I met after getting out of supermax!" he says, beaming. "What a coincidence!"

"That's cool," I say, smiling, relieved by his friendliness.

"How come your shit's not on the bottom bunk?"

"I prefer the top," I say, without disclosing why. Reading on the bottom increases my vulnerability, whereas if I'm on the top, facing the door, I can use the height to kick an assailant in the head. "Take the bottom. It's all yours."

"Where's your TV?"

"I don't have one."

"I'll get you one."

"It's by choice."

He stares as if I'm crazy. "What?"

"I read all day."

Shaking his head, he smiles. "I've got a book for you." He grabs a property box from a cart outside the cell and produces *Tender Is the Night*. "It's the last book F. Scott Fitzgerald ever wrote."

I admire the green cover with a portrait of a well-dressed couple staring in opposite directions. "Since reading Hemingway, I've wanted to read Fitzgerald."

"Yeah, those guys were alcoholic hell-raising homies."

"Well, thanks for this."

"I've got *The Fountainhead* by Ayn Rand, too. It's my all-time favourite." It's hard to figure a person out immediately, but someone who enjoys the classics of American literature can't be all that bad. Stood by the narrow window at the end of the cell, Long Island is praising the prose of Ayn Rand when an object flies in and ricochets off the wall like a bullet. "What the fuck!" he yells, picking up a battery. "Where the fuck did that come from?"

"Bud upstairs. We used to be cellies."

He rushes to the door and glares at Bud stood on the balcony. He asks, "What's with the battery?" While I explain my history with Bud and Ken, his brow clenches and his breathing grows louder. "That battery could have hit me. I'm gonna have a word with those assholes!" He darts up the stairs and charges into Bud's cell. I hear arguing, but can't make out what's said. After five minutes, he emerges and sneaks into the other side of the building. He returns to our cell with Ken, whose presence makes my pulse jump.

"Look, dude, I didn't mean to fuck your visit up like that," Ken says. "When I don't take my meds, I snap sometimes."

Surprised, I say, "You messed my back up pretty good."

"I'm sorry, dude. I used to kickbox. I just don't know my own strength."

"I appreciate you coming to say this. I accept your apology."

I shake his hand, relieved, grateful to Long Island. "At least you didn't dangle me off the balcony by the neck." Ken smiles.

"That asshole, Bud, ain't gonna fuck with you no more either," Long Island says.

"Thanks, celly," I say.

"Bud put me up to smashing you," Ken says, confirming my suspicion.

"So, what you in here for this time?" Long Island asks Ken.

"Stabbing the missus, but it was an accident."

"How the fuck did that happen?" Long Island asks.

Ken sits on the stool. "I'd been up for days on meth, working on my boat. I was on my bed, naked, except for a towel wrapped around me, cleaning my nails, when some of my wife's friends stopped by for a couple of ounces of meth. It was hidden in my boat, and I didn't really want to get it, so my wife started yelling, 'If it was your fucking friends, you'd be out there by now!' So I said, 'Fuck you, bitch,' and threw my knife at the dresser, but it missed and stuck in the side of her knee through her pants. She pulled it out and there was a little fingernail-size hole gushing blood, and a little bit of meat came out. I pushed it back in, and we had fun making butterfly stitches. Her friends buying the dope wanted to call it in, but my wife said she was all right, and we partied all night long. That was on April 11, 2003 at Alamo Lake.

"A week later, on the way back from a trip to LA, we got in a fight. Her kid wanted to go to Taco Bell, but there's no Taco Bell in Beverly Hills. The kid's screaming. I'm trying to drive, and my wife attacks me, so I stopped, grabbed her, and threw her out of the truck, but she got back in. Shit just got crazier after that. I'm driving home, my wife's flipping out, and I start hallucinating. The first troll I saw—"

"Troll?" I ask, astonished.

"Yeah, troll. Look, it's made my nipples hard just thinking about it." He points at a nipple and rubs it. "The first troll was at the side of the road, putting a chain on a bicycle, going *he-he-he-he*. It was an evil little bastard, about two-foot tall, wearing a green flannel jacket, with long brown hair. Driving home, the trolls started ripping up those yellow lines painted the roads. They were trying to trip my truck up. Back in Alamo Lake, there's trolls everywhere, destroying cars, and I imagined – it seemed real at the time – that our neighbours were screaming and yelling at the trolls. At home, my wife took off. I went looking for her at her dad's house, and he called the cops. I was seeing trolls everywhere. I'm driving home past a cop. He looks at me, hits his lights, and does a felony stop. 'Driver, pull the keys out, put your hands in the air!' I asked him why I was being arrested, and he said, 'For assault and battery of your wife.' I told him, 'She ain't charging me. That was over a week ago,' and he said, 'She doesn't have to charge you, her dad did.' So, I got busted, and she got busted for drugs, and they threatened to take her kid away if she didn't testify against me, so she did, and I got five years for aggravated assault. I've lost two wonderful marriages thanks to crystal meth."

CHAPTER 10

In the chow hall, biting into a peanut-butter sandwich, my teeth connect with something inflexible. Aware of prisoners getting injured by things placed in food by their enemies – broken glass, infected syringes, mercury from thermometers – I panic and drop the bread onto the table. Opening the sandwich, I spot carefully folded paper. I crane my neck both ways to see if the culprit is watching, but the prisoners are busy eating. Unfolding it, I read:

Englandman, as you know you're engaged to me so don't be cheating on me because I'm a jealous guy. I've met a couple of Cheetos [transsexuals] here in Florence supermax, but all they do is flash their white asses through doors and that ain't no fun 'cause I can't get none. I want someone I can make love to. I'm more than sure that I'll go to Buckeye soon.

The note ends with a winking smiley face pulling tongues. I recognise the handwriting as belonging to Frankie, a Mexican Mafia hit man I met in the maximum-security Madison Street jail. He first approached my cell just when my trousers and boxers were down, and I was applying antifungal ointment to the bleeding bedsores on my buttocks. He peeped through the plexiglas and disappeared, but a few hours later, I received a note slid under the door, saying he'd seen my "sexy booty" and proposing we have a gay prison marriage. He added, "I'm looking forward to shampooing your hairy ass on our honeymoon in San Francisco." I wrote about him at Jon's Jail Journal on May 20, 2004:

Frankie, a Mexican Mafia hit man – who charges $50,000 for a contract killing – instigates most of the madness in

our pod. He's a recent arrival from the jail's infirmary. Last month he was playing cards in a maximum-security pod when someone stuck an eight-inch shank into the back of his neck. Unfazed, he extracted the shank, and was about to return the gesture, but a guard blinded him with pepper spray. Frankie was dragged from the pod with blood gushing from the wound.

Frankie looks and acts like Joe Pesci. He wears his thick black hair slicked back, and his arms are heavily tattooed. He overcompensates for his Napoleonic height with a cocksure manner, and the inmates have warmed to his lewd wittiness. During a 17-year sentence, he became a chess heavyweight. On my hour out, I usually play a game with him by holding the board up in front of his cell window. His piercing hazel eyes and fiendish grin animate when he attempts intimidation tactics:

"Eat dat fucking pawn!"
"Let me fucking teach ya something!"
"Eat dat fucking bishop!"
"Watch dis! Check! Trick move! What'd I fucking tell ya!"
"Don't do it!"
"Move my bitch [Queen] all da way up!"
"Check-fucking-mate! Boo-yah!"
"Nobody fucks wiv da champ!"

My new neighbour, Yum-Yum, an 18-year-old transsexual, looks like a malnourished teenage girl. Yum-Yum has black curly hair, speaks like a female, and has stirred up the love-starved inmates. Frankie is leading the pack. Every day, Frankie has offered Yum-Yum sweets to move into his cell to "make ma cell look good." Frankie complains that his cellmate, Cup Cake, will not participate in "sword fights" (sexual acts). He seems confident that Yum-Yum will be more obliging.

I pocket the note and scan the area, hoping to spot the sandwich filler. *Frankie must have a lot of influence to make a letter materialise when he's locked-down in a supermax prison over 100 miles away. Being around him in lockdown – where we were out of our cells at different times – was one thing, but being around him here – where we're out at the same time – is another.*

When George – who now insists I call him Jeeves – finishes cleaning my cell, I consult him about Frankie.

"Huh! He calls you Englandman, eh?" George says, scouring over the letter. "I don't know, Englandman. If he managed to get a letter in here, into your sandwich, without a trace, I'd say he's pretty serious, buddy. He's hunting for bear." He nods decisively.

"Hunting for bear, Jeeves?" I say, sat on the stool.

"And a little British bear, I believe. This is pretty serious stuff," he says, waving the letter. "What on earth did you say to him?"

"Nothing."

"Perhaps you were practising your Spanish on him and it didn't turn out very well."

"I never led him on, Jeeves."

"Perhaps you said pass the chorizo and that flipped his switch. As one gay man judging another, I believe that if he ends up on this yard, you may need some protection."

"Protection! For what?"

"Your Hershey highway."

"Am I detecting jealousy, Jeeves?" Tilting my head forward, I lift my brows.

"Hell yeah!" He slaps the letter onto the table. "I don't ever get to see Mr Willy, and he gets to ride the Hershey highway. I don't think so!"

"It's not like I want to give my anal virginity up to him!"

"I hope not. Wouldn't you rather have someone lick the willy instead of Frankie cramming his dick in your ass?"

"Neither!" I say, puckering.

"But you're gonna end up with one or the other for playing with people's emotions like you do."

"I haven't promised anyone anything."

"Evidently you have. Getting a message in your sandwich from someone who's in another prison is pretty fucking serious! This guy knows what he's doing, and he must have plenty of help."

"He may be kidding?"

"*Noooooo*," he says. "This is beyond kidding. It's ... It's ... It's ... love! You may be laughing now, but when his dick is in your ass, you're gonna be singing a different tune."

"So how do I get out of this? You've got to help me!"

"As soon as you see him, you need to tell him, 'I've found somebody else. You're too late.'"

"*I've found someone else!* Are you bloody crazy? What if he doesn't accept that, and it just eggs him on because he thinks I swing both ways?"

"You may want to phone the British Embassy, and tell them to mail you a diplomatic pouch with prophylactics."

"Jeeves, surely there's another way out?"

"As serious as he is, I doubt it. You need rubbers, so that when his dick is in your ass, you don't get any diseases or become pregnant. Accept your fate."

"That's not very helpful, Jeeves."

"Accept your fate, and don't encourage him anymore."

"Is that the best you can do?"

"Yes, and I'm off to clean elsewhere now, so tally-ho, Englandman."

CHAPTER 11

"I've got an interesting person for you to write about: Two Tonys. Old-school Mafia. Irish Italian," Long Island says over a game of chess in the day room. He is proving to be a great cellmate and is always making blog suggestions. Knowing a lot of people, he spends most of the time out of the cell, so I have plenty of quiet to read, write and study. While he's the biggest customer at the illegal tattoo shop Bud runs out of his room, Bud has a vested interest in not causing us any trouble. Long Island has also shown an aptitude for finance, so I give him daily classes in the cell, using books and newspapers such as *Investor's Business Daily*.

"What's Two Tonys in for?" I ask, without taking my eyes off the board.

"Mass murder. He's never getting out."

Startled, I raise my head and stare at Long Island. "Wouldn't that be dangerous writing about this guy?"

"Nah. You'll see. He's a good guy. He's got a lot of respect from everyone. I'll go get him. He'll play you at chess."

Before I can stop him, he disappears. *Play chess! If I beat him, he might want to kill me. If I let him win, he'll know I let him win and want to kill me for deceiving him.*

Long Island returns, chatting with Two Tonys – a bespectacled man in his 60s of medium build and height with tenacious hazel eyes, slicked hair greying at the sides, a broad bulldog chin, and the charismatic accent and manner of a mob boss. I catch the tail end of their conversation:

"They've only got me for whacking some of the motherfuckers – the rest they still ain't found. They were all pieces of shit though. Just like I told the judge at my trial, 'Your Honour, I never killed anyone who didn't have it coming.'"

"This is Shaun from England," Long Island says.

"An Englishman, eh!" Two Tonys smiles.

"From near Liverpool." I shake his hand.

"Oh, the bloody Beatles," he says, impersonating an English accent.

"Shaun wants to play you at chess."

"Only if you want to," I say, hoping he declines.

"I'm not much good, but I'll give it a try," Two Tonys says.

I gulp. With downplaying skill the opening gambit of a hustler, I assume he's either an expert or too honest. Hoping he doesn't notice my trembling hands, I move a pawn. Before he makes each move, he voices his thoughts, openly debating what to do. I know better than to let him win – his judgement of my character is on the line – so I checkmate him.

I shake his hand. "I won because you kept speaking your mind. It gave me an advantage."

"What do you mean?" Two Tonys asks.

"You wouldn't show someone your hand in a game of poker would you?" Long Island says.

"Me and my big mouth," Two Tonys says, slapping his head.

We laugh. "England writes stories for the Internet."

"What kind of stories?" Two Tonys asks.

"About prison. What we take for granted is a completely different world to the public. They find it fascinating. If you like, I'll show you what an English newspaper published." I fetch a *Guardian* article featuring blog excerpts.

Two Tonys studies it, smiling occasionally. "You've certainly got a way with words."

"Thanks," I say, beaming.

"On the road of life, I've dealt with a lot of cut-throat mother-fuckers," Two Tonys says. "To stay alive, I become a quick judge of character. I like you, England. You seem like a nice guy, an honest person. I also think you've come into my life for a reason. Would you consider writing my story?"

"I'd be honoured," I say, glad for the opportunity to ally

myself with someone at the top of the prison hierarchy. Prisoners command respect in accordance with their crimes. Murdering gangsters puts Two Tonys in the highest category. "Perhaps we should start by putting some of your stories on the Internet." I explain how blogging works.

Two Tonys suggests that we go into cell 2 for privacy, so he can tell a story. I take the stool, so I can write. Long Island sits on the bottom bunk.

Two Tonys remains standing. "One spring morning in Tucson, me and Charlie 'Batts' Battaglia have a body to bury in the desert. Me being a young guy, I'm in awe of the Batts. He's the epitome of a gangster with his hair slicked back, wearing dress slacks, alligator shoes and pinkie rings. If I'm Francis Ford Coppola, and I'm making a gangster movie, I want a guy like the Batts in it. We take care of business and set off back to Tucson at about 7:45 AM. I'm riding shotgun in the Batts' white Caddy Eldorado. The sunroof's down. I'm enjoying the smell of creosote in the air 'cause it's been raining. The sun's coming up through the mesquite trees and the Palo Verdes, which are turning a little yellow, and are in the blooming stage. We're cruising along the roly-poly roads in the Catalina Foothills. The radio's playing, 'Get up America ... we love you,' and all that shit. Earth, Wind & Fire's 'Fantasy' comes on. All at once we rise up a steep hill and hit a dip, and we see a hen quail going across the road with little chicklets behind her, all of them in a straight line. The Batts has got a big Anthony and Cleopatra cigar in his face. He sees the quail family, slams on the fucking brakes, and my head almost goes through the windshield 'cause I ain't wearing no seat belt. I thought somebody had shot the Batts. I'm scared. I'm wondering, *What the fuck's going on?* The Caddy is spinning on the gravel, but somehow he regains control and we head for breakfast.

"At Sambo's on Miracle Mile, over bacon and eggs, I say to the Batts, 'You know, you almost killed us back there for a fucking bird.' I'm looking in the eyes of a stone-cold killer, a guy investigated for whacking motherfuckers from coast to coast, who knew how to get away with it.

"The Batts looks at me and says, 'Hey, let me tell you something: it wouldn't have been the right thing to do. Somewhere out in the desert tonight,' – a smile came across his face – 'a mother quail and her little chickadees are gonna be all together at suppertime, and I'm not gonna be responsible for breaking up their little family and squashing them on the highway.'

"I'm salting my cantaloupe, and I get the impression that the Batts is putting me on. But there's something in his eyes that tells me he's serious. This leads me to believe he justified doing the things he did as just something he had to do. Although I hadn't seen much of it, it was clear that the Batts had a heart ..."

Two Tonys tells more stories. His enthusiasm saturates cell 2. Drawn into his fascinating life, Long Island and I sit, fully absorbed.

CHAPTER 12

"You mentioned that being unable to reach your full potential in prison is a cause of anxiety. What do you mean by that?" Dr Austin asks in his tiny office.

"Because I'm not in front of a computer, trading stocks, doing the work I enjoy the most."

"Do you feel that your behaviour in prison is similar to your hard-working self before your arrest?"

"Yes."

"Describe a typical week before your arrest."

"On weekdays, I watched stocks and did online research. I mostly stayed at home with my fiancée, other than when we went to the gym, skating and the Indian restaurant. Also, I was studying Spanish at college."

"And what about the weekends?"

On the weekends, I'd hear the wolves. "I was a party animal, but I'd met a good woman, so I was phasing that behaviour out."

"In my life," Dr Austin says, "I like to spend a whole weekend day doing absolutely nothing, recharging from the stresses of the week."

"At one time, the weekend merged into one day. A Friday-night rave and after-party all day Saturday. A Saturday-night rave followed by partying all day Sunday, and sometimes we'd go out on Sunday night."

His eyes widen. "How was that possible?"

"I'd take Xanax, sleep like a baby, and wake up crisp and fresh on Monday."

He shakes his head. "You're describing two modes again: the party mode and the reclusive hard worker. So, in prison, you're in the second mode."

"Yes, I'm studying, reading and writing more than ever."

"You said that you were phasing the partying out?"

"I stopped hardcore raving years before my arrest. When Sammy the Bull lit the scene up, attracting undercover cops, I moved to Tucson and tried to live a normal life. My stocks were doing well. Everything was going great."

"Why did you move back to Phoenix?"

"Because I met and fell in love with Claudia. We got a place together in Scottsdale. I only went to two raves in 2002. She wasn't a raver."

"So, you were settling down, and the party lifestyle was on its last legs, you almost had a normal life, and then you got arrested. Most people in that situation would feel bitter about that, yet you seem to take responsibility for what you did?"

"How can I not? The lifestyle I chose led to my arrest. At first I was upset, but now I don't waste mental energy thinking about it. It's counterproductive. My interest in writing and the results I'm slowly achieving, make me think that everything is working out for the best. In a way, I'm glad I'm going through this because it's enabling me to develop as a person."

"How did things work out for you and Claudia?"

"She visited me regularly for a year. Then she was indicted for a prescription pill found a year earlier without a written prescription, a Class 6 Felony, which meant she couldn't visit. She stuck with me for over two years and helped me however she could. My feelings for her grew, but then we broke up and I was devastated. She visited here last week. I think we might be getting back on track," I say, smiling. "She said she's going to visit again."

"How does that make you feel?"

"Happy, but confused. I'm telling myself to go with the flow, see what happens, and enjoy any visits, but not to set myself up emotionally again, so I don't get hurt. But I can already feel intense feelings coming back. Who am I trying to fool?"

"Do you miss raving?"

"I miss the music. I don't miss my behaviour. I see it as a

phase I look back on. Incarceration has forced me to grow up. Previously, I would have mocked someone for listening to Vivaldi or for doing yoga and other things I enjoy now. I'm continuing to change and learn."

Returning to my cell, I'm intercepted by two guards. "Come with us, Attwood!"

Wondering what kind of trouble I'm in, I quicken my pace. They steer me around the corner of a building to a blind spot from prisoners and guards. *They could beat me up or kill me here and no one would know.* A senior guard appears – stocky with a cruel face and inquisitive eyes. He orders the others to leave.

"Attwood, I've been reading your blog, Jon's Jail Journal."

Is he going to tell me to stop blogging?

"I work in internal investigations," he says, referring to the prison police. "It's my job to know what's going on in here. Reading your blog is giving me a general idea of certain things." As I'm careful not to blog anything that might get a prisoner in trouble, I assume he's trying to bluff me. "Although I find your blog helpful, if you'd like to talk to me in a more specific way, I could make life much easier for you, for instance, with certain people you've been having problems with." He smirks knowingly.

He's giving me the opportunity to snitch on Bud and Ken to get rid of them. "I appreciate the offer, but I don't have problems with anyone. If the prisoners find out I've even spoke to you, it's likely to create problems for me."

"That's why I arranged to meet you on your way back from Medical. No one will know."

"I'm sorry. I can't help you," I say, staring at him uneasily, turning a foot away from him.

"Well, keep the blogging up, Attwood."

Shook up, I return to my cell. Long Island says to ignore the guard and not tell anyone.

CHAPTER 13

It's March 6, 2005, and Claudia's due to visit. I wake up early, excited, grinning at Long Island.

"I hope your visit goes well today, dog!" He smiles.

I shave, wait for the cell door to open and rush to the shower. Afterwards, I grab a book and lie on my bunk. Every time names are called to Visitation, I stop reading and hold my breath, listening for Attwood. Surprised my name hasn't been called by breakfast time, I head to the chow hall, but I'm barely able to eat.

Back in my cell, I say, "I wonder where she's at."

"She might be stuck in traffic or something," Long Island says in a concerned tone, but with an expression as if he knows something that I don't.

Unable to concentrate, I squirm on the bunk. After he leaves, I climb down and pace back and forth, wondering where she is. As lunchtime approaches, I assume she's not coming as Visitation hours are almost over. Reasons for her absence fly through my mind. I try not to assume the worst – that she doesn't want to see me anymore – but the worry throbs in my skull, stifling my ability to think about anything else.

Mid-afternoon, I call her, my pulse rising as her phone rings. When she answers, I say, "Is everything OK? I was worried because you didn't show up. Thought you might have been in an accident or something."

"No, I'm fine," she says in a sad low voice that tightens my stomach.

"What is it? What's the matter?"

"I'm so sorry, Shaun, but I can't visit you anymore."

"What do you mean? Why's that?" I ask, raising my voice, prisoners in the vicinity staring my way. "I thought we got along so well at the visit."

"We did, but it's this plea-bargain thing. You know my family is my world. If you can't ever come back to Arizona, the only way we could be together is if I move to England, but with my family here, I wouldn't be able to see them."

"But if you move to England, you could fly back to see them whenever you want, and they could come and visit us, too."

"I can't live that far away from my family, Shaun," she says, sniffling.

I feel awful but don't want to lose her either. "I'm sorry. I didn't mean to pressure you. I totally understand where you're coming from. I just figured we would start our own family in England and you could fly back and forth." Silence. "So, what does this mean for us?" I ask.

"I don't think I can visit you anymore."

"Why the sudden change?"

"I'm not going to move to England, Shaun, and you can't ever come here. I still have feelings for you. I wish you'd never signed that stupid plea bargain that's banned you from America."

"I know, but I can't change the past. Look, you've done so much for me, I really don't want to put you through any more pain. It hurts to hear how sad you are. I'm going to get off the phone and I realise I'm probably not going to see you again." My eyes well. "If your feelings change, then please let me know. You shouldn't be suffering like this. I appreciate everything you've ever done for me. Ok, then, goodbye, Claudia."

"Goodbye, Shaun."

With tears streaming, I return to my cell, shattered by loneliness, aware that it's finally over, hurting as if one of Bud's needles has jabbed my heart.

CHAPTER 14

A massive Mexican American with gold teeth and turquoise tattoos on his skull says at recreation, "Frankie's been approved for this yard." Apprehensively, I drop out of a headstand and take a letter from him:

What's up, Englandman? Did you find yourself another esposo [husband]? How are things going on at your end besides you cheating on me? I thought it was all about you and me. It's all gravy 'cause nobody can lay pipe like me. Tu esposo [Your husband].

The yard has two main buildings, each divided into four fifty-man pods, so the chance of sharing a pod with Frankie is one in eight. There's a one in four chance of going to chow and recreation with him as two pods go together. As I assess the situation, a prisoner approaches – 40ish, average build, pale skin bordering on anaemic, a playful gleam in his dark eyes. "Can you show me some of that stretching?" he asks slowly and clearly with protracted vowels. "I'm Justin."

"Have you done yoga before?" I ask, glad to gain a friend.

"No. Never."

"How about I take you through some basic postures?"

"Let's do it."

After adjusting his alignment for forward bend, cobra, cat, downward dog and seated spinal twist, we lay supine for corpse pose, the sun bearing down from a cloudless sky, baking us like gingerbread men. "Now stand up slowly, so the blood doesn't rush to your head."

"I feel totally relaxed. Thanks, man." Justin gets up, shakes my hand and leaves just as recreation ends.

Walking back to the building, Long Island asks, "What were you doing with that Justin dude?"

"Just showing him some yoga."

"You need to watch him, celly. He was totally checking your ass out."

"No, he wasn't!" I say, blushing.

He shakes his head. "What you consider being friendly can easily be misconstrued in here. Just giving you a heads-up."

The next day when I'm alone, Justin stops by cell 2. "I want you to read this, not share it with anyone and let me know what you think as soon as possible."

"OK," I say, confused. He leaves, so I open the letter:

Hi Shaun!

This is Justin writing from afar. There's been a lot on my mind that I've wanted to share with you. I'm not afraid of too many things in this world, and I usually prefer to look someone straight in the eyes when I'm talking about something that means so very much to me, but in this case, I am afraid. I'm scared to hear you tell me (however tactful) that I'm offending you, or that I've got no chance in hell, and that's where I should go, or maybe you'll be kind and say "... we can still be friends."

Rejection scares me when it comes from someone I admire. Shaun, I'm gay, and until you tell me otherwise, I have to assume you are straight. But ever since I first saw you, first heard the sound of your voice, I've wanted to be closer than just a friendly acquaintance. You are sooo handsome to me, and intelligent, and rather self-confident – a strong man. You have all the things I admire most since I've never seen you with less than shorts on!! Yes Shaun, you know where this is going. Even though people know I'm gay, I do not want anyone to know who I have feelings for, and I do not want anyone to know who I get together with, when, where, or what exactly happens between myself and a guy that's willing to give me a chance to show him excellent pleasures. I've been gay since 12 years old, and I love myself just the way I am. When someone straight tries to understand, it's impossible! Try explaining a colour to someone born blind.

Being in prison for years on end without the sexual pleasures of a woman, leaves most men frustrated and they are left with what they feel is no alternative than to fantasize with some long-ago dream and a magazine in the company of their own right hand. That gets old after years and years.

To finally decide to give a guy like me a chance to do the very same things (most things) a woman can do leaves a guy realizing he should have let me please him long ago.

Since being with you would be our "first time" it's best, if you would give me a chance, to go slow, and show you what I can do for you a little at a time.

When you were out there doing that yoga, and the morning sunrise made all that hair on your legs shine – as I watched you from a distance, I imagined how fine you must look if you were with me and if you let me kneel before you and slowly pull your pants down and the first thing I would see, would be a beautiful bush of soft hair around a huge hard cock. I imagine you're circumcised and 7–8" hard. And how you would say so softly "ohh yeah!" as I took your cock in my hot mouth for the very first time. I would love so very much to give you a blow job, slow and easy and make you come so hard!!!

This would be our secret. This is no work of fiction. If you would ever want this to happen, you know where I live, and the thing to do is to come over here when everyone goes to rec. Shaun, in the privacy of my room, there is nothing (nearly so) I would not do to please you. I have other fantasies too. If you wish, I will write them in my next letter.

I'm touched by his frankness, eloquence and the level of thought put into the letter. Resolved not to hurt his feelings, I go to bed pondering a response. The next day I seek him out at recreation. "Justin, I appreciate your honesty in letting me know how you feel, but I don't sleep with men. I really enjoy chatting with you. You're witty and extremely articulate. But that's as far as this can go. I'd be glad to remain friends and show you more yoga."

We shake hands. "Thanks for your honesty. If you ever change your mind," he says, a smile replacing disappointment, "I'm not going anywhere."

Pleased the situation is resolved, I hope to achieve the same with Frankie.

CHAPTER 15

In cell 2, Two Tonys is smiling at the responses from my blog readers, some of whom are speculating that his phrase, "I never whacked anyone who didn't have it coming," originated in Hollywood. "The characters in these movies are based on motherfuckers like me," he says, his eyes sparkling. "It's not the other way round. They're just actors using lines from real gangsters. This blog shit's pretty fucking cool. I never thought I'd see the day when some schoolteacher out of Singapore would ask me questions about my life. I'm serving 141 years. I never thought I'd communicate with anyone outside these fucking walls again."

"Your stories are generating way more comments and emails than usual," I say. "You're going to have a strong following in no time."

"I like the way you write my stories. You've got skills," he says, patting my shoulder.

Afterwards, marching to the chow hall, crunching gravel underfoot, he asks in a low voice, "Is that motherfucker, Ken, still giving you shit?"

"No. It's no big deal," I say, feeling awkward. "You can't come to prison and not expect people to give you shit. Anyway, he apologised and the beef's squashed."

"Whatever he does to you, give it right back. If he hits you, hit him back. If he kicks you, kick him back. It's the only way to deal with motherfuckers in here."

"I know, but the last time he snuck up behind and caught me off guard. I'm way more aware now." He nods as if plotting.

Inside, he sits with Ken and Cannonball, Ken's burly and intimidating cellmate with yellow-jaundiced skin on a big round face resembling a poppadum. I sit on the next table and eavesdrop.

"If they cut your ass loose in Mall of fucking America, what would you loot?" Two Tonys likes to pose hypothetical scenarios.

"I'd hit the diamond stores," Cannonball says.

"Smart," Two Tonys says. "Lots of small pricey shit. Diamond rings and gold chains. What about you, Ken?"

"I'd go where the big money's at: the banks." Ken lifts his dark-circled eyes from his slop as if seeking approval.

"Get out of here!" Two Tonys says, flexing his brow. "How the fuck would you get in a locked bank vault, motherfucker?"

Ken recoils. "I dunno. I'd figure it out."

"You couldn't even break out of your own fucking cell. If they locked you in, you'd die in there. You know nothing about locks or robbing banks."

"What should I be looting then?"

"You'd do well looting Los Angeles."

"Why's that?" Ken asks, hope in his eyes.

"'Cause of all the fucking porno stores. If Korean snipers didn't cap your ass, you'd be cleaning out the sex stores. I can see you running down Hollywood Boulevard with a backpack full of dildos – big black ones."

I stifle laughter as Ken's face sours. With the prisoners paying attention, I worry about the situation escalating as Ken is twice Two Tonys' size.

"How come Cannonball gets to be a diamond looter, and I got to be a fucking dildo looter? What're you trying to say?" Ken huffs and slaps his palms on the table as if about to rise.

"I'm saying there's something about you that exudes fucking dildo looting. Cannonball would be snatching diamonds, and you'd be grabbing big black double dildos."

Ken grabs Two Tonys' neck.

"Hey, motherfucker! Don't fuck with an old man doing two fucking life sentences!" Two Tonys' face turns red. His eyes protrude.

Ken releases the chokehold. "You fucker! I should have choked you out."

Coughing every few seconds, Two Tonys says, "If you're gonna choke me for clowning you about dildos, then we're not fucking playing anymore."

After chow, I'm waiting in cell 2 to give Long Island his stock-market class when he bursts in. "Two Tonys just asked me for a shank. He's boiling water, waiting for Ken to come in, so he can throw it in his face."

"Why don't we go over there and talk to him to get his mind off Ken?" I say, worried about losing my friend to the hospital or punishment block. "We can postpone our stock-market stuff till after lockdown." The highlight of our day now is the arrival of the financial newspapers, so we can check how well we're doing in hypothetical trading accounts we're competing against each other in.

"Yeah, and if Ken tries to start any shit, we can stop it."

Rushing to leave the cell, we almost bump into Ken. Long Island steps in front of me and tilts his head back. "You can't beat Two Tonys down. He's too old. You'll kill him."

"I promised him I'd never hurt him," Ken says, "but after what he said today, I don't care. I can only be pushed so far."

"Look, he's shook up right now from you choking him. At least let him calm down tonight before you go and talk to him."

"OK." Ken leaves.

We find Two Tonys in his cell, boiling water with a heating filament called a stinger. After he vents about Ken, I ask for a story. In case Ken changes his mind and decides to pay Two Tonys a visit, we remain there until lockdown, satisfied no harm has come to him when we leave.

CHAPTER 16

"Why did you start taking drugs?" Dr Austin asks.

"When I was a teenager, I was shy," I say, facing him, hands on my lap. "I'd go to clubs and pubs, but wouldn't really talk to people other than my friends. I never had the nerve to strike up conversations with girls. I was too self-conscious to dance. But when raving came around, I took Ecstasy and speed, and I'd party with complete strangers all night, talking to them, hugging them, telling each other our life stories. It got to the point where if my hometown friends didn't want to go raving, I'd go to the party on my own because I knew so many people there. It was all I could think about all week long. Raving became my religion."

"What do you remember about the first time you took drugs?"

"I'd been told drugs were bad, so I was really nervous, but once the high hit, I felt like I'd entered a whole new dimension of pleasure. I couldn't stop dancing. On Ecstasy, I was dancing on the main stage, smiling at hundreds of people, wearing psychedelic colours and a silver cowboy hat, not giving a damn about what anyone thought about me. I loved it. I've always had some anxiety. Some nights in childhood, my thoughts would race, worrying about stuff, keeping me awake for hours. On Ecstasy, for the first time in my life, I felt completely relaxed. I didn't have a care in the world."

"How did your drug habit get so out of control?"

"It's never as good after the first time. You're always chasing those early highs. You have to do more drugs to keep the high going, or you step up to harder drugs, or you mix drugs up. Drugs put a cloud in my head that I didn't know was there until I was arrested. When the cloud lifted, I saw the danger I'd put myself in over the years. I realised how lucky I am to be alive."

"To address the anxiety you experience that drives you to drugs, a compromise must be found. You have a need for relaxation and pleasure, for good mental health, which you're not addressing if you believe that you 'have to get this done and have to get that done' to achieve your goals. Let me take a guess: you probably spend 70 per cent of your time working towards your goals and 30 per cent on relaxation and pleasure?"

"More like 90 per cent plus on my goals, and 10 per cent or less on pleasure." My lips tighten.

"It's worse than I thought then," he says, raising his brows. "Instead of rising up rapidly and having a massive need for play at the crest of your wave, you should try to obtain your goals more slowly, by letting steam out from time to time on the way up by engaging in pleasure and relaxation."

Confronting the issue generates a sinking feeling. "What you're saying is true, but I don't want to achieve my goals slowly." My body tenses, shoulders rise. "Part of my goals are the time parameters I set," I say, raising my voice. "I view the road you're describing as mediocre performance."

"Unless you change that belief and let out steam gradually as your stress builds, you'll have the same problems that you've had in the past."

His caring tone cuts through my hostility. "So how do I change that?" I ask, my voice softening, shoulders relaxing. "I've got something inside that drives me relentlessly. I don't understand where it comes from."

"I need to go deeper into your psyche to find out what has shaped your core belief system." His face turns serious. "But sadly, that's not possible because I've been assigned to work at another prison," he says, compassion in his eyes.

"Oh, no!" I say, lifting my hands. "Just when it seemed we were making progress."

"Do you feel that you've benefitted from the sessions we've had?"

"Yes, but I feel we were about to make progress, and now you're leaving."

"But there's a new guy, Dr Owen. He might not do my stuff though. He's more into cognitive. I believe you can change the way you think, and that's what our sessions have been about."

"I appreciate your help. It's meant a lot to get a professional opinion and to have you to speak to." Having never tried to analyse myself with someone at this level before, I leave disappointed to lose Dr Austin, and wondering whether I'll be able to establish such a level of rapport with Dr Owen.

CHAPTER 17

At recreation, I gag on the stench of sewage coming in waves on a hot breeze, and walk around Slingblade. He is alone on the field, topless, sweat streaking down his belly, his body glistening, his arms folded tightly across his chest, staring blankly into space, occasionally muttering, cackling and shaking his massive fists at the sky. I wonder if his convulsions are due to mental illness or side effects from the pills the nurse brings him three times a day. I wish I could help him somehow, but I worry that if I approach him, he may have a flashback.

"You come here!" a member of a gang of Mexican Americans shouts at me.

My body tenses. "No, you come here!" I yell in my deepest voice, not wanting to show any fear.

"Don't give me that shit! I want to tell you something," he says, veins bulging from sweaty biceps.

"What you got to tell me?" I ask, bracing to fight.

"Something from Frankie." Relieved, I approach him. He leans forward and whispers in my ear, "I've been told to tell you that Frankie's here in Building 2. He wants to meet you at early-outs lunch tomorrow."

"OK. Thanks," I say, wary yet excited.

Two Tonys shows up, panting from exercise. The Mexican Americans nod and raise their eyebrows in a respectful way. "You look outnumbered by my friends, my English buddy!" Smiling, he bumps fists with the gang.

When the gang leaves, I ask him, "How's your day going?"

"I'm having a wonderful day," Two Tonys says. "It started when I got up this morning and cleaned the house and had a hot coffee. I went to the chow hall, and they had my favourite fucking breakfast: French toast, grilled potatoes and hot cereal. I thought I was in the fucking International House of Pancakes for a minute. I was looking for a waitress to order some cheese blintzes. I walked a bit, played some baseball and ate some ice cream. The biggest decision I got to make today is whether to go to fucking dinner or not."

I can't stop laughing.

"There was a time in my life when I had to make fucking decisions. Do I want to pay this guy or do I want to pay that guy? Do I want to whack this guy or do I want to whack that guy? I'm having a much better day than some of those rich motherfuckers I knew living on Camelback Mountain. They were worried about making their mortgage payments, or their wives banging the pool cleaner, or worried about their high-school daughters smoking crack with some rapper, or their boys turning into hoodlums. Life is good. A guy my age can actually take nice naps in the afternoon. I've got it made."

On the way to meet Frankie, I'm looking forward to seeing my chess partner, but nervous about repelling his sexual advances. I feel a strong bond with him because we both endured the cockroach-infested maximum-security Madison street jail. Frankie and Junior Bull are the only two people I knew here before coming to Buckeye prison. It's such a lonely place that the arrival of a familiar face is comforting.

I line up for chow and spot Frankie at a table, waving, smiling and blowing kisses. Blushing, I smile back. I receive a tray – bland boiled navy beans – and join him. "Englandman!" Frankie stands.

"Great to see you." We hug. "Pity we're not in the same building as I really miss our chess."

"You know who's the greatest." He flexes a bicep.

"We'll see about that. I've been reading chess books."

"I write chess books, homey!" he says, shaking his head. Everyone at the table laughs. We sit down. "Englandman, my wife's stopped visiting me," he says, his expression grave, "causing me to turn straight gay."

Here we go.

"If I get moved over to your building, we can be cellies, Englandman."

"I hate to disappoint you, Frankie, but I've got a good celly."

"You guys doing sword fights yet?" he asks.

"You know I don't fancy men."

"Englandman, you're in denial. Haven't you even had a blow job off a cheeto yet?"

"No."

"That's not even considered gay in here! Everyone's doing it. I'll find you a real nice cheeto if you let me watch."

"It's not going to happen!" *If everyone's doing it, will I eventually? Try not to think about it. Masturbation will see me through. Be strong.*

"Englandman, after five years you'll be getting blow jobs just like the rest of us."

"I doubt it." *But the lack of sex is painful. If it gets worse, will I go with a transsexual? Stop thinking about it!* "Can we get back to chess, please?"

"When I move buildings, it's on! I'll crush you like this." He drops a bean onto the table, and squashes it under a thumb. "In case you've been cheating on me, Englandman, I'd also like to read what you've been writing at Jon's Jail Journal."

"No worries. I'll send the printouts over to your building."

A few days later, I receive a note from Frankie.

Para mi esposa [For my wife]

After reading about George in your journal, I'm very anxious about him. As you know I'm a very jealous man and you are engaged. Don't this guy know that I will set the dogs on him and make him pee? You better tell George about Caesar, I go way back and I love the back door. By the way tell George that it wasn't your Spanish that led me to fall in love with you, it was your yoga exercises that caught all my attention, and that one time at Madison Street jail when I caught you rubbing cream into the bed sores on your ass. It was love at first sight! Also, if you need to know anything about your Hershey highway that's my department. I'm an expert in that area. I'm also a certified pipe layer. Well my friend, I'm hearing that we're being moved to dorms ... It will be really cool if we end up in the same dorm. Now that will be really nice Englandman.

I'm going to close now but not forever.

Much love and respect, Frankie

ps Tell George I'm the number one in your vida [life] and that we're engaged. By the way I want to meet this guy so introduce him to me. Take care and forget me not!

I take the note to George, whose face drains of colour. In a nervous high-pitch, he says, "Tell Frankie I've left the country."

CHAPTER 18

"Lockdown! Special count!" a guard announces at 6 AM on July 11, 2005, almost eight months into my stay at Buckeye prison.

Long Island springs off his bunk and peers through the door window. "We're leaving. The guards are handing out blue bags for our property!" Prisoners are moved every so often for security reasons such as breaking up gangs and foiling escape plans.

Unnerved, disorientated, I climb down from the top bunk. *Will it be cells? Will it be dorms? Will I lose Long Island?* My mind goes into overdrive. With guards barking orders and refusing to tell us where we're going, I hurriedly load my belongings onto a trolley, and wheel it to a warehouse for an inventory check.

"I'm taking my shit over there." Hoping to avoid the confiscation of extra books, clothing, magazines and cassettes, Long Island joins a line for a guard he considers less strict.

As I have no excess property, I join the shortest line; it's for the hard-nosed internal-investigations officer who attempted to recruit me as an informer.

"Attwood. The British blogger." He opens the boxes and starts recording my property. "When I was growing up my favourite bands were The Smiths and New Order," he says, flicking through a book in search of razor blades, syringes and drugs.

"Both from Manchester. Near where I'm from," I say, hoping no one has stashed anything in my property, a strategy prisoners sometimes employ on their enemies.

"I also used to go to the Blue Iguana and the Works Club," he says, referring to rave clubs I attended.

Shocked by him divulging information about his private life – most unusual for a guard – I suspect he's tried Ecstasy. I keep my mouth shut – the best policy around staff.

"Good luck in Tucson, Attwood," he says, handing back a form:

Inmate Property Inventory
1	Radio clear tech Walkman
1	Headphones
1	Corded electric razor without case
1	Reading Lamp with bulb
1	Fan
1	Box of legal material
1	Box of checkers
7	Books
1	Bulb 'Phillips'
15	Cassette tapes 'Learning tapes'
1	Box of toiletries
1	Box of crackers
1	Jar of peanut butter
1	Tumbler
1	Bowl
1	Cup
1	Sunglasses

With my property on its way to transportation, I return to my cell without pen and paper. Accustomed to writing letters and blogs, I feel part of me is missing. I don't quite know what to do with myself. From the few books scattered around the day room discarded by prisoners, I end up reading *Revolutionary Guerrilla Warfare* and Buddhist literature.

The next day at 3 AM, the cell door clicks open. "Roll your mattresses up, put them in the day room and proceed to the chow hall!"

Half-asleep, I drop from the top bunk. The commotion of mattresses being thrown revs my heart up.

Guards escort seventy-five of us to a warehouse. With no privacy, ten at a time are lined up in the middle, and ordered to strip naked. Awaiting their turn, dozens of prisoners heckle each ten with comments like, "Bend over, big boys." My turn comes. Nervously, I disrobe next to Ken.

"Who's got the smallest dick?" Ken yells at the onlookers, waving his arms, wiggling his hips, radiating armpit and crotch odour. We laugh.

"Put your arms in the air. Open your mouth. Raise your balls. Turn around. Bend over. Spread 'em. Cough."

The mockery and jeering escalate as a guard moves down the line, inspecting our stretched-open behinds for contraband. I blush. *Come on. Get it over with.* "OK. Get dressed. Proceed outside."

Fearful of what might come next, I exit the warehouse. "Line up against the fence!" Guards affix hand and leg cuffs that cut my skin, restrain my movement and increase my weight. "If you've got your cuffs on, get on the bus!"

Stood at the foot of an old school bus with grid metal over the windows, a transportation guard yells, "Number!" so aggressively it hurts my ears.

"1-8-7-1-6-0." With the bus almost full, I sit behind the driver, next to Blackheart, the Lakota Indian who ate the caterpillar from my salad when I first arrived, almost seven-foot tall, serving life for murder. The bus leaves.

While the bus cruises at 80mph, I wonder about our destination. A kennel-style gate separating us from the two guards rattles like gunfire, raising my anxiety. The driver picks up a gallon of water and takes a swig. Staring at its Safeway label, I long to shop for groceries and to have a choice over what I eat.

Excitement sweeps through the bus when we spot what appears to be a forest fire, giant flames dancing along the top of a mountain range. "It's not fire. It's the angle of the rising sun," a prisoner says. Amazed, I gaze at the vivid red and yellow lighting up the darkness.

At Casa Grande, the bus joins the Interstate 10 to Tucson – a section of road where at the peak of my drug intake I once saw imaginary wolves howling to come out and party. *Where are my wolves now? Crushed by the system or hiding inside, biding their time, hoping to run wild again?*

A transportation guard dozes, one leg down, the other propped up by the front of the bus and a double-barrel shotgun, his face peaceful as if he's drifting into a pleasant dream. The bus swerves and skids and we get thrown around. I bounce off Blackheart. The inmates curse the driver, waking up the other guard. Startled, he turns his head and stares back at us, his eyes widening as if seeing hell.

At Picacho Peak, hundreds of giant cacti appear to be marching up the mountain, attempting to join those climbing the cliff face. Entering Tucson, we pass the Ina Road exit – the turn for my former million-dollar mountainside house. Wondering if fate is trying to teach me a lesson by converging the past with the present, I get a desperate sad urge to rewind the clock, to be in my sports car, blasting music, heading home. The signs **Wilmot Road Exit** and **Arizona State Prison 4 Miles** mark the journey's end.

At Tucson prison, the guards order us off the bus. The 10 degrees Fahrenheit difference in temperature is a relief. Our chains are removed. After hours cramped in outdoor holding cages, we're escorted to a prison consisting of four buildings: A, B, C and D, each a flat L-shape, built in a diagonal row, so that D is at the far end of the complex. Each has two storeys of cells opening to an outdoor area with a basketball court built on an impoverished stretch of dirt and dust. There's no indoor day room like at Buckeye. A prairie dog pops up from nowhere and checks us out on its hind legs, amusing us. Long Island and I are assigned to D-11 at the back. Overjoyed not to be separated, we high-five and hug.

We take our property to an upper-tier cell with thin hot walls, smelling of sewage and old metal. The doorway overlooks an outdoor area with reverse-charge phones, workout stations, a chow hall, and in the distance – as if to rub in how much I lost – the mountains where I used to live. Through the narrow back window is a view of the perimeter fence, desert cleared so escapees can be shot, and brushland. Long Island takes the bottom bunk, which runs along a side wall. I take the top bunk, bolted to the back wall above a table I aim to turn into an office/blogging command post. The cement floor space is ten by three foot, sufficient to do push-ups. Our mattresses have their charcoal-grey foam fillings bulging out as if disembowelled. Under mine, I discover an old razor blade, syringe parts, and a small transparent scorpion, which I secure in a plastic cup and discard through the few inches the window opens. We despair over the swamp-cooler vent not blowing. We can't plug our fans in because one electrical socket isn't working and the other is hanging off the wall. We spend the rest of the day locked-down, sweating in the concrete oven, wearing only boxers.

At night, exhausted, I collapse onto the mattress without any bedding, and start to drift off, but a noise rattles the building – *crrrrrkkkkkksshhhhh* – jolting my eyes open. Tucson prison is between Davis–Monthan Air Force Base and Tucson International Airport, used by the Arizona Air National Guard. Every so often, a commercial or military plane thunders over, shaking the building. I try to raise my head, but my sweaty cheek is stuck to the vinyl. I detach my cheek, bang my head on the ceiling and climb off the bunk to use the toilet. The flusher button requires two thumbs and all of my strength. I make earplugs by sealing wet toilet paper inside of pieces of plastic bag, climb on the bunk and pass out.

CHAPTER 19

Early the next morning, the yard comes alive. Trusties hand out bedding and towels. Electricians fix sockets. A plumber, a friendly murderer with a hillbilly twang, unblocks drains. Long Island joins a long line for a shower.

I'm glad to see George with cleaning supplies. He rests the mop against the wall and salutes. "Jeeves is here to report for cleaning duty, governor."

"You didn't waste any time tracking my cell down," I say, sat on a plastic chair at the desk bolted to the back wall.

"Of course not, governor. We wouldn't want the royal willy to go unwashed now."

I rotate my chair to face him. "You're not coming near my willy."

"That's a damn shame because you have so much foreskin to offer," he says, leaning against the wall. "You act prim and proper, but you were a rave king, and I know that a lot of ravers are bisexual, so you were the head kink because you ran them. I'm surprised you didn't have glory holes at your raves."

"We did have some kinky after-parties," I say, regretting it immediately. His eyes expand to the limits of their sockets. He steps closer and leans forward. *Oh shit!*

"I bet when you were hyped up on Ecstasy and in mood-enhanced deliriums you probably licked a penis or two."

"Never!"

"Don't be ashamed. You should be proud of these things, and you should flaunt your penis to those who want to see it."

"Including you?"

"I would like to see him erect, saluting Queen Elizabeth, or anyone who wants to look at him." He tilts as if about to dive between my legs.

"I'd starve to death before I'd let you suck my dick," I say, pointing at him threateningly.

"OK, governor." He stands to attention and salutes.

Walking from the cell onto the balcony, I hear yelling. "Where's my fucking chair?" Stood outside of the rec room – at the end of the run on the bottom tier where inmates play cards and gamble – Ken swivels his head, scanning the yard. Someone points at a chair with wet orange trousers draped on it, drying in the sun. Ken grabs the trousers just as a well-built prisoner emerges from a cell.

"What the fuck do you think you're doing with my chair?" Ken roars.

"What the fuck do you think you're doing with my pants?"

"I'm taking my chair, motherfucker!"

The man marches towards Ken. In a tug-of-war, each grips the chair and trousers. Ken rips the chair from the man and throws it into the rec room. "Don't ever take my fucking chair!" Ken leaves for his cell. By the time he returns, the chair is back outside, and the man about to put his trousers on it. "What the fuck are you doing?" Ken yells, scowling.

"You don't own this chair! Fuck you!"

Ken marches to the man and drops his forearms on the crotch of the trousers, forcing the man's arms to twist and cross. He punches the man under the jaw, launching him into a wall. With blood gushing from his tongue, and struggling to stand, the man sways. Ken slams him against the wall, and he falls. "What you gonna do now, motherfucker?" The man tries to get up. Ken kicks him in the head. "Let's see your punk ass do something now!" Again, he tries to stand. Slam. Fall. "I'll beat your bitch ass, motherfucker!" Slam. Fall. Ken stomps. The man writhes, blood pouring from his nose.

At the beginning of my incarceration, violence was shocking, but I've seen so much, I'm desensitised – just like everyone else in here. Comparing this to what Ken did to me, I count my blessings. Prisoners pull Ken off. He grabs the chair, places it in the rec room and sits proudly, ready to play a card game called pinochle.

CHAPTER 20

In prison, mail is gold. Hours before mail call, prisoners hover around the guard station, gazing through the plexiglas at the stack of envelopes on the desk, hoping to spot their names as the guards sort through them. Some even recognise the handwriting, so they know who the letters are from. When large manila envelopes bearing stamps with Queen Elizabeth arrive, I'm informed by prisoners anxious to read the printouts of my blogs. Between my blog readers and my story occasionally being reported in the news, I receive regular mail. The letters raise my spirits. I feel connected with the outside.

Out of three letters today, I don't recognise the return address on one. To solve the mystery, I rip it open:

I am writing you because your story has touched my heart. I want to get to know you no matter what you done in the past. I am a 6 feet 1 inch tall single 26-year-old blonde from Nevada, and an attractive mom of two boys. If you want a good girl in public and a whore in the bedroom, I'm her. I am looking for a long-term thing and I hope you like kids ... I want more.

Touched, I smile and put it down. I reply to everyone, so I'm thinking of telling her that I do like kids but we won't be running off to Las Vegas to get married anytime soon as I'm banned for life from America by the Department of Homeland Security.

The next letter is from Jade, an American I met in 1999 in Tucson who has been studying criminology in England for three years. She loves fantasy art by Luis Royo, and her letters often include his calendar pages. Although we get along great, neither of us was single over the course of our friendship, so no romance developed. She's been writing since my arrest. Earlier on, she was upset that I'd been incarcerated just when I'd stopped dealing Ecstasy and was getting back to a normal life. In our correspondence, we often bear our souls. Although she has a boyfriend of three years, since my break-up with Claudia, her letters have contained an undertone of feeling and attachment. Opening the letter fills the cell with a sweet perfume. I close my eyes and inhale deeply. She says she's going to visit here for the first time. I grin at the cement-block wall. Still smiling, I'm reading the third letter when Two Tonys walks in.

"Just got a letter from my sis in London," I tell him. "She says I fall in love too easily, and that I need to stay single for at least a year when I get out, and to date various women. What's your take on love?" I sit down on the plastic chair.

"I'm almost 66," he says, sitting on the bottom bunk, "and as a sailor, I had a girl in every port. The only thing that cliché missed was that the girls wanted gratuities on the way out – and sometimes on the way in. Love is an entirely different animal. I can't compare love with running around full of testosterone, with my pecker hanging out, trying to bang everything in sight. If you wanna talk about love, I think I've been in love, but if I was, wouldn't I still be in love?"

"I think love is something you go in and out of."

"Who says?"

"From my own experience," I say.

"Were you ever in love?"

"I thought I was," I say.

"Therein lies the problem," he says. "You thought you was. You're not in love now are you?"

I think of Claudia. It's been several months since she ended things and my pain is fading. "No," I say.

"I'm saying when you feel true love, you never fall out of it. It overcomes sickness, desertion, death and separation. You don't quit loving her just 'cause she left you."

"But it fades," I say.

"Now we're going into the realm of time, which heals all wounds, or so the poets say. But does it?"

Not wanting to reignite my feelings for Claudia, I decide to cite my ex-wife. "In my case it did," I say, relishing the opportunity to share my feelings with Two Tonys. "I was deeply in love with my ex-wife, Amy, but those feelings are long gone. It's the same for most of my girlfriends, going all the way back to high school. Although, saying that, I still do have a certain level of affection for them."

"And mine, too. But when you were in love and the separation came, I bet nothing felt worse."

"That's so true," I say. "There were times when I couldn't eat or think straight, and lay in bed, depressed, day after day. There were times when the pain was so unbearable, I tried to deal with it by going on a drugs rampage. I didn't care if I lived or died. I overdosed on GHB, put my head through walls, just missing a nail below the plasterboard one time, and woke up caked in vomit, wondering how I'd got there and what I'd done. I was lucky my friends took care of me. Anything could have happened. I look back now and wonder why I behaved so insanely."

"I've been shot, stabbed, had my ass beat numerous times," Two Tonys says, "my parents have died, my siblings have died, and I've never felt any sense of complete aloneness or excruciating mental pain as when someone I loved left me. But love is strictly a remedy for loneliness."

"I disagree," I say. "I think it's about the joy of sharing your life with another person."

"Why?" he asks.

"If the chemistry's right, it feels great to get to know and care about someone, and to share the adventure of life. Over time you grow closer and the love gets stronger. Waking up next to her, that certain look in her eyes and smile she has for you, even her smell. You get a feeling of your life being complete when you're with the right woman."

"But you can't do any of that alone!" he says. "You do it 'cause you're lonely. You don't wanna look at the Grand Canyon by yourself. You don't wanna go to Niagara Falls and ride the Maid of the Mist by yourself. So, you fall in love and you have to pay a price. It's not free. It's expensive – in terms of emotions. Your mom and dad are in love, right?"

"Yes," I say. "They fell in love when they were in their late teens and have been together ever since."

"Sooner or later one is gonna have to pay one hell of a price when the other moves on. I'm talking about death. I saw my ol' man pay the price. It was pitiful. We've come to the age-old question: is it better to have loved and lost or not to have loved at all?"

"It's better to love, to take chances, to experience life to the fullest, including the ups and downs. Even though I went through some rough break-ups, I was also the happiest I've ever been in my life when I was in love. But I also attracted women who were materialistic like myself, and I got my just deserts."

"Were you doing drugs with them?" he asks.

"Most of them."

"You need to stay away from that, but what does your sis expect you to do? Go to St Paul's and find some cathedral chick? Get on the computer and fill out some Internet dating application? Mr Matchmaker, I like my coffee with two lumps of sugar. I like to wear argyle socks. I like soccer. I only pick my nose when nobody's home. Are you gonna rely on some devious teenage whizz-kid entrepreneur sending you an email, saying he's found you some chick who likes soccer and argyle socks? Of course not. I don't think you can fall in love like that. I think you become in love. In the movies, a guy sees a woman across a table and they fall in love. You meet a woman at a lonely point in your life and you become in love. Before you were arrested, were you ever on your own?"

"No. I've been in back-to-back relationships since I was a teenager, none of which lasted longer than three years."

"Then you don't know what being lonely means."

Not wanting to hold anything back from Two Tonys, I decide to put my feelings about Claudia on the table. "I do now. Claudia not visiting hurts. When she finished our relationship at the jail it was one of the loneliest times in my life. The sheer helplessness of being behind bars and unable to see her made it worse."

"When I was a fugitive on the run in Waikiki and Maui, living in a beautiful house on the slopes of an extinct volcano by myself, I was lonely. Even in here, it's nice to have a friend like you."

"Thanks. It's great to have you to speak to, too."

He smiles. "To be alone is a brutal thing."

"I hope love lasted longer for you than it did for me," I say.

"I don't think I ever loved any of my wives! I remember being in Vegas with my wife and new-born baby, looking at townhouses. And a red light was going on. I knew in my heart and soul: *Look, motherfucker, if you buy this townhouse, you're gonna end up sleeping in the back of your car, paying the mortgage, while she's in there with her next husband.* I saw a gangster one time in The Walls, who'd stand on a mound for hours on end, for six or seven Saturday Visitation days in a row, looking for his old lady's yellow Caddy to show up at the prison parking lot. And you know what? She never turned up. She gutted him while he was in the joint and he never regrouped. He was always a shell of a man after that."

"So what kind of a woman do you think I should look for?"

His brow crinkles. "She's got to be a caring and gentle person. Maybe a bit of an intellectual or at least a reader. But let me give you one piece of important advice: if she don't care for you, don't be afraid to get the fuck on down the ramp."

CHAPTER 21

The day of Jade's visit, I rise at dawn and bounce around the cell. As some chow items create bad breath, I check the breakfast schedule to avoid repelling Jade. Hot cereal. Biscuits. Grilled potatoes. Three ounces of cheddar cheese. *Toothpaste won't even disguise the cheese smell. I'll give it to Slingblade.* I gaze at a $1 mirror – a piece of tinfoil on cardboard. Holding my shaver, I ram the corner of its beard trimmer into each nostril to excavate my nose hairs. I wash my face and ears with a flannel – a piece of cloth ripped from an old towel. I check my clothes. Trousers pressed by George. New boxers bought for $3.50 and a new T-shirt for $5. Tube socks. White Riddell sneakers. *I'm set.* To prevent my orange outfit from getting sweaty, I sit in boxers, reading, aiming to get dressed when the visit is called.

Four hours later: "Dog eleven, you've got a visit, but it's headcount, so you're going to have to wait!"

Wow! She's here. My heart gallops as I dress. Unable to leave, I stew for thirty minutes like a sprinter at the block waiting for the pistol to fire. The door clicks open. *Go! Go! Go!* I bolt out and charge down the stairs, heckled by prisoners.

"Look at 007 run!" Bud yells. "Must be some fine-ass chick come to see him."

"Have a nice hand job!" Booga shouts. "And don't forget to save some jizz for me."

Swerving around Slingblade – with his hands in the garbage rummaging for food – I almost run into Ken, who tries to grab me, but I race away like a greyhound.

"Shall I place medical staff on standby in case you get too excited?" yells Officer Rivero, a baby-faced Hispanic.

"It might not be a bad idea," I say.

At Visitation, I arrive at the guard station and await clearance to join Jade, but the guards are busy dealing with other people. The large room contains chairs, circular tables, vending machines, a microwave oven, board games and a food smell that provokes instant hunger. Outdoors are picnic tables under a wooden roof surrounded by chain-link fence. I spot Jade at a table, her long curly raven hair in a half ponytail pulled back from a face that's a combination of American beauty and Irish mischief. She's wearing a black Polo shirt, trousers and flip-flops. She sees me and smiles. I wave. After five minutes, a guard takes my ID, cautions that the visit will be ended if any sexual contact is made and tells me to keep my hands on or above the table at all times.

Approaching Jade, I admire the freckles across her nose and cheeks spread out like a bird's wings, and her sparkly peachy-pink nails. She stands and we hug. "Thanks so much for coming," I say, sitting down.

"You're welcome," she says, blushing. "I was so nervous coming in. I had sweaty palms. I was late because I went to the wrong prison."

"The wrong prison!" I say, gazing at her big eyes.

"I went into the lobby of the federal prison and asked them where the state prison is. They said, 'It's a little further down the road.' Their lobby is nice and then I got to this shabby place. Parking, I was thinking, *I'm here. Oh my God! I can't believe I'm actually voluntarily going into a prison. Shaun better know how much he's worth it.* I had to stand up against a chain-link fence while the dog went by. I felt violated. Then some guy with a teardrop greeted me when I got to the building. What's the teardrop mean?" she asks loudly, staring at the tattoos on the prisoners.

Smiling, in a gentle voice I say, "You've got to stop looking at other tables, and please don't talk to anyone at other tables or else the guards will end our visit."

"Oh. Sorry."

"The teardrop means he's killed someone."

"Oh my God! And there I was just making conversation with a convicted killer."

I chuckle. "So out of all of the people I know, what made you start writing to me at the jail?"

"I really like writing letters and cards, and sending things through the post, so you're a great pen pal. Stuck in here, you're forced to write." She grins like a pixie. "What made me really sad was when you told me that absolutely no one other than your family and Claudia was contacting you when you were first arrested. But I didn't do it out of pity. I did it because I'm a loyal friend."

"How are things going with Theo?" I ask, referring to her Greek boyfriend.

She stiffens. "I'm unhappy because he's very controlling. I feel like I've given up everything for him. I moved to England. I do all his laundry, cleaning, cooking, grocery shopping and he won't even give me a ride down the road. He'd rather sit and watch sports and not do anything. I have to walk two-and-a-half miles to get home because my boyfriend won't give me a ride."

"Wow. That's insane," I say, shaking my head, outraged, feeling sorry for her but wondering why she puts up with him.

"I have to take a bus to the grocery store that takes up to fifty minutes, when it would take ten minutes in his car. I have to text or call him when I'm nearly done, and he meets me at the checkout, and pays for it. No woman should have to tolerate this."

Restraining myself from criticising, I reply, "I can't believe what I'm hearing!" A thought pops up – *If only I were free and she was with me* – that clashes with my feelings for Claudia. Guilt and my awareness of the difficulties of maintaining a prison relationship shake off the notion. *I don't want to put her through the same as Claudia.* But the more we sit and laugh and talk with intense chemistry – our eyes shining with something beyond friendship – I can't stop thinking what a great girlfriend she would make. *Stop it! She has a boyfriend. She's just a friend.* We discuss her goals and ambitions. She wants to do a master's and a Ph.D. She intends to return to America and maybe work for the FBI. When the visit ends, I stand and give her a quick kiss on the lips that sends an electrical charge through me.

After the strip search, I walk across the field, flustered. *Have I lost my mind? My sister's right about me falling in love too easily. What's wrong with me? Is this what happens after almost four years inside? But it feels great! What was the chance of us getting along like we did? But it's no good because I'm in here and she has a boyfriend. Everything is stacked against us.* As I approach my cell, the fantasies keep unfolding.

I walk in to George sniffing my boxers that he was supposed to have washed, and stroking his crotch. "What the fuck are you doing?" I yell, snatching them.

"Governor! Governor! I heard you traded me in for a little floozy?" he yells, distraught.

"Calm down, Jeeves. She's in no way, shape or form a floozy. She's a criminologist."

"Then let her come and do your fucking laundry, tidy up your room, wipe your royal ass and count your scrotal moles!"

I raise a hand. "Jeeves, slow down. What's come over you? You should be glad I had a nice visit."

"You've got female company in here: She-Ra and Mochalicious! What's wrong with them?" he asks, referring to two transsexuals, throwing his hands up.

"There's nothing wrong with them except they have penises."

"But neither of them want their penises, so, it's like not having one."

"Sit down, Jeeves. Relax," I say, pointing at the chair. "It's not the same." I sit on the bottom bunk.

He pulls the chair close to me, sits and leans forward. "So that's why you spent thirty minutes in the shower when you came back from Visitation!"

"I've not showered yet!"

"You must have whacked your tallywhacker! I bet you went to town on it, you little perv," he says, flicking his gaze from my face to my crotch.

"The visit wasn't about that."

"Puh-leeze! I bet you got a boner out there."

"I must admit when she leaned towards the vending machine, I couldn't help but admire her rear and—"

"That must have pumped up your Prince Harry!" he yells, shaking and raising his head. "What would the Queen Mum think if she knew you were running around Visitation with a trouser tent pitched?"

"The visit wasn't about sex, Jeeves. Jade is intelligent and great to talk to."

"If she's such a good conversationalist, why were you gawking at her ass?" He squints in disgust.

"'Cause I'm only human, and she's an attractive woman. You wouldn't understand, Jeeves, but for us heteros, being without a woman is one of the hardest parts of prison."

"You make me sick! What kind of woman likes pale, bald-headed, pernickety Englishmen?"

"I'm hurt, Jeeves," I say, shaking my head, faking sad eyes. "I thought you'd be happy for me, but instead you're trying to put my day down."

"I wish you all the happiness in the world, but I don't wanna be hearing about her all the time, or to find you staring into space, daydreaming about her ass, getting boners, pitching tents."

I smile. "I'll try not to. I certainly won't bring her up around you again."

"Actually, it's nice a person visited who floats your boat. I would never stand in the way of the governor's happiness."

George leaves. I start a letter to Jade, but Frankie bursts in. "Englandman, I decide who you kiss and who you don't kiss! This Jade has to have my approval. I wanna see a picture of her in a swimsuit."

"Are you jealous?"

"Why should I be?" He puts his hand on my shoulder. "I've got you real close."

I twist away and stand. "It was only a kiss. No need to be jealous," I say, grinning.

"I'm not a bad guy, Englandman. In fact, I'm a nice guy. I'm into open relationships. But you'd better recognise, I'm always the man in the relationship. If she's gonna visit you again, you need to start practising your kissing with me. I'm down to practise, Englandman. I'm game." His eyes rove over my body, widening, narrowing, lingering on parts men avoid. His lips alternate between a half kiss and a sleazy smile. His tongue slithers across his bottom lip. "*Mmm-mmmm.* You know this ain't my first rodeo. I know how to do these things. I'm easy to please. Besides, homey, I'm gonna practise on the back of your neck one of these days." He opens his arms and leans forward.

"In your dreams!" I fold away from him into a plane-crash position, hands on my head.

"Englandman, you know you're gonna give it up one of these days."

"Never." *Concentrating on Jade will keep my mind off resorting to sex in here.*

During the lockdown for headcount, I get the quiet I need to finish the letter to Jade:

I'm writing this shortly after the visit. I'm at an emotional peak, and I'll probably write stuff I'm embarrassed about later on, but I feel these thoughts need to be captured, so I'll get this written and in the mail before I change my mind.

Thanks so much for braving the prison to see me. You are great! We chatted and giggled like little kids in the midst of a prison-visitation room surrounded by poker-faced people, some of whom didn't even appear to be talking to one another. I feared this would happen. I hoped it would, and hoped it would not as I fear we can have no future, and it breaks my heart. You're an incredibly beautiful and intelligent woman. I'm electrified – still – just from being in your presence. The emotional explosion is oh so real. As you probably noticed, I couldn't take my eyes off your eyes. It was as if our eyes were speaking in a language of their own. You definitely have a magnetic pull over me. I'm left wondering what it all means. I'm stunned.

I hope these words of affection don't put you off me in any way. I'm not fishing for a relationship. There's just a massive battle raging in my soul. Seeing you was like winning a prize of four hours of bliss and happiness in this hell. I'm still drunk from that.

I am stubbornly loyal to those who have done extraordinary things for me like you, writing since my arrest and now visiting. No matter what happens for the rest of your life, I'll be there for you.

Let's keep things as they are – exactly as they are. And I'll try not to blow any gaskets in the meantime.

The next day, I debate whether to post the letter. *If she doesn't feel the same, I might put her off. You never get anywhere in life unless you take chances.* I send the letter and wait, my hopes high.

CHAPTER 22

"Give it me! I wannit!" yells She-Ra – a tall transsexual with long flowing blonde hair. In cut-off shorts, She-Ra's hips swing as she strides towards Bud, who is crouched over dirt, holding a scorpion by its tail.

"You can have it." Squinting at She-Ra, he drops the scorpion and leaves.

She-Ra picks the scorpion up by its tail and puts it on the back of *her* hand. As it stings one of *her* fingers, She-Ra laughs. *She* carries the scorpion towards fifty or so prisoners awaiting the opening of the chow hall, their orange clothes giving off a radioactive glow under the intense sun. Noticing the scorpion, the prisoners split in half.

"Look at She-Ra's crazy ass!"

"She's nuts!"

"What's wrong with you, She-Ra?"

"Wow! That's a big-ass scorpion!"

Curious, I stop walking the yard and follow She-Ra, who's been asking in a playful tone since Buckeye prison if I want to party. I've always been attracted to colourful characters, and She-Ra is off the scale. *Her* random outbursts soften the danger-ous atmosphere and get everybody laughing. *She* shares a cell with *her* boyfriend and protector, who's never lost a fight since I've been here. "Does it hurt where it stung?"

She-Ra cranes *her* neck and stares down through large com-passionate eyes that are different colours, one blue, one green, which add to *her* supernatural aura. "It hurts like a motherfucker, but it'll stop hurting soon." *She* raises the scorpion to chin height. In a motherly tone, *she* says, "I know you didn't mean to sting me like that. You're just scared. I still love you, little buddy. I just wanna take you home with me, but I can't." *She* squats and frees the scorpion. It hides under a rock on the outside of the fence.

"You wanna see Dog, my pet tarantula?" *she* asks, *her* thin brows arching encouragingly.

"OK," I say, captivated by *her* enthusiasm, but wary of the spider.

Inside *her* cell, *she* opens a cardboard box strewn with dirt and insect pieces. "That's Dog!" *she* says proudly, smiling at a spider so big I step back. From a bulbous body, Dog's eight hairy legs extend almost as wide as my hand. His beady eyes in the middle are surrounded by three more on each side. She-Ra coaxes Dog onto *her* hand. "Here, let me put Dog on your arm," *she* says politely as if offering a cup of tea.

"But he has fangs. Big ones!"

"Doggie won't bite you," *she* says, stepping towards me. "Don't be scared."

"Unlike you, She-Ra, I like to keep a safe distance from scorpions and spiders."

"Dog's very docile. He's beautiful. He's always pleasant and great to play with. I wash him and give him baths. I've put his fangs on my skin and pushed his head down. He wouldn't bite me. I wanted to see what being bitten felt like, but he wouldn't do it."

"Knowing my luck, I'll be the first he bites."

"Don't be such a chicken-ass, limey!" *she* says, shaking *her* head. *She* points at the chair. "Just sit there and let me put him on your hand."

Not wanting to disappoint *her*, I volunteer my left arm. My pulse rockets as *she* manipulates Dog onto my wrist. His gentle feet – blue-green iridescent pads – tickle my skin. Dog moves so slowly and lightly, I start to relax, enjoying the sensation of him plodding up my arm, dissolving my fear of tarantulas.

"What do you feed him?" I ask, flinching as Dog approaches my shoulder.

"Crickets. I keep him stuffed, so he won't want to make a meal out of me."

"What else do they eat?" Dog disappears onto my neck.

"Other tarantulas."

My head trembles as Dog tickles the back of my skull. "Other tarantulas! How does that work?" I clamp my eyes shut as Dog crawls over my nose.

"It's mostly females eating males during the mating season after they have sex. I'd be a homosexual if I was a tarantula. Hey, I am a homosexual!"

Hearing my name called for mail, I ask She-Ra to remove Dog. Hoping to receive a letter from Jade, I dash across the yard and slice through the ring of prisoners hovering around the control tower watching the guard lift each envelope from the pile, all of them stood still, rigid and tense, their eyes shining with expectancy like zoo animals at feeding time. Receiving only *The Wall Street Journal*, I walk away, dejected, wondering whether the outpouring in my letter has scared Jade away.

CHAPTER 23

I first spot Shannon walking to his cell on August 24, 2005, cursing a *Criminal and Addictive Thinking* workbook. I feel an immediate bond with him, almost the same height and build as me, but with a bit more weight, short-brown hair, friendly eyes, his arms covered in tattoos and scars. He tells me that he's 30 and is serving eleven-and-a-quarter years for stealing $800 worth of property that was returned to the victim by the police. His first suicide attempt was at 7. He stuck a knife into an electrical outlet. His mother abandoned him at 12, and the State of Arizona put him on Ritalin. The scars on his head are from shot glasses his dad smashed in drunken rages. He spent his adult life either trying to kill himself – he slashed his wrists, tried to shoot himself with his dad's revolver, ate glass and razor blades – or in jails, prisons and psychiatric units for committing petty crimes to get drugs. About two thirds of the prisoners have hepatitis C, and Shannon's has developed into stage three liver cirrhosis. The last time he was released, he was hoping to live a normal life. He filled out the forms to continue to receive the same psychiatric medication he received in prison, but the company in charge of the decision, ValueOptions, denied the application because his behaviour had been normal in prison – true, but because he was on medication. He reverted to petty crimes to finance drugs. He believes his long sentence was punishment for him refusing to sign a plea bargain and exercising his right to a trial, which cost the State of Arizona tens of thousands of dollars.

To qualify for hepatitis C treatment, he has to complete a therapeutic course. "I don't need to be in these stupid support groups and courses!" he yells, frowning, negativity pouring off him. "How do I know it's legit? The book says I sacrificed goals because drugs and crime were more exciting, but that's not true, because after a while, drugs and crime weren't exciting."

"I think it's true," I say calmly. "My ex-wife, Amy, was at the University of Arizona, and she wanted me to go there to do a master's degree. And what did I do? I sacrificed a positive goal to run round Phoenix doing drugs, which seemed more exciting. If you're going to reject the whole course because you disagree with the wording, don't you think you might not benefit from what it has to offer? People do drugs for excitement – especially in the beginning – and they do sacrifice family, education and work goals."

"But it's not because those goals aren't exciting!" He throws the book onto the dirt.

"Maybe not, but doing drugs and crime are more exciting. Why don't you stop fighting the book? It's not done anything wrong." I pick it up. "Why don't you focus on helping yourself instead of finding small objections to reject the whole course? What disorders have they diagnosed you with?"

"Bipolar. Antisocial. Borderline."

"Don't you want to get the most from this course to help you stay away from crime?"

"Sure. If it's legit info."

"You're familiar with the letter of the law and the spirit of the law, right?" I ask.

"Yeah."

"Then why don't you stop seeking problems with the letter of the course and go with the spirit of it?"

"I see what you're saying," he says, easing up. "But why should there be double meanings to things?"

"Your mind is creating double meanings. If you choose to get stuck on objections, you won't benefit."

"Maybe that's why I am who I am?"

"But don't you want to change that? Isn't that what this class is trying to achieve for you?"

"I need a course that'll teach me not to resist courses. Of course, I'd try and resist that course, too." We laugh.

"The bottom line is you've got to want to help yourself. It's got to come from your heart," I say, patting my chest.

"But it's a joke how they're doing courses here. It's supposed to be done in a live-in community with in-house counsellors where everybody's doing the same course."

"I'd like to do yoga in an air-conditioned fitness centre on a mat instead of the concrete floor. Do I quit because of these things? No. I adapt. With no mat, I do headstands off a deck shoe. Why don't you try and make the most of the course in spite of the environment?" I hold out the book.

He takes it and visits my cell in the evening. "I stand corrected. I'm a word quibbler. It says so in the book. I employed a diversion strategy – a way to divert attention rather than understand."

"It sounds like you're doing better."

"Yeah. I'm gonna give it a try, but can I come talk if I need help?"

"I'd be happy to help you." I smile. "You want to read my blog entries?" I hand him printouts of Jon's Jail Journal. He sits down and studies them, concentrating intensely, chuckling every so often. For hours, we discuss the blog-readers' comments.

"What's it cost to start a blog?" he asks.

"It's free. Anyone can start one, but you need outside help, and it's a lot of work. My parents do it for me, typing blogs up, printing them out, moderating comments, responding to emails. You want to start one?"

"Hell, yeah! I'd like to expose what's going on, especially the lack of medical treatment for guys with hep C, and maybe get a few pen pals along the way. Has the prison ever tried to stop you blogging?"

"A sergeant pulled me out and said the Deputy Warden had received complaints that I was using the real names of prisoners and guards. He'd been commissioned to read all of Jon's Jail Journal. He said it took him a whole weekend, he laughed his arse off because he thought the writing was funny, and it was interesting to see the prison through the eyes of a prisoner. He told the DW no real names were used. Besides, expressing ourselves like this is protected by freedom of speech under the First Amendment of the Constitution. The American Civil Liberties Union won a lawsuit against Arizona, enabling prisoners to write for the Internet."

The first state to ban prisoners from the Internet was Arizona – after the widow of a murder victim read an online pen-pal ad in which her husband's murderer described himself as a kindhearted lover of cats. A law passed in 2000 carried penalties for prisoners writing for the Internet. Privileges could be taken away and sentences lengthened. The American Civil Liberties Union challenged the law. In May 2003, Judge Earl Carroll declared the law unconstitutional, and no other state tried to follow suit. But even with the law repealed, any inmate writing openly runs the risk of retaliation from staff and prisoners – a risk that I live with as I feel it's important to let the world know what's going on.

"What about problems with prisoners?"

"I've had a few burst into my cell and say stuff like, 'Don't ever put anything on the Internet about me or else I'll smash you!' I always explain to them that whatever I put on the Internet is with the full consent of the prisoners I write about. They read everything, and usually a few changes are made before I mail the blogs to my parents."

A pen pal of mine, Sue – who discovered Jon's Jail Journal and wrote for advice after her son was arrested for accidentally killing his best friend in a drunk-driving accident – kindly offers to start a blog for Shannon called Persevering Prison Pages. Sue's son had been sentenced by a judge who was eventually convicted of taking cash for kids he had sentenced to private prisons, which the media reported as the kids for cash scandal.

In each other's cells and walking to the chow hall, Shannon and I discuss blogging endlessly, creating a special bond. He spends hours daily working on a lawsuit against the prison. He introduces me to the prisoner who guides him on legal issues.

Weird Al is short and grey and doesn't seem to belong here. He has big blue eyes and a broad smile. Before prison, he was a real-estate investor and flew planes.

In his cell, Weird Al describes how he ended up inside. "A failed suicide-by-cop attempt," he says, sat on the bottom bunk, holding a bag of nachos. "It's a coward's way of committing suicide. You get the police to shoot you because you don't have the nerve to do it yourself. My girlfriend had recently died from lung cancer, and over four or five months, I became increasingly depressed and crazy. I bought a book by Dr Death, Jack Kevorkian, and tried his method: a bottle of vodka, sleeping pills and a plastic bag over my head. It didn't work. I woke up in hospital after my neighbours called the police because I was knocking things over. The police found me with a garbage bag over my head, and after a visit to hospital, I was sent to the nuthouse. After staying in bed for a few days, an idea came to me: rob the bank and the police will come and shoot you. I slept great that night. I woke up happy and watched *Regis and Kathie Lee* because my bank didn't open until ten. I wrote a note: *I have a gun. I am here to rob you.* And I put, *This is not a joke*, so they'd know I was serious. I went to my local bank where I'd done business for eight years.

"When I walked inside there was a line of people. You'd think I would of gone straight to the front. If I was gonna get shot, why stand on manners? But I'm a polite person. I stood in the line, waited, wondering which teller I'd get. I got a familiar lady clerk. She said, 'Hello, Mr Miller. How are you today?' I gave her the note and her eyes went as big as saucers. I kept my left hand in my pocket, pretending I had a gun. She opened the drawer real quick. I grabbed the cash, put it in my pocket and walked outside to sit on the curb next to my car. I figured that the police would screech into the parking lot at any second and shoot me.

"But they didn't come right away. It took ten minutes. I was getting pissed off. I was expecting a big scene and an adrenaline rush. I wanted to go out like Bonnie and Clyde. They didn't screech into the parking lot. They calmly got out of their cars without their guns drawn. I thought, *Wait a minute. Something's not working here.* One cop said, 'Mr Miller, I'm telling you right now, we're not going to shoot you.' 'But I have a gun,' I told him. 'You don't have a gun.' A second cop said, 'What in the world's going on here?' 'I robbed the bank.' 'Yeah, we know that. But why? You have more money in the bank than you stole.' I had fifteen thousand in the bank, and I stole seventeen hundred.

"It got worse from there. They arrested me, and took me to Tempe Police Department. The FBI came down, took one look at me and said, 'Forget it. We don't want him. He's all yours.' I thought I had an original idea, but the police said it happens all the time. That people try to get the police to shoot them, usually in hostage situations. I thought, *Son of a bitch. I should have took a hostage.*"

"How much time did you get for that?" I ask, moved by his sad story.

"Three-and-a-half years."

Almost daily, the three of us sit in the chow hall. I warm to Weird Al's intelligence and deadpan humour. He's had hepatitis C for so long, he jokes that the first thing he's going to do when he gets released is bid on eBay for a Chinese liver. He's at an advanced stage of the Siddha Yoga philosophy course that I've been studying for a year. Daily, I look forward to our discussions that range from the pursuit of enlightenment to the latest scandal on the yard. With Shannon and Weird Al to talk to, I feel less lonely.

CHAPTER 24

A week after Jade's visit, I'm called for mail. At the control room, I shuffle through several letters. My eyes light up when I spot one from her. Fretting over whether she's receptive to my outpouring or has backed away, I dash to my cell and lock the door.

I can't describe in words how great it was to see you and spend time with you. As nerve-wracking as it all was in the beginning, it was worth any trouble. I could never have imagined how much I would miss you until I had to leave you behind there. I was overwhelmed with unexpected emotions upon my departure. I was incredibly happy and there was gleeful anticipation of seeing you again and determination to make it happen. I even sat there thinking that I need to go shopping to find the perfect top for the next visit. I couldn't stop thinking about you and wishing you were out and hanging out with me. I have missed you intensely since the visit.

Insanely happy, I want to leap up and down and run around the prison waving the letter. It's the best news I've had in years. My smile expands as I read:

It was odd how normal it felt to sit and chat with you. I felt like we weren't in prison at all. I am still amazed at how remarkable our conversation felt given the circumstances. I felt so at ease with you that the surroundings were only minutely noticed. I have not been in prison, nor deprived of attention from the opposite sex, and I still felt that way. It leads me to wonder if you would feel the same if you weren't in prison.

I don't know what's wrong with me. I am still in the process of analysing and sorting my thoughts and emotions. I apologize if this letter and its contents are somewhat incoherent and muddled up. I hope you understand the loop you have put me in. It seems appropriate to remind myself and you that although we could have some wicked times together and that there is definitely something there between us, it is something that shouldn't happen. I could easily list why you are so wrong for me, but maybe that is counterproductive. At the same time, I feel like you have lit a spark inside me.

I will undoubtedly be thinking of you and wanting you so much more than I should. Missing you loads! Hope you miss me too.

Take care of yourself,
     Jade
ps I was wearing Guess Perfume
pps This was sprayed with Hugo Boss Woman

Pondering her description of us as something that "shouldn't happen" – which I attribute to her boyfriend – takes the edge off my euphoria. But only for a minute. *He treats her so badly, I have no respect for him.* I reread the letter, soaking up every heartfelt sentence, my soul filling with joy to bursting point. I grab my notepad and frantically pen a response:

Your letter received this evening managed to add to the intoxication I've felt for several days – SEVERAL DAYS! – after your visit. I'm feeling it right now as I write this. The parallels in your letter and how I'm feeling are uncanny. Now a battle rages in our souls. You quite rightly pointed out that "us" shouldn't happen. So what happens now? Hmmm ... Here's what I think about us not happening: you could put me in the visitation room with 100 women, and I doubt I would have felt like I did with you. It was more than a deprivation reaction, and it's not just your beauty. It's your personality and intelligence and much more that I can't put into words. Also, look at what's happening at your end. Why are we suffering joint madness? I can find no reasons to break us up before we ever get together.

I can't stop looking at the pics you sent. I wanted to kiss you properly so bad, but I didn't want to be presumptuous in any way. I've been fantasizing about kissing you all week. I'm grateful you came, and I'm happy about the madness raging in my heart because it's added a new and unexpected dimension to my life. Every day this week when I went to mail call, my heart sank until this evening.

Although I'm physically unobtainable, you've obtained me mentally. I can't deny that. Perhaps unobtainability has a role to play in all this?

It's late, so I'm going to wrap this up. Have sweet dreams. I hope I'm fortunate enough to dream about you.

Each day drags until mail call. I feel the pain of the men hovering around the control room, pining for letters. If I wasn't so busy reading and writing, I'd join them in the hope of spotting one from Jade. It takes a week for another to arrive. Opening it, I'm excited but worried her feelings might have cooled. I'm relieved to discover that she feels the same. I can't believe my eyes when I read:

I broke up with Theo. I told him that the only thing keeping me in England is my studies. Because he's so controlling in our relationship, I only have a couple of friends there. He's never allowed me to bond with other people. He never wants me going out.

I know it's selfish, but it's a happy moment. I start counting down the days to her next visit.

CHAPTER 25

In Dr Owen's office, a mini metallic-blue boom box is playing a Mozart concerto. *Nice touch.* Dressed in a royal blue shirt and black trousers, he is about a decade older than Dr Austin. His brown hair, greying at the front and above the ears, is parted and flicked over at the fringe. His beard is white across a narrow chin, with traces of auburn above the mouth. His height and dark hypnotic eyes give him a commanding presence. Under the influence of his penetrating stare, I instinctively feel that he's observed things that most will never see. He greets me slowly, concisely, and introduces himself as a cognitive behaviourist and neuropsychologist. He begins by reading a homework assignment he sent after a brief chat we had at Medical:

Look at what you are doing with yoga, and how you use it to confront mental-health issues. How could you do better?

My emotions seem to depend on two things: activating events and my interpretation of those events. Mental yoga has taught me that I have the power to choose whether or not I become upset about events over which I have no control, and that activating events are necessary to restore karma. If something bad happens, I shouldn't mope. If I suffer a depression, I can wallow in self-pity and exacerbate the condition, or I can choose to recognize – and maybe even rejoice – that I'm restoring my karma.

This approach is similar to the Stoic philosophy taught by Epictetus, who pointed out that people are disturbed not by negative events, but by the negative views they take of them.

If I feel stressed, I use yogic breathing (full belly with active exhalation as opposed to shallow chest breathing) to calm down. Concentrating on breathing instead of a stressful event enables me to relax.

I am striving to do better by following Socrates' advice "know thyself." I've discovered that one of the causes of my wild partying may have been the need to self-medicate depression and anxiety problems I never knew existed until I received professional help after being arrested. I aim to do better by learning and putting that knowledge into practice.

"Do you ever feel you're a fish out of water?"

Surprised, I pause. "In here or before my arrest?"

"Whichever."

"Yes. Since I was a teenager."

"How was your family life?"

"Normal. Great parents who raised us well and a younger sister who I teased a lot. They encouraged our interests and further education."

"Why did you do drugs?"

"I don't know all the reasons. Maybe so I wouldn't feel like a fish out of water. My drug taking increased to dangerous levels during relationship breakdowns."

"Which drugs did you use?"

"Club drugs. Ecstasy. Special K. Speed."

"Do you know how Ecstasy works?"

"It raises serotonin levels in the brain, so you get a blissed-out feeling."

"Correct. How long have you been doing yoga?"

"Since my arrest. Almost four years now."

"Yoga systems have been around for over 5,000 years. Yoga can help the brain," he says. "The Dalai Lama had neuroscientists monitor the brain-wave activity of Buddhist monks, and they found increased gamma-wave activity. By exercising the brain through techniques such as yoga, we know that you can restructure certain parts of the brain."

"Neurogenesis?"

"Yes. The brain is malleable in small but significant ways. For example, a brain scan of a musician listening to music will show more biochemical activity in specific areas of the brain than when you or I listen to music. And that's what you've been doing with the yoga you've written about. What are you looking to get out of these therapy sessions?"

"I want to understand myself better. I don't want to go through life having runs of success followed by knocking everything down. If I can understand my past mistakes, I'll be less likely to repeat them."

"Yoga and psychotherapy should give you a growing awareness of yourself. You must learn to be happy in the present – with or without success. You certainly shouldn't be beating yourself up – whether consciously or subconsciously. I'm going to have you do a personality test this week, and we'll go from there. Do you have any questions?"

"Will you be here for the foreseeable future?"

"I'd like to say yes, but frankly, with DOC, you never know. DOC is like a glacier moving incredibly slowly, and every now and then a fragment chips off, and you never know if you'll be in that fragment." I leave impressed by his knowledge, and eager to analyse more of my thoughts and feelings with him.

CHAPTER 26

"Here's a motherfucking good read," Two Tonys says, entering my cell, waving a book.

"What is it?" I ask, writing at the desk.

"*One Day in the Life of Ivan Denisovich* by Solzhenitsyn."

I put my pen down. "I'm not even going to try to pronounce that." I stare at a thin worn-out copy.

"Check it out, and let me know what you think."

"I'll start it today," I say, keen to discuss it.

Ken barges in past Two Tonys, destroying my good mood. "We should be cellies when Long Island leaves." Long Island's release date – December 10, 2005 – is approaching. A few prisoners have asked to move in because I'm not a troublemaker.

"You're kidding, right?" I ask, recoiling.

"No. I'm serious. All you do is read and write. You don't smoke. You don't do dope. You don't get involved in drama. You'd be a good celly."

"You're too volatile," I say, my voice tense. "I need peace and quiet to write. You snap when you don't take your meds."

"Are you saying you don't wanna be my celly?" he asks, hands on hips.

"Listen, Ken, this ain't fucking happening," Two Tonys says, shaking his head.

Ken turns towards him with an expression that says, *What's it got to do with you?*

"Dating agencies make fortunes matching motherfuckers," Two Tonys says. "I'm looking at his profile and looking at your profile. No fucking match!" I breathe easier as he backs me up.

"What do you mean?" Ken asks, scowling.

"You're too fucking crude for him. He'll be writing and trying to do his fucking yoga, and you'll be farting and giggling all fucking day long. You're gonna have to forget about it."

"Says who?" Ken yells.

"It ain't gonna work, Ken. In the mornings, this guy runs a fucking office in his cell with all his blogging. How's he gonna do that with you taking a shit every five minutes?" I stifle laughter.

"I got to shit when I got to shit," Ken says, knitting his brow.

"And the last celly you had, all he did was read his fucking dictionary. He made Daniel Webster look like a fucking chump. And you almost choked that motherfucker to death, too!" Two Tonys says.

"So, who do you think would make a good celly for Ken?" I ask, hoping to steer him elsewhere.

"He can live with killers, robbers, psychos – any violent motherfuckers, but really he needs to be by his fucking self."

Ken shakes his head, turns and looms over me. "I'm moving into this room when your celly leaves!"

"I don't think so," I say, looking him squarely in the face, emboldened by the presence of Two Tonys.

"You ain't got no fucking choice!"

"Yes, I do. I have to sign the move slip."

"Not if your arm's broken." Ken smiles and nods, slowly, victoriously. He leaves.

"Don't sweat that piece of shit," Two Tonys says. "He ain't gonna do nothing. I'll fucking see to it."

I dread the return of Ken, but the next day, he shows up in a good mood after knocking someone's teeth out. Flaunting the wounds on his knuckles – skin hanging from bloody indentations at the top of thick fingers that look like hairy sausages – he doesn't mention moving in. I suspect he's trying to schmooze me. Frankie arrives to play chess. Nodding at Frankie, Ken says, "And I'm gonna knock this motherfucker's teeth out soon if he doesn't pay back the five dollars he owes me."

Frankie's eyes widen. "You're gonna do what?"

"We're gonna have problems if you don't pay me back that five bucks," Ken says, swelling his chest.

Frankie's jaw flexes. "You've got me fucked-up talking like that." His lips harden until they almost disappear. My breath speeds up as I brace to deal with mayhem.

"You better pay up, motherfucker."

"Why? What are you gonna do?" Frankie asks.

"You'll find out."

"Try me. You'll find out, motherfucker." Frankie steps forward. Almost chest to chest, they yell at each other.

"Hey, come on, guys." I spring off my chair, wedge myself in-between them, raise my hands, and rotate my torso to push them apart. "Let it go, guys. Frankie's just come here to play chess." For a few seconds, their eyes bulge, locked in a death stare, and my heart pumps louder.

"You better pay up, motherfucker, and England, I'm still moving into this cell!" Ken leaves.

"I'm gonna teach that motherfucker a lesson one of these days."

"Him moving in here is my worst nightmare," I say.

Frankie squats and slides the chess set from under the bottom bunk. "Englandman, are you ready to play strip chess? Whoever loses each game strips something off." We sit on the floor, cross-legged.

"No, Frankie," I say, rapidly setting up pieces. "I don't want to see you naked. You know I'm straight."

"That's not what She-Ra said." He gazes up from the board.

I laugh. "What did she say?"

"That you guys were making tortillas."

"Tortillas!"

"It's when you flip-flop. One guy goes and then the other guy goes. That's two guys making tortillas."

"She-Ra would never say that about me."

"Ha-ha. Gimme a little taste then."

"Of what?"

"Chicloso. You know, prison pussy."

"What's wrong with you? Aren't there enough cheetos for you in here?"

"There's never enough."

"Not getting any play?"

"Hell no! Justin offered to come in and get freaky, but he ain't all that. He told me he could suck a dick real good. He's too fucking old. He's lost all the rubber bands holding his asshole together, and he calls himself good. I'd have to kidney punch him a few times to tighten him up and then his asshole would look like this." He coils a forefinger to a thumb.

"What about George?"

"I was thinking about having him do my house cleaning. Naked."

"How much would you pay him?" I ask, amused.

"A twenty-five-cent soup, and he'll be lucky."

After chess, Frankie leaves, but quickly returns, panting. "Englandman, I need toilet paper. Two dudes just fought like bears in my neighbours' cell. I need to clean the blood up."

I grab a roll from under the bunk. "Here you go."

Twenty minutes later, the yard is locked-down. Guards – aware of the fight – go door to door checking knuckles.

CHAPTER 27

"I can't believe you broke up with him," I say in a sympathetic tone to Jade at Visitation, barely able to contain my excitement at seeing her.

"He was a jerk to me for way too long."

I want to ask what the break-up means for us, but don't want to come on too strong. "I don't blame you. How's he reacted?"

"He's kissing my ass now, calling all the time. But it's three years too late!" She rolls her eyes.

"Three years is a long time. You must be pretty sad."

"I am in a way, but also relieved. Did you get the calendar pages?" she asks, referring to pictures she mailed of women in gothic settings by Luis Royo.

"Oh, yes," I say, smiling. "Thanks."

"I love dark artwork, the sensual undertone. Art should be provocative. I've always liked books about vampires and darker fantasies and storylines."

"You've got that vampire spirit like me."

We laugh. "Nosferatu!" she shrieks, referring to my portrait on the front page of the *Phoenix New Times*. "I've watched vampire stuff since I was a child. By eighth grade, I was reading Anne Rice, which is full of all kinds of indiscretions and complex dark relationships."

"So, does my dark side appeal to you?"

"It does. But it's not your dark side that I love. I think that you're very intelligent. You and I can converse on a level that I can converse with very few others, ever, in my entire life. The banter between us creates a unique type of chemistry."

"I've noticed that about us," I say, grinning, soaking up her energy, her laughter, the warmth in her eyes, feeling cherished and secure.

"I find you attractive, but it's definitely – and it may manifest itself in a physical form – a mental and intellectual level that we identify with each other on."

"I agree," I say, imagining leaning over the table to give her a kiss. "I'll never forget when I first saw your pale mischievous Irish-looking face, and I said you look half-Irish terrorist."

We laugh. "You called me a terrorist for a really long time."

"Why don't we walk along Lovers' Lane," I say, hoping to kiss her outside. "We can hold hands around the picnic tables."

Outdoors, I take her hand and intertwine our fingers, gripping her tenderly, the physical connection making me feel closer, causing a shiver of delight. I'm proud that the heads of prisoners and guards are turning towards her, yet frustrated because the attention makes kissing impossible. We walk several laps until people aren't staring at us. I suggest we sit at one of the picnic tables furthest from the building. Below the table, our legs touch, starting ripples of pleasure that go to my head and combine with her scent, looks, eyes, freckles and lips to multiply my urge to kiss her, to abandon all caution and run the risk of disciplinary sanctions and the visit being cancelled. Kissing requires the guards to be distracted and the security camera to be pointing elsewhere. I scan the area. The three guards seem to be looking everywhere at once, robotically. The camera is moving this way and that. I sigh. But eventually, the guards approach a table and accuse a prisoner of inserting drugs into his anus.

"We should kiss now while they're busy," I say, rubbing my knee into her inner thigh.

"I ain't keystered shit!" the accused prisoner yells.

"But they'll end the visit!" Jade says, pressing her leg against mine, provoking semi-arousal.

"You need to come with us to a dry cell!" a guard yells – a dry cell holds a prisoner under observation until he excretes the drugs.

"People get away with it all the time," I say, heating up. Jade stares with the same reluctance as the accused prisoner. "It's now or never," I say, leaning forward. Two guards grab the prisoner.

"Come on," I say. "Let's go for it now while he's getting dragged out."

"Fuck you guys!" the prisoner yells.

"OK." Jade starts to lean …

"Attwood!" yells a sergeant I hadn't noticed, stood against a wall far from my side, slightly behind us. "Come here!"

"Shit," I say. Jade's face fills with fear. The visitors and prisoners turn to watch us. Embarrassed, I stand and approach him.

"How about I write you up and end your visit, Attwood?" he barks, scowling.

"What for?" I ask, shocked.

"What's going on under that table?" he asks.

"Nothing," I say, assuming he thinks I'm smuggling drugs.

"Why's your leg touching hers so much?"

"I didn't know it was."

"Don't lie or I'll end your visit!"

"OK. Sorry. We'll go back inside."

"I'm warning you verbally this time, Attwood. Any more physical contact and your visit will be ended. Resume your visit."

Back in the building, I say to Jade, "He must have X-ray vision to have noticed our legs like that."

"We'd better stick to the rules, then," she says, shook up.

Now's the perfect time to bring out the surprise. "I've got something for you. I'm going to go get it."

"What is it?" she asks, her eyes brightening.

"You'll see." At the guard station, I request what I pre-ordered. A trustie fetches a bouquet – flowers grown in a garden tended by prisoners, including She-Ra. African daisies. Bachelor's buttons. Xenias. A long dwarf sunflower. Admiring the vivid colours, sniffing the petals, Jade blushes and beams.

When the visit ends, we stand. Commotion erupts as the visitors hug and say goodbye. Noticing plenty of prolonged kissing, I hug Jade. I kiss her and she responds. A charge runs through me. I want to close my eyes and get lost in the kiss, but I have to observe the room to ensure we're shielded by the flow of visitors obstructing the view of the guards. The warmth of her lips and their taste soar my spirit to the day's high.

In my cell, I write to my mum, telling her that Jade has all of the characteristics I could ever want in a woman. I write to Jade:

Developing feelings for someone in prison is a road I swore not to go down since the Claudia heartbreak. With that said, I must admit I'm falling in love with you. It's something I didn't expect to overwhelm me as much as it's doing right now. I've got all the classic symptoms. Thoughts of you make me happier than anything. Your pics soothe me, and cause me to smile. When people here ask who the "gorgeous chick" at Visitation was, I feel so proud. Reading your mail gives me a warm and fuzzy feeling.

I don't believe this crap about reacting to you because I haven't been around a woman in a while. Sparks were flying between us like I've never felt before. Things we both wrote parallel how we each feel with pinpoint accuracy, and I'm still gob-struck. At the visit, I wanted to convey the intensity I felt for you, but I couldn't do it. I was afraid, and maybe too proud. It seems I'm much better at writing these things down than having the balls to say them to your face. Perhaps that will come if I'm lucky enough to see you here again.

Your visit changed my world. Things for me now can't be exactly as they were before. I'm not going to fight how I feel for you. I'm just going to let it happen come what may.

A few days later, I receive a response:

I put your flowers in water as soon as I got home. They are still sitting next to my bed. I even took some pics of them so they will never be forgotten. I cannot wait for you to get out of prison and see you in the outside world. I am looking forward to our future conversation and banter. Hopefully your prison exit is sooner rather than later. I miss you and will be waiting for you on the outside. Until then, keep safe and stay healthy.

Take care of yourself,

Jade

CHAPTER 28

The most terrifying thing about prison is rape. Although I've avoided it, I've met victims and heard horror stories. There are times – such as when Bud's associates were joking about raping me – that I felt particularly unsafe. Trying to gain knowledge in the hope of avoiding it, I ask She-Ra in my cell, "Why do prisoners rape prisoners?"

"Two reasons: sexual desire to perform the act and anger," *she* says in a sombre tone, sat on the bottom bunk.

"In what proportion?" I ask, sat on a chair.

"I'd say more than half are out of anger or hatred."

"Hatred of themselves or their victims?" I ask.

"Probably both. Taking anger at themselves out on their victims."

"Do you know anyone who was raped in prison?"

"Yes."

"Who was it?"

"Me."

"Oh my God, She-Ra! I'm so sorry."

"It was a long time ago," *she* says, *her* expression blank. "I'd like you to post what I'm about to tell you to Jon's Jail Journal, so that public awareness is raised about prison rape."

"Are you sure?"

"Yes."

"OK, but feel free to stop at any time."

"The first time was a gang rape. The Aryan Brotherhood beat the shit out of me. It was definitely motivated by anger. They stuffed things inside my body, beat me until I was unconscious, raped me while I was unconscious."

"Stuffed things inside your body!" I say, grimacing.

"Yes, a broomstick," *she* says, retracting *her* feet to lock *her* ankles.

I press my legs together. "If you were unconscious, how did you know they were raping and sticking things inside you?" I ask, my heels jerking up and down.

"When I had to excrete afterwards, I could tell by what came out."

I gag. Stunned, I exhale loudly, shake my head and search *her* eyes. Horrified, I'm thankful for not experiencing anything like that.

She-Ra nods, *her* face grey.

"Should we continue?" I ask gently.

"Yes."

"What did you do after being raped?" I almost whisper.

"I sat in my cell for two weeks waiting for the physical scars to go," *she* says, clasping *her* thighs. "I got moved to another yard where the same thing happened. They beat the shit out of me, raped me, and used me afterwards as a sex toy, a prostitute, a punk. There's no recourse, no one to talk to. Someone who's raped can't go to Admin or they'll throw you in the hole for months or years in a dungeon, and they'll say it's for your own protection. A person can do absolutely nothing other than kill the perpetrators. There's no way to have someone prosecuted. The victim is labelled a rat and a punk and considered less than human."

"The guards won't help you?"

"You can't snitch. If you snitch, you get killed. Besides, who would believe you? Even Admin won't believe you. They think you're playing games."

"Did you think about killing the people who did this to you?" I ask, imagining I would at least die trying.

Staring at the floor, rubbing *her* neck, *she* says, "I thought about killing myself first. I wanted to. I still do sometimes." *She* raises a hand and wipes away tears. *She* presses *her* eyelids shut. *Her* head and shoulders collapse. *She* sobs.

With tears welling, I join and hug She-Ra tightly. *She* puts *her* arms around me and rests *her* head on my shoulder. We sit in silence. Feeling *her* pain, I never imagined I would ever share such a tender moment with anyone in prison. I appreciate *her* telling me something so personal. It speaks volumes about how much *she* values our friendship. I'm starting to believe that I was meant to meet certain people such as She-Ra and Two Tonys, but I don't know where it's heading. I want to alleviate their suffering, but all I can do in here is offer my friendship and write their stories. *When I get out, I'll be able to help them in other ways.*

Unable to talk, She-Ra leaves, but returns the next day. "I've got more to tell you."

"Are you sure?" I ask.

"Yes. I'm OK now."

She sits on the bottom bunk. "When prisoners are being used for sexual purposes they're told to appear like men – to grow moustaches, to shave their heads or to be clean-cut – so nobody believes that so-and-so is using them for sex. The belief that we're treated like females is a false one. Looking how you're told to look is denying who and what you are."

"Does this happen mostly to youngsters?"

"Yes, it does. But it can happen to anybody. I've seen it happen to big bad dudes, skinny, even the ugliest in the world. People who come to prison who aren't street smart, who don't understand the mentality of the ghetto life, they get preyed on the most."

"How did you stop it?"

"I took the abuse for as long as I could, and then I started fighting. I won most of the fights. When I stood up and told them that I didn't care about getting killed, it stopped. You've got to be ruthless. People who don't stand up for themselves get killed."

"You knew people who got killed?"

"Yes, I had a friend, a youngster on drug charges, who had no one looking out for him, and no family support. The Aryan Brotherhood held him down, took turns raping him, then cut his head off with a shovel, which isn't easy and takes some time."

"Are you fucking serious?" I ask, clasping my head.

"When his head was finally off, they picked it up, and took it, and positioned it in an area of the prison where the rival gangs would see it to make the point that they were the most violent and ruthless gang. I also had a friend who was gang-raped, then they took a light bulb, shoved it in his ass, and smashed it while it was in there. He committed suicide afterwards."

For the rest of the day – haunted by She-Ra's story – I feel sick. Wondering how *she* deals with it overwhelms my mind. I write a blog in the hope of raising awareness of prison rape. *Perhaps sharing such a terrible experience in the hope of helping others will be therapeutic for She-Ra.*

The next day, walking to the chow hall, I'm grabbed from behind. I spin around to Bud. "What're you doing messing around with She-Ra in your cell?" he asks.

Why's Bud spying on me? "What're you talking about?"

"I saw you hugging *her*. You'd better be careful. Your new best friend's an extremely dangerous homosexual. She-Ra's served twenty years for kidnapping and violent crimes. They won't let *her* out 'cause *she's* classed as a sociopath."

That's rich coming from you. "She-Ra's been one of the nicest to me in here. We're writing about prison rape."

"I bet she didn't tell you how she stopped it."

"Yes, she did. She started fighting back."

Bud rolls his eyes. "There's more to it than that."

"Like what?"

"If I tell you, and you tell She-Ra, I'm gonna have to smash you, 007."

"Look, Bud, I don't want any problems with you. I won't say shit to anyone."

"OK. If you don't think She-Ra's dangerous, check this out. *She* was reading a medical book back then. Them queens all study that shit, so they can slice their nuts off without killing themselves, so they can be more like women. Anyway, studying anatomy gave *her* an idea." Scrutinising my face, Bud steps closer and intensifies his gaze. "The next two times the Aryan Brotherhood came to rape She-Ra, the first one to put his hand on *her*, She-Ra plucked his eyeball out, so it was dangling from the socket by the optic nerve." Slamming my eyes shut, I almost fall over with shock. "Can you imagine seeing someone with an eyeball dangling out? Even with the help of a doctor, putting the eyeball back in ain't easy either. They might never see properly again or even be blind. It can cause a brain haemorrhage or the fluid cushioning the brain might leak out through the hole."

CHAPTER 29

"What the fuck's your problem, you old motherfucker, telling me I can't move in with England?" The question, swung like a battle-axe by Ken, halts the conversation on the yard between Two Tonys and some Mexican Americans, including Frankie, who I'm talking to.

"Don't fuck with me," Two Tonys says, shifting to face Ken. "I kill Californians, motherfucker."

"Why don't you find someone else to move in with?" I ask, strengthened by the presence of Two Tonys and Frankie.

"Shut the fuck up, England!" Ken swaggers over from a gang of whites. My heart bounces. I brace, resolved to follow Two Tonys' advice – retaliate to whatever he does. If I don't respond – "show heart" – then I'll lose respect. Ken closes in, raises his hands and shoves my shoulder. I push him back. He punches my body. With my chest absorbing the blow, I reel backwards. Rather than repeat my earlier mistake of remaining too close to him, I spring forward, roundhouse-kick him in the thigh and back off. He looks amused and surprised.

"Hey, Ken," Two Tonys says casually. "Have you looked under your nose lately?"

"No. Why?" Ken asks, touching his mouth as if something is wrong. Grateful for Two Tonys' interruption, I study Ken.

"Your moustache looks like a broom that you haven't washed since you've been down. I can see nits in it and lice crawling round your fucking head." Everyone laughs.

Ken marches and snatches the ID off Two Tonys' chest – a piece of plastic we must wear to the chow hall, clipped to our shirts showing our photo, name and DOC number – and squeezes it in his hand. Enraged by the sight of his ID getting bent in half,

Two Tonys steps forward, hitches a leg behind Ken and pushes his shoulders. Ken, caught off guard, stood on a curb, loses his footing. He falls. His heavy body slams against the ground. He stays down, too startled to speak, too stunned to rise. Amazed, we gaze in disbelief at Ken.

"Why'd you grab my ID? I warned you never to lay hands on me, motherfucker!" Two Tonys snatches his own glasses from his face, throws them down and raises his fists. "I'll kill you, motherfucker!"

"I told you a long time ago that I'd never hurt you," Ken says, getting up. "Well, fuck all that. Come on, motherfucker! Get some of this, old man!"

"Come on, motherfucker!" Two Tonys says, rotating his fists as if deciding which one to throw. "Let's do this. I ain't scared of going to the hole. I've been in every hole in Arizona's state prisons." The whites pull Ken away. I help the Mexican Americans extract Two Tonys. I go with Two Tonys to his cell. "I'm gonna get a shank and kill that motherfucker. I know what he's up to. He wants to get close to me, so he can give me a sucker punch …" It takes a while for him to calm down. "You know what though? Putting him down like that made me think about the sweetness of life."

"What do you mean?" I ask.

"There's people my age driving around Sun City in fucking golf carts right now, and here I am – 65 years old – putting down a 35-year-old, a big motherfucker. That makes me feel fucking great."

"I'm glad you put him in check."

"The motherfucker had it coming."

Reading the latest blog printouts, Two Tonys smiles at the record number of comments and questions about his Mafia life, which we discuss at length. With a contemplative sparkle in his eyes, he dictates his responses. I read them aloud, and he adjusts them until satisfied. Although impressed with blogging, he wants us to start on his life story. Feeling honoured, I tell him that I'd love to do it. We go over the logistics. It'll take months. Daily, I'll have to sneak into his cell to write for hours. Cell visiting isn't allowed, but we generally get away with short visits as there are too few guards to enforce the rule. Prisoners can stand at cell doorways and talk, but setting up shop in Two Tonys' cell risks getting a disciplinary ticket, which could affect my release. He says he'll station prisoners outside who'll warn us about approaching guards.

The next day, I take a pad and pen to his cell. He says his biography is going to include some unsolved murders. With no statute of limitations on murder, he doesn't want anything I write that could be used against him legally to come to the attention of the guards. He's not worried about getting time added to his 141-year sentence, but about being moved from Arizona for a murder trial. I agree to write in a scrawl that only I can understand, and to mail the manuscript to England via the British Embassy, so it's classified as legal mail, which the guards can't open. I show him my scrawl, and he seems satisfied. As an added precaution for certain murders, he requests that I write that someone other than him did it, but verbally he'll say the truth and I can add that in later on. I sit fascinated, writing rapidly, while he describes his upbringing in Detroit, and how his first dealings with the Mafia involved shining their shoes. Every time a guard does a security walk, I have to rush outside. I get caught in the cell a few times but we manage to schmooze my way out of a ticket.

He gets a stream of visitors throughout the day, all paying respect, during which the writing halts. Being present while they chat gives a clearer picture of how popular he is. He tells his visitors that I'm his official biographer, a role I'm proud to concede. I feel some of the respect they harbour for him rubbing off on me in my new role. I appreciate him sharing his friends and raising my stature on the yard. I don't judge him for what he's done, but rather through the lens of his kindness to me.

Even though he has the court paperwork to prove it, it's difficult to imagine him murdering someone. I trust him so much,

I ask him how he'd murder me right now. Without hesitating, he grabs a heating filament, wraps the electrical cord around my neck and squeezes it. As I was expecting a verbal response, I'm stunned. Confident he's not going to kill me, I don't resist. My breath is cut off. After holding my breath for a bit, I gasp and start to panic. He squeezes just long enough for me to regret asking the question. He releases it as expertly as he applied it and grins. Shook up, panting, massaging my throat, I manage to smile. He reveals that there are people he's whacked in Arizona who have associates in the prison system, so he's in a perpetual state of readiness to kill anyone who attempts to snuff him out in his cell. Spending so much time with him and listening to things that I imagine he's never shared before brings us even closer together.

CHAPTER 30

In my room, I'm in a headstand, eyes closed, when I sense a presence at the doorway. Used to people sneaking up on me while I'm in a headstand – Ken managed to push me over a few times, and Booga almost pulled my trousers off – I open my eyes to Slingblade a few feet away, breathing heavily, his nostrils dilating, his eyes roaming for food. A sharp stink I grew familiar with living next door to him – sweat laced with chemicals from high dosages of psychiatric medication – saturates the cell.

I drop down and stand up. "How can I help you?" I ask, trying to sound calm even though I'm scared.

"Peanut butter?" he grunts.

Feeding Slingblade will guarantee his return, but wanting to understand and open dialogue with him, I reply, "Sorry, I'm all out. I've got crackers though." Anticipation flickers in his eyes. I crouch and rummage under the bottom bunk. He draws near – his spherical physique monopolising the limited space – until I can feel breath first walking up my back, neck and head, and then enveloping my body. *He's close enough to crush the life from me.* Tension fans out from my solar plexus. My lower regions churn. My scalp rings with sweat. Trembling, I grab the crackers and stand. His face is blank. Gazing at his big brown bloodshot eyes, I sense his trauma. I try to imagine what he went through in Vietnam and twenty-five years in prison, and how it's affected him. Although I want to help him, his proximity is overwhelming. Knowing he could have a flashback at any second and lash out, I want him at a safe distance, and for my heartbeat to slow down and things to return to normal. I hold out the crackers. For a few seconds, his face twitches. He stares as if trying to communicate, but no words emerge. He snatches the crackers, grunts and leaves.

Exhaling loudly, I towel sweat from my face. I rush to the doorway and watch him shove crackers in his mouth, the inmates on the balcony scurrying out of his way as if a rhino is coming at them.

As expected, he returns every few days. Each visit, I grow slightly less afraid. Before giving him food, I ask questions. Most of his answers are senseless. Over time, I learn that he's eligible for parole, but has no one to help him process his release. Weird Al says that Slingblade needs an address to be released to. I put a request on the Internet for help from an organisation that could facilitate his release, but no one responds.

CHAPTER 31

George enters my cell, topless, the grey hair on his chest receding towards his gut. "I still think you're bisexual."

"Why do you say that?" I ask, resting a book on my bunk.

"'Cause in the past you willingly experimented with drugs, which leads you down the same path as experimenting with sex."

"Drugs just made me hornier in a heterosexual way." Wearing boxers, I drop down from the top bunk face forward, so he can't grab my rear. I put shower sandals on and sit on a chair. She-Ra walks in, frowning at George.

"You're experimental," George says, "but you're afraid your bisexuality will diminish your manhood."

"Being experimental doesn't make him bisexual," She-Ra says, rolling *her* eyes.

"George is trying to convince me that I'm bisexual, and that receiving oral sex from him is in my best interest."

"Huh! I know Shaun's not bisexual 'cause he doesn't hit on me," *she* says. "Everyone else hits on me. George hit on me once. He offered to buy my penis."

"George, is that true?" I ask in a stern tone. Silence. "She-Ra, how much did he offer you?"

"Four-hundred dollars."

"Four-hundred! George, that's twice what you offered me!" I yell. "You've gone and made me feel all cheap now!"

George cringes. "I know, but I wouldn't have paid that. I was only trying to get She-Ra enticed."

"You dirty dog!" I yell.

"Slut!" She-Ra shouts.

George sweeps his eyes up and down She-Ra, who squints, folds *her* arms and thins *her* lips as if he isn't worth a second thought. George lunges and tries to wrap his arms around She-Ra, whose long limbs spring open and entangle him like a spider grabbing a fly. He strains to free himself, but *she* shoves him towards the doorway and ejects him onto the balcony. "Get out of here and never come back, you hairy-ass human tarantula!" He scurries across the yard.

I pick up blogs I wrote about *her* antics in the chow hall that made everyone laugh. "You're getting as many comments as Two Tonys now."

She reads them and asks to take them to show *her* boyfriend. Smiling, *she* pats *her* hands excitedly on *her* lap. "So, what's the deal with you and Jade?"

Dreading the question, I bow my head. "It's been a month since the last visit, and I still haven't heard from her." Shortly after I saw her, Jade went to stay with her mother in Wisconsin. She was going to write with her new address. As I haven't heard from her, I have nowhere to mail letters to, so our correspondence has ceased. Not knowing how she feels is making me miserable and moody. Thirty mail calls in a row, I've felt disappointment and heartache.

"Why's that?"

Maybe she lost interest or found someone else. "I don't know. She's probably busy," I say, staring at the floor. "Prison relationships never last. I was dumb for getting overemotional. I appreciate that she went out of her way to visit. I should know better than to have high expectations while I'm stuck in here." Talking about her increases my sadness.

"Well, I've got a new *girl* for you to meet on the yard!"

"Who?"

"My friend, Gina, just arrived. And does *she* have a story for you!"

"Like what?" I ask, sitting up straight, hoping the story takes my mind off Jade.

"Outside of prison, Gina wanted to have a vagina, but they wouldn't give *her* a sex-change op because *she's* a felon. To get the op, *she* had to wait seven years without committing a crime. *She* ended up back in prison, so *she* cut her nuts off and flushed them down the toilet."

"Ouch!" I yell, curling forward, pressing my knees together. "How on earth did *she* manage that in a cell?"

"Give me a pen and paper." I pass them to *her*. "*She* cut open *her* sack like this." *She* draws a circle with a vertical line down one side. "Then *she* severed *her* vas deferens with a razor blade."

"What's the vas deferens?"

"It's a vein, nerves and a tube that carries the sperm. It's attached to the balls. *She* cut that, popped *her* nuts out and flushed them."

Shuddering, I arch forward and claw my thighs. "So, the vas deferens is a branch holding the nuts in the sack?"

"Yes. The branch was severed. The nuts were free. Then *she* used a cigarette lighter to cauterise the wound and a sewing needle and thread from inmate hobbycraft to stitch *herself* up."

"Holy shit!"

"But *she* got caught because the wound got infected. *She* was wheeled out on a stretcher all strapped down."

"Was *she* happy with the end result?"

"Kind of. *She* said *she* lost a lot of weight, and now the nuts are gone *she* overheats a lot."

"What about *her* penis? Does *she* still have one?"

"Yeah, and *she* still gets erections. *She* gets excited sucking someone's penis or taking it in the butt. *She* doesn't like erections though. The sack's shrunk quite a bit, and *she* gets sensations where the sack's at, but *she'd* be much happier with a vagina."

"Do you want to have a vagina, She-Ra?"

She-Ra jumps up. "We're all gonna get vaginas! Fuck it! I wanna get a vagina on my right hand, that way my fingers won't get tired. I'll be able to fuck someone with my hand and tickle their balls at the same time." *She* bumps my shoulder with *her* hip, licks *her* armpit and sits down. "I don't really wanna vagina, but I do believe that if someone wants to change themselves or their lifestyle, and that will make them a better member of society, they should be free to choose those changes."

"How do they make the penis into a vagina?"

"They slice the penis in half and fold it into the body."

I cringe. "Do they still get enjoyment afterwards?"

"The incoming penis would rub against the prostate, and they get the same pleasure as getting fucked in the ass, but just from the other side."

"Wow!"

"To make it look like a vagina, they take the urinary tract, and they place it to look like a clit, and it works the same way."

"But the clit contains nerve endings," I say.

"And there's nerves in the prostate."

"That cause jollies?" I ask, my mind boggled.

"Yes! Anyway, let's go meet Gina."

"Am I allowed to ask her stuff?" Enthusiastic, I'm wary of coming across as impolite.

"I already told Gina about your blogging, and *she* doesn't mind sharing *her* story. You can ask *her* whatever you want."

I follow She-Ra across the yard. Spotting Gina, I can't believe my eyes. *She* looks like a woman – a short thin attractive Italian one. I search for signs of masculinity – everything is feminine. *Her* small head, *her* heart-shaped face and thin chin. Long lustrous black hair. Narrow olive-coloured hands and long nails polished dark red. Sculpted brows. Eyeliner tattooed around large eyes the colour of lychee stones. Full sensuous lips tattooed red. A round behind narrowing towards a tiny waist. Toned hairless legs in cut-off shorts. *She* even smells of perfume.

"Meet Gina," She-Ra says.

"Gina, how do you do?" I ask, smiling.

"Very well," Gina says in a female voice. While *she* bats *her* long eyelashes and smiles flirtatiously, I'm surprised to feel the stir of sexual excitement I feel around an attractive woman. "I need to tell you I'm an Anglophile," Gina says.

If this was a woman, I'd have it made. "So, you like all things

English," I say, without giving it much thought, realising I'm flirting.

"Yes. And your accent is making me feel like I'm talking to King George III in his coronation robes."

Oh boy! I'm in trouble. "The pleasure is mutual," I say, responding as if on autopilot – a situation so unfamiliar and bizarre, I don't know where it's heading. "What made you become an Anglophile?"

"When I first saw a drawing of George III in his coronation garb, I was hooked. The crown, the robe – *ooh la la!*" Gina rolls *her* eyes. "I knew I was an Anglo at heart, and tracing my family tree revealed that England is the home of my ancestors. Another exposure was when they taught us about the colonies and independence. From the start, I've loved America, but it's England that I fell in love with."

With Gina feeding all of the right signals to my eyes, ears and nose, I'm unable to stop my thoughts: *I'd only be putting it in* her *mouth and* she *looks like a woman …* Reminding myself *she* has a penis, I blush.

"OK!" She-Ra yells. "Now tell him why you cut your nuts off."

"Ovaries – I like to call them," Gina says in a posh voice. "I cut off my ovaries to feminise myself. Testosterone is the sex hormone responsible for the production and maintenance of pubescent male characteristics such as body hair, having a deep voice and the major contributing factor to male pattern baldness."

"Are you happy with the results?" I ask.

"Yes. Since removing my ovaries – or, as my beloved puts it …"

Beloved. She's taken. Damn! I wonder who the lucky guy is that's getting some almost-female action as opposed to nothing. I can't believe I feel a pang of jealousy. I wonder whether I'm turning gay. I'm unable to stop the sexual charge that's heating me up from Gina's proximity and the way *her* eyes are gazing so invitingly.

"… my underies – my voice has softened, my skin is softer and less … much less oily, even the large spider-like veins in my arms became 100 per cent unnoticeable. Plus, I'm not subject to getting colon cancer."

"So, how does it feel to be in a men's prison in your situation?" I ask.

"Being in a blokes' prison without Lenny and Squiggy is a plus. I am a woman. My orchiectomy sets me apart from the error nature made and moves me closer to the woman I am within. When I get out, I want to have breast augmentation. I can reach a B-cup, and I look hot when I jack my stuff up a cup higher – especially with my little waist."

My eyes drop to *her* waist and linger on *her* hip curves. *If Gina looks like a woman, speaks like a woman, moves like a woman and smells like a woman, what's the difference?*

"I plan to have rhinoplasty, teeth-whitening procedures and then to move to England. It must be London. I love rain and fog. It's so sexy to be in a field of tall grass with someone you love, inconspicuous to others. As for the fog, it's the same scene as being in tall grass in the rain, but when the fog lifts. Yes! England and a soulmate are my obsessions. By the way, you're the first English accent I've heard face-to-face." Gina flicks *her* hair. *Her* beautifully made-up eyes stare affectionately.

I shiver with unanticipated and uncontrollable pleasure. My face reddens. "Really. And you're the closest to an attractive woman I've seen in prison," I say, smiling giddily. *Thank God George and Frankie aren't here.* Realising that Gina and She-Ra are tuned in to my aroused condition, I stiffen my expression.

"Gina!" a voice booms across the yard. We turn our heads to Bud waving Gina over.

"Ah, my beloved," Gina says. "Au revoir."

Bud! Visualising him with Gina makes me want to laugh, but I stay composed to avoid provoking Bud.

Charged up with sexual frustration after flirting with Gina, I head for the shower to masturbate in the hope of preventing myself from overstepping any boundaries. With all sexual acts being illegal in prison and subject to disciplinary sanctions, the shower cubicle is the safest place from the guards.

Masturbating surrounded by chaos was hard when I was first arrested, but I've managed to improve my concentration over the years. In 2002 at the medium-security Towers jail, I shared a pod with forty-five men. At the end of the bottom tier, the shower area consisted of three showerheads in a row, separated by privacy divides so small I could see the rear of the person showering next to me, and if he was masturbating, his elbow jerking. Every now and then, I'd run into an exhibitionist like Booga, who'd yell my name and wave his penis. Having another prisoner stare at your penis in the shower was so common, I learned the expression for it: peter-gazing. As the gangs preferred to attack and murder people in the shower out of view of the security cameras, getting from erection to ejaculation when showering next to two inmates, with fruit flies and mosquitoes whizzing around, required discipline.

In 2003 at the maximum-security Madison Street jail, the inmates were considered so dangerous, the shower area was open plan, in the hope that no one would get murdered out of view of the guards in the control tower. There was a space the size of a small room at the end of the lower tier, with a railing in front. Not only did the guards have full view at all times, but so did the prisoners in the day room. The frosting on the windows adjacent to the corridor had been scratched off, enabling predators in the next pod to watch, blow kisses and play with themselves while I showered. I followed protocol by masturbating with my back facing the guards and the day room, so that it looked like I was giving my man parts a prolonged scrubbing. In here, the showers so far have been self-contained cubicles – like telephone boxes without windows – but the doors don't lock.

With so many barriers to a pleasant experience, it's a wonder why I bother. Going without sex for days, weeks, months, years, the pressure builds like Chinese water torture. To remain sane, the pressure must be released. Many heterosexuals view no sex as the hardest part of incarceration. When I was first arrested, the shock of the situation overrode everything, but over time, the demands from my sex drive intensified. Almost daily, I felt a yearning in my loins that made my hips quiver that combined with hot flushes, restlessness and flashbacks to previous encounters to render me incapable of concentrating on reading and writing. After showering, the antidote of orgasm reset my stress clock and the docility enabled me to resume my routine.

Being committed to hand relief for years means that we heterosexuals – the minority in here according to She-Ra – must innovate to spice up our sessions. Known as "going on a date," we sometimes tape sexy pictures protected by a clear plastic bag to the semen-spattered shower wall, either cut from magazines or photographs of partners. After a few years of using my right hand, I tried my left, which although suboptimal in terms of speed and eloquence of rhythm still added an exciting new dimension as if someone else was doing it. In the Madison Street jail, Frankie recommended a "fee-fee bag," usually a hot, wet sock, lubricated with soap or lotion, but a creatively folded towel also suffices. I tried it and enjoyed the texture, heat and moisture, but the end result was messy, so I didn't make a habit of it.

I'm in the shower masturbating when I hear the door open. Through the curtain, I see the silhouette of a tall long-haired figure. "Shaun, where's that book you've got for me?" She-Ra asks, referring to a book one of my blog readers sent *her*.

Surprised, amused, I yank the curtain back. *Is She-Ra coming onto me?* Even though my erection is dwindling, I obtain a strange thrill from She-Ra looking me up and down as if a woman is checking me out. "It's on my bunk."

"All right," She-Ra says, smiling as if something unspoken is happening.

I giggle. "How about lending me some tapes? I'd like to listen to some music."

"I'll get some for you." She-Ra leaves, closing the door behind *her*.

Within the hour, George bursts into my cell. "So, you were in the shower grooming the willy when She-Ra came in with some lame-ass excuse, eh?"

He's quickly followed by She-Ra, who drops *her* trousers, and wiggles *her* thick and lengthy circumcised penis at George. "Look, I'm hung like a boy hamster." Having never thought I'd end up in a situation that requires staring at a penis, I'm compelled to look at the tattoo of a colourful butterfly on She-Ra's. Thankfully, I feel no sexual pleasure, just curiosity.

"Yeah, a twelve-foot one," George says, unable to detach his eyes. "Let's have sex."

"I can't 'cause you're a girl just like me," She-Ra says, playing with *her* penis, "and I don't have sex with girls. Besides, I heard your anus smells like halibut."

I laugh. "What turns you on so much about She-Ra, Jeeves?" I ask.

"*She's* cute, and *she* has a beautiful penis. I'd like to see it erect. It'll only take me a couple of minutes."

"It takes hours for me to get hard," She-Ra says.

"I'll massage it until it's as erect as you found his Prince William in the shower," George says, his face glowing with lust.

"And when it gets hard, I pass out," *she* says.

I cackle. "It is pretty big."

"Actually, it's not that big. It's the same size hard as flaccid."

"C'mon, let me try it!" George yells, purple patches exploding on his face as if all of his blood has gone to his head. He dives, mouth first, wide open, at She-Ra's penis.

She falls backwards, knocking the door open to a guard, Officer Ronson, a hillbilly with a haggard face, a wart on a cheek, a crooked nose, an elongated chin and sinister slitty eyes who's always coming onto She-Ra in front of everyone in the chow hall. I quickly climb onto the top bunk. About now, any other guard would be issuing us disciplinary tickets for sexual acts. I'd be the laughing stock of the yard, and officially out of the closet in the minds of many such as Frankie. I pray Ronson doesn't write us up. With Ronson being excessively intimidating and unpredictable, I brace for what might happen.

"What the hell's going on in here?" Officer Ronson asks, admiring She-Ra's penis. "You told me you and She-Ra weren't an item!" he yells, scowling at me.

She-Ra puts *her* penis away. George stays on the floor, panting.

"I'm just up here minding my own business," I say unconvincingly.

"You leave!" Officer Ronson yells at George, who jumps up and disappears.

"So, what's She-Ra doing in your room?" he asks in a threatening tone. "And don't try and bullshit me, Attwood, by saying you're writing about *her*."

To buy time to think of an answer, I climb down from the bunk. I try to diffuse the situation with humour: "Well, you know how She-Ra likes a little English muffin on the side."

"I knew it!" Officer Ronson yells, smiling, his beady eyes sparkling as if turned on.

"Actually, I *was* writing about She-Ra," I say, afraid of him making sexual demands.

"Your hair looks nice, She-Ra," he says, stroking *her* hair, ogling *her* rear.

"Thank you," She-Ra says cautiously.

He winks at *her*. "I'm gonna work the night shift one of these days. Stay away from my woman, Attwood!" He leaves. Staring at each other as if we can't believe we didn't get in trouble, She-Ra and I smile and hug.

CHAPTER 32

Dr Owen's listening to Beethoven and reading *Synaptic Self*. He checks my homework: a thought journal detailing my recent nightmares about being chased and shot, and a description of the anxiety I felt when picked to speak in front of a group of prisoners at a SMART Recovery class. I expect him to disclose my personality-test scores, but he asks, "Why do you do yoga?"

"For better balance in my life," I say, taking notes.

"Yoga means union. In the context of universal energy, you need to increase your awareness of the universality of your life."

"How does that relate to my problems?"

"What do you want to do with your problems?"

"Get rid of them."

"All energy is constant through the universe, psychic energy or whatever. If you get rid of your problems, then you must consider what you're going to put in their locations. You must clarify your thinking and consider multiple solutions to your problems. Do you have hermit fantasies?"

"It's funny you should ask that because my friend, She-Ra, recently called me 'the quintessential hermit.' I certainly don't come out of my cell very often. I spend as much time as possible reading and writing."

"Using phrases, you can redefine yourself and challenge your assumptions. You can redefine your language using yoga, by changing your thinking, and thinking comfortably."

"How did I do on the personality test?" I ask, eager for the scores.

"Primarily, you showed an anxiety disorder, and also social detachment, which is an inability to socialise, not antisocial. In the subcategories, physiological stress shows, and anxious thinking.

Inability to relate to others. Your need for attention is high. Sense of importance is quite high."

"High enough for delusions of grandeur?" I ask, attempting a joke.

"No. Just high. Take the *quite* off. Your level of looking for cheap thrills is high. You have poly-substance abuse, anxiety and borderline tendencies. You have a fear of being abandoned."

"How high?"

"High enough."

"If I have a poly-substance abuse problem, yet drugs are readily available in prison, then how come I'm not doing them?"

"Your problem is in remission due to prison. Getting arrested was a slap to your head. You realised, *Holy shit. What have I been doing?* If you hadn't been arrested, would you still be doing rave parties?"

"I honestly don't know. I'd tapered that activity off, but who's to say whether I'd get stressed out and party hard again. My life has been a pattern of that."

"You obtained a definition of who you were through partying. On drugs, your anxiety went away. You surrounded yourself with folks in similar situations, and there's generally no true bonding in those environments. The club drugs you did caused a cascade of neurotransmitters. With huge amounts of drugs in the system, the brain operates at another level. Studies of substance abuse have shown volumetric reductions in the limbic system and short-term memory areas."

I've got some serious problems to sort out. "When I was asked to read at SMART Recovery, I felt I was drowning. All that existed was me and the booklet I was reading. I ended up gasping for air, and my nose started running. I've only got like that in recent years. After I was arrested, at Towers jail I volunteered to read a passage from the Bible in a packed room. I did it easily and coherently, and I was praised by the priest. Ask me to read in front of people now, and I become a basket case." I shift in my seat.

"Are you familiar with the fight or flight response?"

"Yes. When you feel threatened, the chemicals in your body prepare you to either fight or run for it."

"What about the third response: freeze?"

"Like the deer in the headlights?"

"Yes. This happens with most primates. During freeze, all that exists in the world are themselves and the thing they're looking at."

"Like the pages I was struggling to read."

"Yes. The situation seemed worse than it was. You needed to step back and breathe. You weren't breathing effectively."

"But it was pages long, and I was trying to get through it as quickly as possible to end my discomfort."

"Then you should have stopped for a deep breath at the end of each paragraph. Your discomfort was a state of mind. Your classmates were not going to beat you up because of the way you were reading. The situation was in control and you were not. You must learn to be able to say to yourself, *I'm going to do what I can do today, no matter who is in front of me*."

"OK, I'll try. From looking at my results, can you tell me where my mental-health problems sit in comparison to an average person?"

"If I told you that, I fear you'd use it as an excuse to think, *That's who I am*."

"But I'm trying to learn about these problems, including doing a psychology correspondence course to help understand myself and to get better," I say, hoping to impress him.

"Do you think a medical student doing a correspondence course could successfully perform an appendectomy?"

"No, of course not," I say, offended. "But at least I'm trying."

"I don't want you to beat yourself up with labels. I want you to be able to say to yourself, *I am perfect*."

"Isn't that egotistical?"

"No. I would like you to consider that in the context of your yoga texts. Read about your connection to the universal. And for your homework, I'd like you to observe and to write down positive and negative thoughts. Don't do another nightmare journal. I'm trying to raise your awareness of your thinking."

"You've begun to do that already by making light of my panic in the classroom. I really appreciate your help."

Enthused, I return to my cell and study a Siddha Yoga lesson in the hope of learning more about myself. It says that I'm a small part of something vast: the universe. Back when I threw parties, my ego was so large I thought the universe revolved around me. It's clear that my attention seeking was ego driven, but I can't understand my wild and reckless behaviour. *Why did I get so deep into drugs? I could have got attention in other ways without living so dangerously.* Staring at the bare cell, I feel disconnected from the universe. *This airy-fairy new-age crap is dumb.* Repeatedly, I tell myself that I'm part of the universe, but nothing happens. If anything, I feel abandoned by the universe. I recall being high on Ecstasy and feeling connected to nature and everyone around me; how breathing felt divine as described in yoga. *Why can't I feel like that without drugs? Will yoga teach me to feel that way? I trust Dr Owen. If the sessions are able to continue, he has a good chance of getting to the bottom of things and helping me develop as a person. If I don't decipher my nature, I'm doomed.*

CHAPTER 33

In the chow hall, Two Tonys and I are discussing *One Day in the Life of Ivan Denisovich*, below dozens of flies stuck to strips of yellow tape dangling from the ceiling, some dead, others twitching. The red pots at the bottom of each strip are swaying to the rhythm of air blasting from a fan rattling as if it's about to fall apart, showering us with the stink of poison and the fragrant adhesive on the tape that attracts the flies. The insect zapper attached to the back wall is crackling non-stop.

"Reading what Ivan endured makes me grateful for the conditions here," I say, looking around at 100 prisoners cramming food, rushing to eat in the fifteen minutes allowed, half of them swatting away flies.

"There's always some motherfucker worse off," Two Tonys says, smiling. "At least we're not being worked to death in Stalin's gulags."

"It was so cold their spit froze mid-air." I spoon lentils and bite a piece of bread.

An insect explodes in the zapper, attracting everyone's attention. "Damn! Some big-ass bug!" Bud yells.

Grim – a giant with flames, skulls and satanic symbols tattooed on his head and a patch over where an eyeball once resided until a cellmate stabbed it while he was asleep – sits next to us. "Did you see the ambulance outside of Building 2 last night? Some guy blew his asshole out while taking a shit."

Two Tonys' face puckers. "Hey, Grim, I hope my slurping my fucking chicken noodle soup doesn't interfere with your discussion about assholes and taking fucking shits. I'm trying to fucking eat. Do you mind?"

"What's wrong with talking about shits and assholes?" Grim blows a fly off his food.

"It's not just that. It seems like every time I sit down to eat my fucking chow, you come around, and the conversation goes straight to shits and assholes and nasty stuff that's unappetising to me. We don't have to talk about splitting the fucking atom here, but we could at least have a normal fucking conversation." I laugh.

"You've been down plenty years," Grim says. "You've heard worse than shits and assholes."

"Yeah. And I was in the navy for fucking years, keeping the Red Chinese from snatching your fucking ass."

"That's before my time," Grim says. "If you'd fought on the Ho Chi Minh Trail, you'd get my respects."

"I was in fucking Blood Alley, Formosa. If Chairman Mao had got his way, you'd be speaking Chinese and eating noodles with chopsticks, motherfucker."

"I love Chinese food."

"You would, you bizarre-looking motherfucker. When you get out, I'm gonna send you to the coast for lunch with Francis Ford Coppola. But when you talk to him, don't mention people taking shits and blowing their assholes out, and you might get a bit part in one of his movies – as a fucking monster."

"I can't go to California," Grim says. "I've done too many repetitive dangerous crimes there."

Laughter erupts around us, attracting everyone's attention. "They just got busted having sex!" a prisoner yells. Through full-length windows, I spot a sergeant escorting two prisoners from a cell: Frankie and Mochalicious, a petite Mexican-American transsexual with purple lips, black shoulder-length hair and sculpted eyebrows fashioned with a fifteen-cent razor in the sparse style of Jennifer Lopez as seen in the latest issue of *People* magazine. Holding disciplinary tickets, they enter the chow hall. Our laughter intensifies and a torrent of abuse – revolving around whether Mochalicious was "swallowing swollen goods" – pours down.

After chow, Frankie reveals his ticket:

Offence: B10 Indecent Exposure or Sexual Acts

I came upon cell D-8 on Yard 4 that had paper on the door window. There was a gap in the paper, and I could see inmate [Frankie] who lives in C-9 standing while inmate [Mochalicious] was knelt in front of him. The inmate who lives in D-8 was manipulating inmate [Frankie's] penis as if to get it erect. Inmate [Frankie] appeared to allow the other inmate to do this until I stopped them at approximately 17:47 hours. I verbally put the inmates on report.

The next evening, the prisoners are threatening to riot over foul-tasting spaghetti.

"I'd sooner eat red-hot barbed wire."

"They're serving us liquid shit, literally."

"I wouldn't give it to my dogs or worst enemies. If we bury it all in a mass grave, it'll show up on a satellite as a radioactive spot on earth."

"They should use it on *Fear Factor*," Two Tonys says, shaking his head at his tray. "They should be offering fifty grand to people to eat this shit."

I pocket an apple, join the line of prisoners donating their spaghetti to Slingblade and sit next to Two Tonys, excited to resume our discussion about literature without Grim around. "I appreciate you introducing me to Tom Wolfe. *A Man in Full* is now my favourite work of contemporary fiction. There are few modern authors who hold my interest."

"Average authors are churning out junk food," Two Tonys says. "Compared to their hamburgers, Tom Wolfe's books are Beef Wellingtons."

"My parents have been trying to get me to read more contemporary fiction. They sent me some Stephen King. I enjoyed *Rita Hayworth and Shawshank Redemption*."

"Stephen King's running a fucking McDonald's franchise," he says. "He's pumping out books like quarter-pounders. It took

Wolfe eleven years to write *A Man in Full*. Wolfe's so fucking good, he's got a war going with those other authors: Updike, Irving and that fucking thug, Mailer. They're jealous of his skills."

"Weird Al gave me some Tom Robbins books. What do you think of him? My writing turned surreal after I read two Robbins books back-to-back." After enjoying *Jitterbug Perfume* and *Still Life with Woodpecker*, I started describing things so bizarrely that a reader of Jon's Jail Journal asked if I'd resumed drugs.

"I'm not familiar with this Robbins guy. I'll tell you something though: he's got to get up real early in the fucking morning to sharpen his pencil to be in the same league as Tom Wolfe."

Grim joins our table. I brace for him to open his mouth. "I saw She-Ra coming out of the shower," he says. "That girl's got a big-ass schlong. Anyone ever notice that shit?"

I sit back and watch, keen to admire how Two Tonys handles the situation. I could listen to him all day long. He puckers, leans away from Grim and puts down his apple. "What is it with you, Grim? We're over here trying to have an intellectual fucking conversation about books we've read, and you've got to come along and talk about schlongs. Have you got some kind of fucking fetish for talking about schlongs and assholes when I'm eating?"

"But it's true," Grim says. "I've been down a long time, and I've noticed that gay guys have bigger than average schlongs."

"Listen, Grim, I've been down twice as long as you, and I'll be honest with you, I'm not in the habit of checking out men's schlongs. And the fact that you're bringing schlongs up while I'm trying to converse with my British friend, I'm finding fucking insulting. You wanna talk about schlongs, sit at a fucking child molester or sex-pervert table. This table's for crimes of integrity, like homicides for motherfuckers who were asking for it."

"I saw She-Ra's ass as well," Grim says.

"Hey, Grim, you know my reputation. I don't fuck with these gays, now or never. I don't look at men's asses. It's a case of each to his fucking own. I can imagine taking you to a fancy joint like the Four Seasons. The maître d' gives us a choice table, and you wanna talk about the Guatemalan bus boy's ass or the shape of the maître d's schlong. That's why I can't ever envisage taking you to a five-star restaurant, Grim. You're strictly McDonald's – drive-thru material." I laugh.

"This spaghetti sauce looks like some Marines took a shit in it," Grim says. "Straight fucking Panama water."

"That's because of your sick fucking mind," Two Tonys says. "Come hotdog day, you're gonna be seeing the hotdogs as schlongs and cock-heads. You're stuck on phallic fucking symbols."

She-Ra approaches. "Hey, guys! Who wants a table dance?"

"Me and my Brit friend don't," Two Tonys says. "But Grim'll see you in a private booth. He'll meet you at your cell later on."

"I was just telling the fellas about your big-ass schlong," Grim says.

"Not that I asked for that info," Two Tonys says. "'Cause, to be real honest with you, I don't give a fuck if you're hung like the Incredible Hulk."

"Two Tonys, are you sure you don't wanna see my swing set?" She-Ra asks.

"No, I don't care to. But if the day ever comes when I do, I'm hoping you motherfuckers will snuff me out by smothering me with a pillow first. Like at the end of *One Flew Over the Cuckoo's Nest*. After that, I'll meet you motherfuckers in hell, 'cause that's where we're all heading."

CHAPTER 34

I'm so happy, I could kiss the guard handing me a letter from Jade. Hoping it answers the questions on my mind, I rush across the yard. I want its perfume to burst out and linger in the cell. I tear it open. No perfume. *That's odd.* My stomach tightens. It says that shortly after the last visit, Theo flew from London to America in a desperate attempt to win her back. She initially rejected him, but his behaviour changed. He proposed marriage and she said yes. My heart hits the cement floor and shatters into pieces. Stunned, I sit and read the rest. Her apology is irritating. When the shock wears off, I feel angry and betrayed. I snatch a pen and write furiously:

From my experiences in relationships, I know that when some-one has the upper hand emotionally, and for some reason feels they're losing the upper hand, the person's ego feels the greatest challenge in the world. I'm not going to give up on you because it seems to me that Theo doesn't love you for you, or accept you for you because the only thing that made him change his behaviour was the possibility of losing you, which isn't about love, it's about control. Him proposing to you isn't based on how much he cares because he hasn't cared until now. It seems he only cares about himself. You don't deserve to be mistreated in this way. But, alas, love is blind, and my analysis of the situation will be rejected by you because of the hope that's been raised in you by him by some petty expression of grief and some behaviour that is normal in the sense that this is how he should have been treating you during the last several years. He failed to give you the love and respect you deserve, and now he acts like a normal boyfriend as he sees you gaining the upper hand, and you jump like a little dog through a circus hoop. Beware of the ego's crocodile tears.

Wow, I'm sounding bitter. The bottom line is that I love and respect you as the beautiful, intelligent and witty woman that you are. Theo doesn't deserve you. You'll find the right person eventually. If fate pushes us both together again somehow, which wouldn't surprise me, then perhaps we can apply the brakes on our emotions synchronistically, so I don't go making a fool of myself again.

When you visited, I opened my heart to you – against all of the reason and logic in the world. Hearts seem to know things instantaneously, and then we clutter how we really feel with logic, and sorting out our feelings and all that crap. I can't say that I'm surprised by you stating how you felt at Visitation as being under the influence. You were under the influence. When you feel so good around a person so naturally, your brain releases hormones into your system. I was under the same influence. But we can't explain away the sparks of love that flew between us.

I'm glad that you seem happy in your letter. I think I sound childish in this one. I'm tempted to rip it up. I'm trying to pretend that I'm not peeved, when really I am. Is that selfish of me?

Wishing you happiness. With all my love with bells and whistles and brakes on.

Long Island arrives. Picking up on my agitation, he asks what's wrong. We often discuss our relationships, so he knows about Claudia and Jade. He has an ex that he's not quite written off. I tell him about Jade's engagement and let him read my response. He says not to send the letter and to reread it tomorrow when I've calmed down. I don't know what to do. When he turns his TV on, I reread the letter, growing uncomfortable at how I've expressed myself. *If I don't send it now, I'll reread it in the morning and bin it.* Still fuming, I storm off to mail it, convinced Jade deserves to read my gut reaction and not a diluted version. *What does it matter if I've lost her anyway?* After sending it, I march back to my cell, glad darkness has arrived to disguise my damp eyes.

CHAPTER 35

On the eve of Long Island's release – he's served fifty-six months – his apprehension, excitement and my sadness at losing him are palpable. He's come so far in his stock-market studies, the profit in the account he trades on paper exceeds mine. When I announce the result, he stops doing handstand push-ups against the door and paces around the cell, yelling, "Yes! Yes! Yes! I beat you!" pumping his arms in the air, showering the cell with sweat, his head and neck roped with thick veins. Impressed by his enthusiasm, I hope he puts the knowledge to good use, and the passion he's developed for trading steers him away from crime.

"How does it feel to be getting out?" I ask, sat at a desk scattered with stock-market newspapers, charts, books and our trading records. *I wonder how I'll feel when I'm getting out.*

He sits on the bottom bunk. "I'm extremely scared ... anxious ... nervous ... more than I ever thought I'd be," he says, his face contorting, his eyes as wide and wild as when I first saw him – the stress of entering, exiting and changing prisons pushes inmates to psychological extremes.

"Surely you're happy?" I ask, leaning forward, smiling. "Fuck, I'd be over the moon."

"Yeah, of course I am, but other emotions are overshadowing my happiness right now," he says, reaching to rub his neck, flexing a bicep recently tattooed with bright colours by Bud. "I'm not getting out expecting to fail like other guys who are happy to rob, get high and come back to prison. I'm happy to get out to build a life, and that's gonna take everything I have. Becoming a stockbroker is gonna take a lot of hard work." Inspired by chapters I wrote about my stockbroking career, he is determined to repeat my success. "There are prejudices out there that I'm gonna have to

145

face or manipulate my way around. I'll need to keep my wits about me. I owe my family and others who've supported me financially and emotionally to not let them down for putting trust in me. I'm wondering whether to contact the girl I was with, but I'm scared that might set off a chain reaction of things I don't want to deal with right now." He puts his hands on his lap and stares blankly.

We discuss relationships. When I mention Jade, he shakes his head and offers sympathy. Not wanting my heartache to taint his release, I ask, "What's the first thing you want to do when you get out?"

"Have dinner with my family," he says, relaxing, turning up his palms. "And I'd like to sit at a bar and have a drink alone. Hopefully, a nice little barmaid will bring me a Stoli tonic." He tilts his head and smiles.

"What's the work plan?"

"I want a stockbroker's licence within six months," he says, wiping sweat from his head. "I'd like to be pulling six figures within three years."

"Are you staying in Phoenix?"

"Absolutely," he says, nodding.

"Any further education?"

"I've got sixty-five college credits, which is an associate's degree. I need another sixty to get a BA."

"Will you keep me updated on your progress?"

"I sure will. You created me!" he says, a smile lifting his eyes. "Now I just have to go."

"What do you mean by that?" I ask, grinning.

"I've tried to glean as much knowledge of the financial markets as I could from you. Now I just have to apply it. You've transferred a wealth of knowledge to me. It's like you said, 'Here, read these books and go and be successful.'"

"But remember," I say, raising my brows, "there's much more to life than the pursuit of money. Look what happened to me."

"I have a lot of catching up to do before I have to think about that."

"To succeed in business, you have to be cut-throat, but crossing the line will land you back behind bars," I say, tilting forward.

"That won't happen," he says, shaking his head. "I'm looking forward to bringing my love for the financial markets and integrity to whatever brokerage position I'm fortunate to land."

"It's been a real pleasure being your celly," I say, sadness welling up, my body leaning further forward. "I'll miss you loads."

"Same here," he says, his eyes glistening with emotion.

"And I'll be disappointed if you get in trouble," I say, failing to sound stern.

"Thanks. If Bud or Ken start any shit again, go to Two Tonys. He really likes you. He's looking out for you in ways you don't even know about." He smiles.

"I really appreciate you introducing me to Two Tonys." We stand and hug. I pray to never see him back in prison. The guards extract him at dawn. I brace for Ken to move into my cell.

CHAPTER 36

Dressed in my best clothes – a sweatshirt borrowed from Two Tonys, trousers hemmed by Long Island, sneakers cleaned by George, socks with no holes – I dash from my cell for the first Christmas 2005 visit with my parents, and power-walk towards Visitation. At the guards' desk, I hug Mum, Dad and Mum again. We sit and chat about how we're holding up and the kindness of family, friends and blog readers. We praise my journalist sister, Karen, for getting an article published in *Cosmo* about having a brother in prison.

"Has Jade visited lately?" Mum asks.

My stomach lurches. "Er … no. I don't expect to hear from her again. She's … er … getting married."

Dad jolts back in surprise. "What?" Mum asks, eyes wide.

I tell them the story. They sympathise. "It's probably for the best," I say, not wanting them to worry. "The ups and downs of maintaining a relationship from prison are overwhelming," I say, even though I'd do anything to get Jade back. Six hours pass fast. Before they leave, they ask if I've had any more problems with Bud and Ken. I say that Ken wants to live with me, but fortunately the counsellor is refusing to approve the move because of his numerous tickets for fighting and drugs.

Afterwards, I join dozens of prisoners cramped in an outdoor cage with no seats, awaiting strip searches. Listening to their conversations, I'm snapped back to reality.

"I gotta take a shit!"

"My sister-in-law wants me to hook up with one of her girlfriends. I told her, 'Hell, no! Are you crazy? Why would I wanna have some chick doing time with me?'"

"I've got three chicks visiting me – on rotation."

"If I need a girlfriend, I grab *Playboy*."

"My stomach's killing. I really gotta shit."

"Why would I wanna put a chick through the misery of falling in love with me when my sorry ass is in here?"

"I've got to get back to my house to take a shit. Would you fellas mind if I get stripped-out first before I have a fucking accident?"

"Fuck that! I'm sick. You ain't jumping in front of me."

"Yeah. What makes you think you're so fucking special?"

"Take a shit in Visitation, homey."

"I can't shit in there. I've got standards."

"You don't have to sit on the seat. Just kind of squat a bit."

"I've really fucking got to go. I'll wait till all the visitors have gone. I don't want them smelling my shit when I open the door."

Thirty minutes later, I'm in a chilly room with a stocky Mexican-American guard wearing rubber gloves. He has a gentle coaxing voice, a stern expression and the watchful eyes of a bird. Facing him, I strip and hand over my sweaty clothes. Searching for drugs, he digs in pockets, runs his fingers along linings and examines my sneakers. He inspects my ears, mouth, armpits and below my scrotum. "Pull your foreskin back ... OK. Turn around and spread them ... OK. Put your clothes on and go back to your house."

During the final visit ten days later, two visitors join my mum and dad: Pearl Wilson, one of the founders of Mothers Against Arpaio – a group of women whose loved ones have suffered or died in Sheriff Joe Arpaio's jail system – and Linda Bentley, a reporter for *Sonoran News*. Since Mothers Against Arpaio discovered Jon's Jail Journal, we've campaigned together against Sheriff Arpaio. Another founding member, Linda Saville – whose brother was coaxed into buying bomb parts by undercover police working for Arpaio in what a jury ruled as a blatant publicity stunt by the sheriff – mailed me testimonies from people affected by Arpaio's jail. Before the visit, I read them and grew incensed:

... my fiancé committed suicide in Madison Street on December 28, 2004.

My brother ... came into contact with what they call "Durango Rot," a foot fungus. They refused him medical treatment for this until one toe became so large with disease that it literally exploded.

... my son has suffered constantly with anti-Semitism. He has been beaten, tormented and denied medical care after a beating by a detention officer ... He suffered two herniated discs and nerve compression in his back. He is suffering from reoccurring staph infections

... He has had heart surgery due to a staph infection that attacked one of his valves. His body is covered with scars due to these infections eating away at his skin.

... a very close friend of mine was beaten into a coma by other inmates in Madison Street jail, and nearly died. Still today, he can barely walk.

My daughter ... at Estrella [jail] ... contracted an infection ... She may lose her leg; they took her [to a hospital] with an open wound, a good 8 inches long, 2 inches wide cut almost to the bone and tissue ...

... my daughter ... saw a woman pepper sprayed because she had been asking and asking for medical help.

My son ... has been beaten (resulting in broken ribs, bruises, cuts) ... The jail is overheated, overcrowded and infested with bugs and lice. Sheriff Joe has NO RIGHT ... to run his jail as a NAZI CONCENTRATION CAMP!

Our grandchildren's father died while in the custody of Sheriff Joe Arpaio. Our grandchildren are without a father

now because of the horrific conditions that Eddie was sub-
jected to.

One lady who was in the holding cell with me ... [her] uterus
fell out while in the tents. She was holding it and told the
sheriffs ... [she was told] it was not an emergency and she
could push it back in.

... his tents aren't saving tax dollars, they are making Joe
rich ... His justice will come just like Hitler's and the rest of
the Third Reich.

Pearl and Linda mention attending an Arpaio function. The sheriff was boasting about solving murders. Linda asked him about
the unsolved murders in his jail. Arpaio said there are no murders
in his facilities. Pearl stood up and said that her son was murdered
in Tent City. Philip Wilson, a plumber with a degree in graphic
design serving two months for violating parole for minor drugs
possession, was beaten into a coma by the Aryan Brotherhood
and died in hospital. The guards who failed to rescue him manu-
factured a story that he was murdered for his onyx ring. Unable
to contest Pearl, Arpaio slandered her and continued his speech.
Listening to Pearl – one of the bravest women I've met – recount
her story, I'm on the verge of tears. Having seen people getting
beaten until they looked dead in Arpaio's jail, I'm aware of how
easily and frequently it happens. I wish there was more I could
do to get the conditions improved and maybe save some lives.
I'm frustrated at how hard it is to expose the truth for us little
people operating in the shadow of Arpaio's multi-million-dollar
media machine, but I'm hopeful that my writing will eventually
expose Arpaio's jail to the world. Pearl finishes with good news.
The maximum-security Madison Street jail that my blog drew
international media attention to is scheduled to be closed down;
however, Arpaio runs six different jails, so we don't see the human-
rights violations ending soon.

When the visit ends, the presence of Pearl and Linda prevents

Mum from getting too upset. Long hugs and farewells fill our final moments together in 2005. I leave the visit grateful for them travelling so far to see me.

CHAPTER 37

Dr Owen's office is quiet. No classical music. On his desk is an article about Susan Sontag: "Melancholy Minus Its Charms." I hand him a journal of my positive and negative thoughts. "I noticed that I bounced between happy and sad until the weekend, then my happiness went off the scale. I think I was manic." His eyes protrude as he reads Saturday's entry:

Overwhelmingly, inexplicably happy. Feel as if I can accomplish anything. Have written for almost 8 hours. My mind is racing with ideas. Creativity and the right words are flowing naturally. I haven't showered, done yoga, or talked to anyone other than ushering a few visitors out. Time is flying. The announcements of rec beginning and then ending (a two-hour period) seemed like ten minutes. I thought I was hearing things when rec ended because time couldn't possibly go so fast. I've accomplished a lot today, and I am extremely satisfied. In comparison to recent happiness, I am way off the scale. Why can't I feel this good every day? I feel like I could walk to the chow hall and back on my hands – and maybe even fly!

"When you reviewed these thoughts after you wrote them, what did you think?"

"I thought, *Oh, no! Now I've got multiple personality disorder*, because Saturday's thoughts seem like they were written by a different person."

"Some writers, when they're feeling great like that, achieve tremendous insights. What was the quality of your writing on Saturday?"

"Words fell into place. My sense of humour was up. I liked what I wrote."

"The reason I ask is because when you are at negative or positive emotional extremes, your critical ability goes down."

"That's true. A lot of what I wrote was rubbish, but I judged my production on things that bubbled up that looked great. Things that I couldn't have written if I wasn't in such a good mood. I simply edited out the rubbish when I'd calmed down."

"Your sudden energy interrupted what you usually do in the day: yoga, taking a shower and dealing with people. What did foregoing those things mean to you?" he asks, his eyes locking onto mine, tilting his head forward.

"That was all secondary stuff. Most important was my writing."

"Is this energy you experience the same as the energy you utilised when throwing raves?"

Staring up, I pause. "I never thought of it like that. It could be. Throwing parties, I switched into a high-energy mode. But it wasn't happy energy that led me to drugs. It was depressions, relationship break-ups, and negative emotions and events. I wanted to get so high that my stress didn't matter. When the high first hit, it felt great, and I'd do more drugs in the hope of keeping that feeling going, but I'd usually end up taking things too far. Looking at the amount of times I overdosed, or had car crashes, I'm ashamed of my behaviour. I wonder why I kept intentionally pushing myself into the danger zone for so long. It's like there was something wrong with me that I still can't figure out. I wonder if I'll always be like that. Thinking about the insane things I did scares me." *Why could I never say no to the wolves?*

"You have to watch your swings. It seems that you don't think of yourself as interesting when you're not manic," he says, raising his hands. "You need to polish your thinking style, and be able to weigh the consequences of your ups and downs. You have a high state of denial. That's something you must remedy if you want to have a normal life." He throws his arms up and I jump as he yells, "I like the highs! I can walk to the chow hall on my hands!"

I laugh. "Here's the rest of my homework." I hand him a page.

What I learnt from yoga about being perfect and my connection with the universal: The universal force is the source of all power. We can do nothing unless it enables it. The ego resists this truth, and we believe we have our own power – which is a fallacy. We are unfulfilled until we discover our inner connection with the universal force. Upon discovering it, we flow with good or bad events, conscious of the dance of the universal force, the power behind all happenings and moods.

"Is that what you were looking for?" I ask, worried the answer – derived from yoga texts – sounds crazy.

"Yes. Yoga means union, everything, good and bad, dark and light. Whether studying Tao, the yin and yang of Chinese philosophy, or Christian theology at the mystical level, all paths lead to union with the universal, including observance of the eight limbs of yoga. Such awareness doesn't demand perfection. Whatever occurs is allowed to occur. The problem is: the mind interferes. The monkey mind. It doesn't stay still. It behaves like a restless monkey grabbing at objects that aren't there. The flow of the mind is the essence of many esoteric doctrines."

"I understand that, but reading it and understanding it are different from being able to apply it."

"It always is. You have to work at it. Look at ascetics, people who have isolated themselves from others. Not bums with their cheap wine and oblivion, but renunciators with their books and bags. Isn't that an expression of intellectual energy? Although it has good and bad to it, it seems to enhance the path for some folks."

"So where am I on that spectrum? I'm channelling my intellectual energy into writing, but I've also spun out of control like a bum into drugs."

"It doesn't matter. My opinion has little to do with it. It's your image of yourself that's important – your insights, your judgements. Can you imagine yourself five or ten years from now?"

"Yes. I have a long-term goal to be an author, to get my story published, and the stories of other prisoners. That's why I try not to waste a single minute in here. I'm happy knowing I'm moving in the right direction."

"But goals change. And rest is important. You need rest to be able to apply yourself to achieve your goals. That's where mindfulness and self-awareness come in. If a Tibetan Buddhist monk lost his legs, he could still achieve his goal of making a journey around the Sacred Mountain. He would do it slower than most, but he would be mindful and self-aware. If your goal is to throw the best rave parties in the Valley—"

"No! Never again!" I say, slapping the table.

"Let's just assume that at one time it was. If you'd been mindful of the bigger picture instead of being excited by one thing and forgetting everything else, then you would have been more aware of the unintended consequences of your actions. Consequences that put you in here."

"True."

"For homework, I'd like you to keep up the thought journal and consider the difficulty you have with good intentions. As the old saying goes, 'The road to hell is paved with good intentions.' Most folks don't think about the consequences for themselves. With your physical practice – your asanas – I'd like you to be more mindful and to consider your bone and muscle alignments. You should also meditate to control your monkey mind."

In my cell, I wonder why getting told to rest by Dr Owen made me uneasy as if he were scratching a sore. I'm open to his advice, yet partially resisting. When it comes to work, I pride myself on my ability to completely focus on a project. I enjoy channelling manic energy into big achievements. As a stockbroker, slogans like "Lunch is for wimps" were appealing. In the session with Dr Owen, I wanted to yell, "How dare you challenge my work ethic!" But on reflection, I can see a strong unhealthy force that results in work extremes. It's separate from the wolves, but over time it leads to them emerging. I seem to have the wolves under control, but not this second force, which is worrying. Pondering the session, feeling as if I'm on the brink of a discovery, I buzz with excitement. Realising I've never searched my soul so deeply, I credit Dr Owen for shining a light on my inner self. *But how can I measure progress? I want results, but unlike a physical illness, I have no way of measuring it such as symptoms being cured. Dr Owen said I have to work at it and cited the legless monk making a slow journey. What if I apply my manic energy to this task? Then I'd be using a potentially unhealthy force for a positive goal.* Delighted with my little breakthrough, I resolve to keep trying to understand myself even if it takes a lifetime.

CHAPTER 38

A burly white property officer wheels a squeaky cart across the yard, observed by prisoners, his presence raising the hopes of some, others watching enviously to see who gets what. He stops below my cell. "Attwood, get your ass down here!" I rush to the end of the balcony and down the stairs, expecting a few new reads, excited to see what's arrived. "How many books is a prisoner allowed?" he asks, his brows arched menacingly above dark sunglasses.

"Seven." *Is he going to confiscate books from my cell?*

"Attwood, the forty-seven books in here are all for you!" he says, pointing at the cart. "You have so many books, I could classify them as contraband, and the prison would destroy them." He juts his jaw and chews tobacco in a circular motion as if to magnify the threat.

Stunned, I swallow. "I've no control over how many books people send," I say quickly. "They're coming from my blog readers." I stare hungrily at the piles of books in the cart.

He spits brown juice onto the dirt – *splat*. "I hear you share your books with prisoners and your donations are filling up the library."

"Yes," I say, aware of inmates clustering to eavesdrop.

"Here's what I'm gonna do for you, Attwood. I'm gonna look the other way, and all these books are gonna disappear real fast. Got anyone who can help you?"

I wave over Two Tonys, Shannon and She-Ra, quickly joined by others.

"Guys, please help take these to my cell and help yourselves to whatever you want to read." Watched by the yard, we carry piles of books like a trail of worker ants. As the property officer wheels the cart away, I'm left with prisoners browsing books like it's Christmas. They select some and rush off to read.

Only one person remains, taking time to study jackets and first pages. "I just love the smell of new books," Two Tonys says, sniffing a copy of *The Electric Kool-Aid Acid Test* by Tom Wolfe.

"Me too," I say, wafting pages, intoxicated by the scent of paper, ink and glue. "What do you think about all these books – Updike, Murakami, Rushdie, Bret Easton Ellis, and your favourite, Tom Wolfe?"

"Let me tell you something," Two Tonys says, adding Wolfe's book to a pile. "I've been doing time since I was a kid – since 1958 – in and out, in and out. Thanks to these books, this is the best I've ever had it. There was a time in my life when the fucking TV meant everything to me. Now I've got these books, I don't even turn the motherfucker on. These books are keeping me alive, keeping me from fucking dementia. From this cell, I'm travelling the world. Whether it's Murakami taking me to the Gobi Desert where the Mongols and a Russian are torturing Japs, or Tom Wolfe taking me to a five-bedroom townhouse on New York's Fifth Avenue with green marble floors, or Robert Fiske taking me to Tora Bora in the mountains of Afghanistan with Bin Laden and the Mujahideen – I'm there, bro. These books are getting me out of the fucking cell."

The next day, I find Two Tonys in his room, chatting to an old Mexican-American prisoner with a weatherworn face, tall, bespectacled, soft-spoken, covered in ink. "Pico, this is my friend, England. He's a good dude," Two Tonys says, rising off his bunk to shake my hand.

"Pleased to meet you," I say, smiling.

"Pico here saw I was reading your book," Two Tonys says, "*The Great War for Civilisation*, and he's wondering if you want to sell it to him."

"It's a good read," I say. "A blog reader sent it to me for free, so I can't sell it. You can have it."

"England's got a good heart," Two Tonys says, tapping his chest.

"That's real nice of you, England," Pico says, his eyebrows rising. "Are you sure I can't give you anything for it?"

"No need. I've got to keep my book karma intact."

"I like you, England," he says in a serious tone. "Listen, if anyone ever fucks with you, you tell me." Pico extracts a bandage from his pocket and wraps it around his left hand. Holding a fist out, he says, "Look, I'm always ready to go. I don't give a fuck who it is. I don't give a fuck what time of the day it is. I'm always ready. I've got your back."

Taken aback, I say, "I appreciate that, Pico." He leaves with the book.

"You just made a good friend with that one," Two Tonys says, sitting down on the bunk.

I sit on the chair. "Why? Who is he?"

"He's Old Mexican Mafia. All the Mexican Americans listen to him. He's one of the most dangerous motherfuckers you'll ever meet. He's doing life for murders, and while he was in the joint, he shanked two guards to death in Cell Block 4. The cops tortured him for years. They denied him medical, and he lost a kidney."

"Why'd he kill two guards?" I ask, leaning forward, wide-eyed.

"Him and some others were high. The guards busted them, so him and his homies cut them to pieces."

"Bloody hell!" I say, rubbing the front of my neck.

"Yeah, he's a killer, but he's a sincere guy, an old convict. No one disrespects him. He's a good fella to have in your corner. Now, out of the books from yesterday, I'm really excited about this one," he says, picking up *The Great Thoughts* by George Seldes.

"What's so good about it?"

Two Tonys flips to the introduction. "It's right here. Blaise Pascal: 'Man's greatness lies in the power of thought.' And Marcus Aurelius Antoninus: 'Our life is what our thoughts make it.'"

Delighted he picked Aurelius, I say, "If you like that quote, you'll love his book, *Meditations*. It really inspired me. It focuses on keeping the mind strong in difficult circumstances. It's ideal for prisoners."

"And here's Emerson: 'Great men are they who see that spiritual is stronger than any material force, that thoughts rule the world.'"

"It's powerful stuff," I say, impressed. "I need to work more on my spiritual side."

"These quotes are making me realise I'm wasting my thoughts hating on people. For me to lay up and hate is like having a goitre on my neck," he says, pointing below an ear. "Sometimes I just lay on my bunk, looking at the wall and ceiling, thinking about motherfuckers I hate. It's a goitre that keeps growing and growing, and I've got to cut it off. I'd like to get it surgically removed, but there ain't no surgeon in the world with a scalpel sharp enough to cut this fucker off."

"So how are you going to fix it?" I ask, smiling.

He puts down the book and throws his arms up. "Aurelius is gonna be my surgeon! Pascal is gonna be my surgeon! Emerson is gonna be my surgeon! Life is nothing but thought, is it? I could go to a restaurant and order a rack of lamb with mint jelly, rice pilaf, French bread, a bottle of Cabernet Sauvignon and, for dessert, Kahlua parfait, and yeah, I'd enjoy it at the time, but I'd also enjoy thinking about it afterwards as well. Just like I can lay on my bunk and instead of hating on motherfuckers and thinking of ways to whack them, I can enjoy picturing when I was on the run in Waikiki and Maui, living in a house on the slopes of Mount Haleakalā and how beautiful it was. It's all about thoughts. This is an epiphany for me. Look, my goitre's shrinking," he says, tapping his neck. "When I feel hate invading my space, I'm gonna combat it by reading this book or whatever else I can get my hands on."

CHAPTER 39

Having not seen my sister since she spoke in court on my behalf in June 2004, I'm counting the days to Karen's visit in April 2006. Despite the hell I've put my family through, Karen – who was understandably initially angry – has stood by me. Although she has little money, she saved up to visit twice at the jail. She introduced me to yoga and encouraged my writing. Dad's coming as well, but not Mum as it's only been four months since she visited and flights cost over $1,000.

I arrive at Visitation to Dad, smiling, healthy and relaxed, and Karen, stood tall with long brown hair and a graceful poise gleaned from years of ballet, her big eyes the same steely blue as Dad's and mine. It's Friday, so Visitation is mostly empty, only eight tables in use. We hug, walk outside in the sunshine, sit at a picnic table and talk. We agree that my incarceration is a blessing. That it's de-railed me from a dangerous cycle that could have resulted in my death. Although I was stabilising prior to the SWAT-team raid, maybe things would have spiralled out of control again. Over four years, I've gone from being angry at getting caught, to acceptance, to feeling saved. Dad and Karen are bookworms, so I tell them about my goal to read over 1,000 books by my release, that I've read seventy-two in the last three months, and I'm on track to read over 200 this year. Dad enjoys Kafka, and has recently visited an exhibition in Prague at Kafka's birth house at the Old Town Square next to the Church of St Nicholas. Karen, who spent four years teaching in Japan, prefers Haruki Murakami, and we both praise the first book of his she sent to me, *The Wind-Up Bird Chronicle*. Thanks to Two Tonys, we're all fans of Tom Wolfe.

"Heard from Jade since her engagement?" Karen asks.

"Nope." Even though it's been months, I still feel the pain. "I wish she'd just let me know how she's doing."

"The wedding's going through then," Dad says.

"I'm afraid so. He's like a bad habit she has a hard time trying to break," I say, almost spitting out the words.

"Where are they getting married?" Karen asks.

"They're back in London now, but I think they're getting married in America in a Catholic church."

"If she's in London, why don't I arrange to meet her?" she asks.

"What a great idea!" While my mind ranges over the possibilities, I sit up straight. "Dad can get her email address. If she agrees to meet you, Karen, you can find out what the hell's going on." The idea lifts my hope.

After the visit, walking across the yard, I hear someone yell, "Why the hell isn't your sis here to visit me?"

I reply, "Piss off, Ken!"

Inside, I work on my journal for Dr Owen:

I have many pleasant thoughts of the visit today. Being in the presence of my sister who I've been unable to have close contact with for years has left me on a high. A combination of good company and sugar products caused my thoughts to race, making the last four hours of the visit seem like one. Departed feeling happy hypo-manic ...

At 4:15 PM, I hear Officer Rivero searching my neighbour's cell, his radio crackling, keys jangling, metal banging, drawers opening and closing, property boxes sliding across concrete with a grating sound. Assuming he's coming here next, I put the clutter from my desk – books, letters, paperwork, financial newspapers – into the drawers under the bottom bunk, so I can't be issued a disciplinary ticket. Ten minutes later, he walks in, his young friendly face struggling to appear serious. "Cell inspection."

"Uh oh," I reply, feigning surprise.

"It's quite clean in here," he says, rummaging around.

"Thanks."

"You're in compliance, Attwood." He ticks my name on a clipboard and continues down the run. At 4:25 PM, I spot him sprinting from the building, out of Yard 4 and into Yard 2. Guards appear from all directions, running towards Yard 2. The yard is locked-down.

There must have been a fight or an assault on a guard.

At 5:40 PM, I overhear kitchen workers – ordered to return to their buildings – yelling at the prisoners locked in their cells:

"We've got another hostage situation!"

"A hostage has been taken on Yard 2!"

My pulse accelerates, palms moisten. *Visits might be cancelled.* During the 2004 hostage crisis at Buckeye prison, inmates were locked-down for days without food. *How will my dad and sister feel if they're turned away tomorrow? Why tonight of all nights? Months of planning and preparation and approval-seeking down the drain.*

6:05 PM. Guards, uniformed and plain clothed, amass on Yard 2. Ladders are set up, stretching above the prison roof.

6:25 PM. I try to read *The Trial of Socrates* but the situation shreds my concentration. *Stop stressing out. There's a chance everything will be back to normal soon. What you worry about often never happens. Calm down. There's nothing you can do. And what about the hostage? A person's life's on the line. Go back to reading. Take your mind off things over which you have no control. It'll be resolved. What would Dr Owen recommend in this situation? To breathe.*

6:34 PM. After staring at pages, but absorbing little, I climb off the bunk to watch developments through the window. Flatbed trucks arrive with members of the Strategic Response Team (SRT) in black battle regalia. They march into Building 2 like robots.

6:37 PM. More SRT arrive.

6:43 PM. A floodlight shines on Building 2 for ten seconds.

6:46 PM. Another truck with SRT arrives.

6:54 PM. The setting sun paints the mountain behind Building 2 pink like Mars. The SRT members unload weapons and equipment from the vehicles.

8 PM. Darkness. Bats swoop around the yard lights, catching moths. More SRT arrive.

8:47 PM. A guard appears at my window. "Are you a regular or a special diet?"

"Diet. I'm a vegetarian," I say.

"We're serving regulars right now, but I gotcha," he says. Assuming I won't be seeing him anytime soon, I eat peanut butter and crackers.

9:30 PM. I shove wet toilet paper in my ears and try to sleep.

5:50 AM. I rise and rush to the window. *Not a soul near Building 2. Good. No kitchen workers in our chow hall. Bad. Mixed signals. Are we still locked-down?*

6:01 AM. *Two kitchen workers and a guard in the chow hall. Good. We must be off lockdown. Better get ready for the visit.*

7:17 AM. *Why no announcement for chow? The hostage situation looks resolved. Are we going to be collectively punished with a long lockdown? Here's the nurse distributing meds. A good sign.*

7:21 AM. *Chow's being delivered to cells. Not a good sign. We are locked-down.*

7:30 AM. A guard walks by, handing out red apples.

"I've got a special visit today. Are we still locked-down?" I ask. "Yes."

"But the situation on Yard 2 is resolved, right?"

"Yeah. But who knows if you'll get your visit." I tense up.

7:36 AM. Breakfast arrives on carts laden with polystyrene boxes. Two flour tortillas. Refried beans. Shredded cheese. Salsa. Two slices of brown bread.

"Do you think I'll get my special visit today?" I ask the guard.

"I dunno," she says. "I can ask."

Knowing what "I can ask" means, I frown and shake my head. I do yoga, hoping to reduce my anxiety.

9 AM. *If I've not been called by now, I'm not getting a visit. If I miss one, no big deal. There's three left. Things could be worse. Perhaps they just need a day to get back to normal.*

9:40 AM. Two enormous white guards appear, collecting trash in plastic bags.

"I'm supposed to have a visit today with my family who flew from England."

"You've certainly got the accent," one says in south-western drawl. "I can tell you're not lying."

"I'm not lying."

"The DW's walking round right now. You can ask her." Pressing my face to the window, I scan the yard and spot the Deputy Warden at Junior Bull's cell, a short middle-aged woman in a grey suit, working her way along the run in my direction.

9:45 AM. The Deputy Warden arrives, grim-faced, her big brown eyes turned to stone.

"My family flew from England and I'm supposed to have a special visit today."

"You won't have it," she says in a tone that leaves no room for negotiation, turning her feet and body away.

Frustrated, I ask, "What about the rest of the week? That's all we've got left before they fly home."

"You're gonna be locked-down for a few days," she says, walking away. "I don't know about the weekend." Before I can respond, she disappears, leaving me with nausea similar to how I felt after being punched by Ken.

I might not be seeing my dad and sister for a while. If kitchen workers are out of their cells, walking around, why can't I come out?

11:30 AM. I reread yesterday's mail, cheered up by comments from the readers of Jon's Jail Journal.

The next morning at 8 AM, the same two big guards bring breakfast. Four pancakes. Hot cereal. Peanut butter. An apple. Milk.

"Did you get your visit yesterday?" the largest one asks.

"No," I say. "The DW said we're going to be locked-down for a few days."

"Damn. That's rough. And they came all the way from England, right?"

"Yes. The trip cost thousands. They only came to see me."

"You should see if DOC will pay for the trip."

"We'll see what happens. I've got visits until the weekend. Maybe we'll get off lockdown by then."

8:47 AM. Reading, I hear an announcement: "Dog eleven, stand by for a special visit. Get ready."

What the hell! The DW must have reconsidered in light of how far they travelled. Maybe they came down here and begged to get in. Whooooee! I throw my clothes on and dash to Visitation. Sat with their arms tight to their bodies, Dad and Karen try to smile, but their thin lips sink.

"How did you manage to get in?" I ask, sitting down.

"I called down here, and they said it was approved," Dad says. "The DW must have given her permission."

"What was it like when you showed up yesterday?" I ask, wiping my sweaty palms on my trousers.

"It was terrible," Karen says, rubbing her forehead. "My stomach was in knots. I was throwing up all day."

"We saw it on TV," Dad says. "A reporter was standing in front of the prison. I thought, *Bloody hell! It's going to be on lockdown and we won't get in.*"

"What did the news say?"

"A female guard," Karen says, "was held hostage for six hours by a prisoner demanding to be transferred to Montana."

"Any weapons involved or did she get hurt?"

"He had razor blades, but he didn't hurt her," Dad says, scratching his neck.

"It's a good job nobody got hurt. Did the news say how it ended?"

"They told him," she says, "they'd move him to Montana, so he gave up, and they moved him all right, straight to the supermaximum-security prison in Florence."

"Maybe he was doing a copycat of the Buckeye hostage takers. One got transferred to Maine. For raping a guard and a kitchen worker, he got seven consecutive life sentences plus 152 years. But if you're already serving life, I guess the extra time is meaningless."

"Well, we got in today," Dad says. "We've only lost one visit, so we didn't do too bad."

"How's Mum taking it?" I ask.

"We told her we'd try and get in today," Dad says, "and that if we weren't answering the hotel phone that means we got in. So, by now she'll know where we are."

When the visit ends, Dad says, "Do you think I should ask Officer Conway whether we need to call the prison before we come tomorrow?"

"If they let you in today, you should be all right for the rest of the week," I say.

"That's no guarantee. We'd better ask," Karen says, her expression fearful.

We approach Officer Conway, a polite middle-aged woman with long dark hair, a new guard with an air of empathy the environment hasn't yet stripped from her. "Officer, do you think we should call tomorrow before we come out here?" Dad asks.

"Let me call the DW and find out." Officer Conway disappears into an office. A few minutes later, she re-emerges, her expression pained. "I hate to be the bearer of bad news but the DW said no."

"No what?" Dad asks, his nose crinkling. "That we don't need to call, or we can't have the visit?"

"That you can't have the visit."

My dad and Karen's faces scrunch. The corners of their mouths turn south. Their shoulders slump. The stress I've felt for the past few days redoubles. Speechless, I stand, trembling, frustrated. "I'd like to speak to the DW," Karen says in a faltering voice, eyes misting.

"Let me call her again. Actually, there she is," Officer Conway says, nodding towards a set of electronically activated metal and plexiglas security doors. "Maybe she'll talk to you in person." Officer Conway hand signals the Deputy Warden, who walks through the doors and joins us.

"Thank you very much for allowing us to visit today," Dad says, his tone pained.

"You're welcome," the Deputy Warden says, hands on hips, thumbs to the rear.

"Is it not possible for us to come tomorrow?" Dad asks, interlacing his fingers.

"The prison is going to be locked-down for the next few days while we do our investigation. I spoke to Shaun, and I was able to give you today's visit, but tomorrow's isn't possible." My dad and Karen both speak, but the Deputy Warden steamrolls over their words with, "One at a time please!"

Karen sobs. She raises her fingers to her forehead, shields an eye with a cupped hand and bows her head. "I've not seen … my brother in two years … That's all I'm here for … just this one week … to see my brother."

"We've had this trip planned all year," Dad says, holding his palms out. "We came 5,000 miles, at considerable cost, just to see Shaun. All of these visits were approved by the prison, and we've already lost one visit."

"Which visit did you lose?" the Deputy Warden asks, raising her chin, dropping her hands to her sides.

"Yesterday's," Dad says, hitching his thumbs into his pockets.

"And when do you go back to England?"

"Monday," Dad says, his eyelids twitching.

The Deputy Warden gazes over our heads as if running a calculation. "Right, here's what I'm going to do. I'll authorise tomorrow's visit, but if anything, and I mean anything, goes wrong on the yard during the visit, we'll have to send you home."

"I understand that," Dad says, his lips reappearing. With our postures easing and smiles emerging on our shell-shocked faces, we thank the Deputy Warden. She departs. We discuss our luck and say goodbye. I head for a strip search.

The next morning, the two oversized guards appear at my cell. "I'm ready for the visit," I say.

"Hold on. We're gonna have to strip you out."

That's odd being strip-searched going out. It must be an additional security measure. After the search, I'm escorted to Visitation.

"He can't come in here! This is my command post!" a burly sergeant yells.

Shit! They're going to cancel the visit.

Officer Conway appears. "I'm going to escort you to a different room, a conference room. And the visit has only been approved for three hours."

The plush conference table in the room brings to mind my stockbroking career. *Pitching shares to clients. The view of Camelback Mountain from the high-rise. Power sales meetings. Rowdy New York Italian co-workers. Receiving awards for setting record commissions.* The window overlooks a garden and a section of desert under excavation, including a series of ditches. Hummingbirds are darting from flower to flower, hovering to sip nectar, competing for air space in the oasis against bumblebees and menacingly elongated wasps called mud daubers. As if desperate to join them, a trapped fly is beating itself senseless against the window.

My dad and sister arrive, their faces grey. We hug. "I thought I wasn't going to see you again!" I say, resolved to bolster their spirits and make the most of things.

"I noticed," Dad says, sitting down. "You should have seen your face yesterday. You turned as white as a ghost, and if you'd had hair, it would have stood on end." We laugh.

"We've only got three hours," I say.

"It's better than nothing," Karen says.

When the visit ends, I say, "This might be the last time I see you in a while. They may not allow your final visit." Their expressions say they've reached the same conclusion. We hug.

"I'll call the prison on Saturday, and we'll see if they'll let us in," Dad says.

"Thanks for coming. It's been great seeing you." More hugs.

"Goodbye, Shaun," Karen whispers, tears running. "Love you."

"Love you, too," I say, filling with sadness. Putting on a brave face, I try to hold my tears in, but some spill. Saturday visits are cancelled. On Monday, I think about my dad and sister flying home, how much I miss them, and whether Jade will agree to meet Karen.

CHAPTER 40

Dr Owen reads my thought journal, documenting my happiness at seeing my dad and sister versus the disappointment and tension surrounding the hostage situation and cancelled visits. "How did you deal with these feelings during that time?" he asks, elbows on the table, pyramiding his opposing fingertips.

"Using cognitive techniques," I say, hands on my lap. "I tried to look at it as an activating event over which I had no control. Something I shouldn't get stressed about."

"Did that work?"

"Yes and no. When it comes to things that upset my family, I get upset."

"Is that normal or abnormal?" He drops his hands to the table and leans back.

"Normal for most people."

"You were looking forward to those visits for a long time. Then something happened, and you had no control over events. Your hormones responded. Did you cope with it?"

"My anxiety was up. My thoughts became depressed. I felt lousy. But I wrote and wrote and wrote. I felt better towards the end of it. After the shock wore off, I tried to go with the flow."

"It's more than just going with the flow," he says, patting the table, eyes narrowing. "Going with the flow is what put you in prison. It's about increased self-awareness. It's about how you express your energy."

"How so?" I ask, confused.

"Let's take a pilot as an example. If a pilot gets into a conflict at home, he's going to take that negative energy with him. If he gets into a conflict day after day then that negative energy is going to compromise his ability to fly safely."

"I see. So, did I express the negative energy of the hostage situation in a good or bad way?"

"What did you do with the energy?"

"I wrote."

"There you go. You answered your own question. Didn't you thrive on chaotic energy in the past?" he says, his voice speeding up. "Isn't uncertainty a theme of the stock market? And partying? Couldn't that have blown up in your face at any time?"

"I do enjoy the wild fluctuations of the stock market. You've previously said a reason for my partying was the need for cheap thrills. But the hostage situation was different. My family suffered, and that was upsetting."

"And how do you feel about that now?"

"I accept what's happened. Because I didn't get to see Dad so much, he's coming back in October with my mum and aunt. So now I've got something to look forward to again."

"When do you get out of prison?"

"I'm eligible for deportation in November 2007."

"A year and a half. It's time for you to start planning."

"Knowing it's getting closer is reassuring. During the hostage situation it was in the back of my mind that I'll soon be out and won't have to deal with all of this anymore."

"All this what? The torrent of absurdities!" he says, throwing an arm above his head. "If someone on the street had to deal with what you're dealing with they'd be running along screaming, 'This can't be! Someone can surely fix this!' Yet in here, things that may be difficult for outsiders to deal with happen all the time. Because of this environment, you've gained skills that will help you when you're released. Your level of resilience is way up. You've matured. You now have an ability to bounce back from all sorts of things. You've learned these things the hard way, but what's important is that you've learned them. Some people may go through life never having learned the things you've learned in here. Something you have to consider for when you hit the streets is that issues you had to deal with before your arrest have been on hold."

"Viktor Frankl compared release to a diver coming up with the bends."

"But his experience was in the late thirties and early forties. He used his prison experience to help people when he got out. His techniques were nothing new. That knowledge has been around for millennia."

"Reading the ancient Greeks, I see how the various contemporary schools of thought in psychology have recycled their wisdom."

"Which Greeks have you read?" he asks, smiling curiously.

"I can't pronounce most of them. The Pre-Socratics and plenty of Plato and Aristotle."

"How does studying them work for you?"

"It increases my critical-thinking skills."

"Excellent," he says, nodding.

"I'm interested in how old knowledge is recycled. The atomists seemed to be early physicists. The principle of conservation of energy, in that it cannot be created, destroyed or divided, ties in with the Hindu belief that everything just is."

"But there's still plenty we don't know. When we thought atoms were the smallest particles, along came electrons, protons, neutrons, and then stuff like quarks, neutrinos, muons, gluons, bosons and all kinds of obscure little elements. We revised Newton. We're revising Einstein. It's an evolving process. At least what you're learning will help you when you get out. Most people go out with what they learn here, and they don't have a lot. If you're willing to accept a broad-based view of yourself and take it to the outside world, you're going to have a lot of potential to do well. It's about accepting yourself, knowing when to hold your head up, and knowing when to be careful."

"I'm used to going overboard," I say, tight-lipped. "I start out meaning well, but I get carried away, and something inside of me that sabotages my intentions takes over." I want to tell him about the wolves. *He'll know how to handle them.*

"But you're learning to affect yourself, to modulate who you are most days. You're not trying to change the lives of thousands of people, which is what got you in prison."

"Isn't that under control because of this environment? I keep myself to myself here."

"That's here. If you ran around grandiosely in here, the thugs would just as soon crush you. It's a good adaptation you've reached. You blend in. You're learning to remain humble, which wasn't your previous inclination."

"I still have to work on it."

"We all do. You have to allow yourself to have humility. You have to put it into practice and not struggle with it. Looking at your thought journal, I can see you're making progress. You're getting a grip on your natural inclination towards grandiosity. When you're on the streets, do you want to be the person who runs to a window and jumps out, or the person who walks to a window, relaxes and enjoys the view?"

"I want to stay sane."

"Keep focussed, day to day, on your ups and downs, realising your emotional shifts like you did during the hostage situation, when the world was screwed up, when there was a crisis, and a response, and a crisis for everyone else. Look at what DOC did. They stopped everything. They assessed the situation: is it safe or unsafe? They determined it was safe and eased up a little bit at a time, gradually. It's the same for you, your gradual ease, your slowly increased ability to think more broadly. And you're starting to do it. The results are clear in your thought journal. You're showing a willingness to be who you are without having to dress yourself up."

"How far have I got to go?" I ask, encouraged.

"The rest of your life. We all continue to evolve, to observe and learn from life's plusses and minuses. Take Viktor Frankl. He got out of Auschwitz. Not unscathed, but he took what he learned to help others. Everything you do affects your brain, including this talk therapy. Until next time, I want you to keep up the thought journal. You're making progress. You're reshaping your brain. And

I'd like you to consider the dynamic interplay of energy when you're doing yoga."

"OK. Thanks for that. I'm learning a great deal from you. You're taking everything to deeper levels."

"No. The person taking it to deeper levels is you."

The hair rises on the back of my neck. *I was destined to meet Dr Owen.* I leave resolved to tell him about the wolves in the next session.

CHAPTER 41

In June 2006, I'm hunched over my desk, writing, when a figure appears in the doorway, completely blocking out the sunlight. I crane my neck and freeze. Wearing only orange sports shorts and shower sandals, the African-American prisoner is almost six-and-a-half foot, with a massive build, head shaved and scars so big he appears to have been chopped up and sewn back together again. He's new to this yard. I don't know his name, but in the chow hall prisoners were jokingly calling him John Coffey after the character in the movie *The Green Mile*. Tense, I squeeze my pen. *What does he want?* I drop the pen and stand.

"Hey, man, I overheard you in the chow hall," he says in a deep voice, lingering in the doorway as if uncertain whether to come in. "Where'd you get that accent from?"

"England," I say, motionless, hands at my side, pulse rising.

"That's cool, man," he says, nodding. "My name's T-Bone."

"I'm Shaun. Pleased to meet you, T-Bone," I say, stepping forward cautiously. He moves closer, filling the cell with his presence. My hand disappears into his. He squeezes the blood from my fingers. *There must be some stories behind those scars.* "How can I help you, T-Bone?" I say, wondering if he's on the hunt for food.

He leans against the wall and folds his arms. "I've always been fascinated by English history."

"What?" I ask, bewildered. "Why?"

He stands up straight. "What intrigues me is the ability of the English to adapt to invaders over the centuries," he says in a friendly tone, gesturing with his hands. "The Vikings came in several times, but the old English, they kept pushing back. And the Romans. Look at Queen Boudicca, a very powerful woman who almost kicked the Romans out of Briton. The Picts and Gauls sent tribe after tribe. The English maintained who they were even though they were subjugated. They showed a lot of fortitude to not be completely enslaved while at the same time maintaining their identity. Do you know what I'm saying?" he asks, his voice switching from professorial to deep and intimidating.

"Yes, I love reading history, especially the Romans," I say with emphasis to show he has my full attention. "Edward Gibbon's *The History of the Decline and Fall of the Roman Empire* is one of my all-time favourite reads. I was fascinated by how the leaders were knocking each other off left and right with no scruples whatsoever, and the public never had a clue."

"That stuff still goes on," he says with certainty. "You English are a mixed lot like most cultures in Europe, but the island has kept you guys to a certain way of thinking."

"You calling me a resilient island monkey?" I ask, smiling.

He laughs. "The Brits are definitely not island monkeys."

Emboldened by his friendliness, I say, "I've never seen scars so big. I hope you don't mind me asking, but were you in some kind of fight?" He frowns, tilts his head back, folds his arms and gazes down disagreeably. The atmosphere thickens. *Oh shit!* "I'm only asking because I write stories about prisoners that I post to the Internet. I bet you've got some good ones. If you'd be interested in sharing them, I'd be happy to work with you. I don't get paid, but the prisoners get pen pals and books sent to them sometimes."

"You know what, let me pray about that and I'll get back to you." He shakes my hand and leaves. The next day, he returns. "I've done a bit of checking around on you. You've got a good reputation. I hope no one's been giving you any shit."

Briefly, I visualise T-Bone smashing Ken and Bud, but I don't say a word as I believe in handling my own situations, and because of the rules of racial division, his intervention might multiply my problems. In the last four years, I've seen prisoners stir up drama and suffer big consequences. "I'm doing fine, T-Bone."

He agrees to tell stories for Jon's Jail Journal and starts with background information. Before moving to Arizona, he was a

Marine. In South America, he saw fierce action, people getting killed. His pained expression piques my curiosity, but I'm afraid to pry. He stresses that he doesn't want to talk about the Marines. He moved to Arizona and made money as a bodyguard, which he invested into cocaine. Due to crimes revolving around cocaine, he's served eighteen years since 1986.

"How many riots you been through?" I ask, sat in the chair, taking notes, aiming to gauge his experience.

"Four big ones," he says, sat on the bottom bunk, fingertips on thighs.

"There must have been some terrible injuries."

"Yeah. I saw people lose their lives," he says, wiping sweat from his face onto a forearm. "Heads get bust open with weights, pipes, baseball bats, picks, shovels. People getting shanked in their eyes."

"In their eyes! Holy shit!" I say, shaking my head. "How did it feel for you being in a riot?"

"You gotta do what you've gotta do. You've gotta get down."

"Have you noticed how the atmosphere changes just before something's going to happen?"

"There's a smell of fear, doubt and stress. There's an instinctual change in body movement and body language. People start positioning themselves in groups on the yard."

"It's hard for me to convey to people outside of here the effect of a prisoner calling another prisoner a punk-ass bitch. If someone calls you that, how does it make you feel?"

He inhales loudly, expanding his chest. "Right away, I'm thinking of death. I'm not gonna go berserk. I'll wait and catch the person alone. The guards can't see it, but I'll deal with it."

"How?"

"It depends on who's saying it. If someone calls me a punk-ass bitch, that's like saying I'm a piece of nothing. I take it up the ass in here. That I'm subhuman and have no honour or self-respect. That I need to be killed. In prison you have two things: yourself and your word. If someone calls me out, I'm gonna handle my business."

"Whites, Mexican Americans and Mexicans make up most of the prison population in Arizona, so you must have endured a lot of racism?"

"Here, blacks are always at the bottom of the totem pole. I've experienced pure hatred 'cause of the colour of my skin. People seething with vile contempt and hate, looking at me like they wanna kill me 'cause I'm black. But I'm wearing the same clothes, doing the same time."

"How do you stay strong?"

"The truth is: I turn to God. God helps me mind my Ps and Qs."

Surprised, I pause. "How cheap is life in prison?"

"It means nothing. I've known people killed for $40-worth of heroin."

"You must have lost count of the fights you've seen?"

"I've seen so many people get annihilated, it's unreal. I've seen cops get shanked – one in the eyeball."

"You must get sick of it?"

"The raping annoys me the most," he says, brow furrowed. "It's the foulest thing anyone can do to anyone. Back in the day at The Walls, every single night someone was getting brutalised. You could hear male flesh pounding male flesh."

A sickly feeling rises in my stomach. "And nobody stopped it?"

"You couldn't snitch. If you couldn't fight back, you were game. Some of the rapers were the size of apes. They'd squeeze the back of the victim's neck to put them unconscious. There was a smell of crap on the run from so many dudes taking it up the ass. Regular dudes, not homosexuals, getting brutalised, punked, and scared to admit they were getting raped. You'd also see big dudes kissing little white boys like they were women. Kissing them on the lips and neck. Then all night long you'd hear the punks getting fucked up the ass, going *huh-huh-huh*."

"It sounds like a nightmare," I say, revolted.

"Worse. Gang members would hold someone down and stick things in his ass."

"Things?"

"Cans, soda bottles, shampoo bottles, broom handles or metal shanks."

Squirming, I exhale as if to expel the thought. "Unbelievable! How many fights you been in?"

He laughs. "I lost count."

"Got a good one for the blog?"

"Yeah. I had a celly who was six-feet tall and about 230 pounds. He had gold teeth and long greasy hair. He was a strong man. A cut-up dude. He was benching 385, squatting 475 and dead lifting 400 or more."

"Holy shit! Why'd you get into it with him?"

"It came about 'cause he was raping people on the yard. He raped a retarded kid with mental problems in our cell. I said to him, 'It smells like crap in here. What's been going on, man?' He said, 'What do you think's going on? I just got me some.' I told him, 'Man, you've got to get your nasty tail up out of here.' He said, 'No. You got to get your tail out of here. You ain't nothing but a punk anyway, and I'm gonna cut you.' He stood up, looking at me all crazy. I hit him with a straight right, and broke his jaw in two places. He lost four teeth. Another blow fractured his eye socket. I hit him flush, and he was out."

"What's flush?" I ask, scribbling fast.

"Flat. Like this." T-Bone flexes a bicep as big as a soccer ball and punches my arm, almost knocking me off the chair.

"I get it," I say, wincing, trying to ignore the pain to keep writing and to not show weakness.

"I thought he was dead. I laid him on his bunk, and took a shower. When I came back, he was still on his bunk, calling for his mama. Some white guys, Aryan Brotherhood, came over who wanted to kill him 'cause the dude he raped was white. I stopped that. He was alone on his bunk, bleeding and groaning, and I looked in his eyes and saw a spark like he was becoming more aware."

"Was he regrouping?" I ask, gripped.

"He *had* regrouped. From the top bunk, I moved my right leg. He jumped up. He had a rod of finely sharpened iron. An eight-inch blade with a rag on one end and a real nice point on the other. I backhanded the wrist of the hand holding the shank. He came at me. His eyes were red with rage. His jaw was swollen up. Blood was coming out of the corner of his mouth. He had death in his eyes: black pupils totally empty and void of emotion and feeling. I still have nightmares about the way he looked. He made his move: a lunge. I hit him in the right eye, and he stumbled back. I kicked him in his right thigh, and I felt my foot penetrate the muscle down to the bone. I knew I had to disarm him. His leg was momentarily numb, so in a split second, I grabbed his right hand with both of mine and twisted his wrist. I broke his wrist and elbow and kicked him in his lung."

"Did he go down?"

"Oh, yeah, he was finished. I put him on his bunk, but he couldn't keep still 'cause of the pain. An hour later, it's count time. A guard comes by. I'm using the toilet. My celly rolled over and blood came out of his mouth in front of the guard. He said I'd assaulted him in his sleep. They took me to the hole. I was charged with dangerous and deadly assault on an inmate. I got a seven-and-a-half-year sentence that ran concurrent with my other time, and the cops thought I was a real bad character after that."

I usually end up growing close to the people I blog about, and T-Bone is no exception. He asks a lot about England, where he dreams of going. He wants to see the ruins of the Roman Empire such as Hadrian's Wall, but fears his criminal record might prevent him from getting a passport. He says that I'm going to be an author someday, and he'll be my bodyguard. We get in heated discussions about politics, US military action and the crisis in the Middle East. His stories quickly become as popular at Jon's Jail Journal as Two Tonys and She-Ra's – who get letters and books sent to them from generous blog readers around the world. I speak to all three daily.

Some of the whites don't appreciate T-Bone in my cell because he's black. T-Bone walks laps around the yard at night, and when I offer to join him, he says to stay in my cell for my own safety. I ask him what could be safer than being in the company of the biggest man on the yard. He laughs and lets me come. As we stroll by the perimeter fence, we attract disapproval from clusters of prisoners adhering to racial segregation. Some heckle us, one even calls us lovers, but T-Bone returns their wisecracks, mostly shutting them up.

CHAPTER 42

A prisoner wielding a foot-long shank passes my cell door, his face obscured by a white towel folded like a cowboy's neckerchief over his nose. I jump up and watch his tattooed muscular physique march towards the perimeter fence, prisoners scattering away, locking themselves in their cells. He yells at a dozen staff members on the other side of the chain-link, including a female filming him with a camcorder. The guards appear to be negotiating, drawing him closer. When he gets within several feet, they open up with pepper spray, painting his skin fake-tan orange. He howls and runs to a shower, strips naked, rubs his face and body with wet trousers and puts them back on. For two hours, he struts around the yard, flapping his arms, flexing his muscles, shaking the shank above his head, shouting at the guards. Wielding shotguns with live rounds, SRT members appear on the other side of the fence, wearing helmets with visors and shank-proof black vests. A female sergeant yells orders at them to line up and take aim.

"Before you kill me, let me talk to you!" he yells, seven shotguns pointing at him.

"Drop the weapon!"

Although I don't want to see him get killed, I'm compelled to watch.

"Just let me talk to you, please!"

"Drop the weapon now!"

For a few seconds, he says nothing, squaring off as if daring them to shoot. I brace to hear gunfire. Eventually, he drops the shank.

"Put your hands on your head and kneel down!"

He complies. Guards charge onto the yard from the chow hall. They beat him flat on his stomach and pin him with their knees until a white van appears. He's transported, heavily chained, to a supermaximum prison.

Due to his actions, days go by with the prison on lockdown. We're strip-searched, and guards wearing rubber gloves ransack our cells. A shank is found in a mattress belonging to Slingblade's old-timer cellmate, prolonging the lockdown. It's obviously not theirs but both are cuffed and dragged off to a punishment block to be interrogated with a view to criminal prosecution. Meals in plastic trays are delivered by guards. With my door electronically locked and the window barely able to open, hardly any fresh air gets in. It's hard to maintain yoga discipline with the constant irritation of sweaty itchy skin. I read with my fan aimed directly at my crotch to soothe where my skin has taken on a life of its own as if ants are crawling on it.

Every day, I look forward to the nightly mail delivery. I receive a letter from my sister, and open it fast. Jade has agreed to meet her in a few days. She'll let me know how it goes. I grin. *If she's meeting my sister then she hasn't written me off.* I ponder the possibilities with Jade until I pass out in a sticky heap on the mattress.

Off lockdown, I greet T-Bone on the yard.

"What's going on with you and Jade?" he asks.

"She got back with her boyfriend. I can't blame her. It was good while it lasted, but how can I expect a woman like her to want to go out of her way to come and visit me in this shithole?"

"It's because you haven't stepped up to the plate," he says, smiling confidently.

"What are you on about?" I ask, confused.

"I forgot, they don't play baseball in England," he says, shaking his head. "They play cricket. You need to stick it in her wicket. Tell her how you truly feel about her."

"When I did that last summer, she backed away," I say.

"And so did you back away. You need to tell her to leave Sancho alone." Sancho is the name prisoners call the man who steals their partners. "Tell her to get back down here, so you can give her a bit of old English know-how."

"I can't satisfy her needs from in here though!"

"It doesn't matter. She's fascinated with you. If she's with Sancho, it's just 'cause it's convenient for the moment."

"She's engaged! I can't expect her to put her life on hold for me."

"She obviously already did. She visited you. Has she found a yoga expert who can get into extreme positions while tickling her thang?" I laugh. "How many times has she visited?"

"A few."

"She's in love with you then."

"How do you figure?"

"For her to be messing around with a guy in the joint like that, she's got to be up to something serious."

"I don't know."

"At least you're not thinking with your thang, but I think you may have stepped on it. Do you love her?"

"In a way. I was head over heels last summer."

"Have you told her what your feelings are, your desires, your aspirations?"

"I've covered it."

"But it must really come from the heart. Put a little soul into it, brother." He points at a bird of prey gliding, slowly, majestically, as if it owns the sky. "That's a hawk. It's a sign for me that the day's gonna be all right. I'll catch you on the weekend." I return to my cell more optimistic about Jade. T-Bone has that effect on me.

CHAPTER 43

Still writing Two Tonys' autobiography, I spend hours daily with him. During breaks, we discuss what's going on in our lives. Proudly, he says he has a daughter around my age and they're finally in touch. She's been sending him books and money to spend on commissary. He's hoping she'll visit soon, and he'll get to see his grandchildren for the first time. He always asks how my family are doing. I tell him they're busy planning my sister's wedding, which, sadly, I'll miss because I'm inside. When I tell him what's going on in my life, I find his frank advice reassuring. I'm confident he wants me to succeed. Sometimes, it feels as if he's infusing me with his spirit because he's never getting out, imparting knowledge he knows I'll put to good use. He's convinced I'll be an author and insists I keep "sharpening my pencil" – practising my skills. Even if I don't win the race, he says I'll always be his horse.

In my cell, sat on a chair, I say, "I'm thinking about asking the shrink for advice about staying away from drugs when I get out."

"What do you wanna know about drugs?" Two Tonys says, stood by the toilet. "I've done them, sold them and killed for them, in a roundabout way, drug debts and shit like that."

"I'm going to ask for some general advice. Dr Owen seems really intelligent."

"How the fuck's he gonna tell you to stay away from drugs?" Moving to the centre of the cell, he throws up his hands. "What does he know? Has he ever been hooked? Ask him that. Does he know the thrill of driving down the highway after you've just blown a motherfucker's jaw off, high on crystal meth? Your mind's tripping hard and fast and you're listening to Pink Floyd's 'Another Brick in the Wall,' thinking you just made the most intelligent decision in your life 'cause you're so fucking smart on drugs. You're high. You're Jet Li, Arnie and Sly Stallone all rolled into one."

Nodding, but keen to defend Dr Owen, I say, "I see what you're saying – the shrink's an academic – but he seems to know his stuff."

"All he can tell you is there's nerve-endings in your head like a little clit that twitches when you do drugs and makes you think, *Man, I'm having a great time. How can I get more of this stuff 'cause I really like this feeling? I'm so smart. I'm so handsome. I'm so tough. They're all looking at me in this nightclub, saying, 'Man, who is that guy?'*"

"So what advice you got?"

"Don't fucking do it! And don't hang around with people who are doing it or else you'll end up doing it, too. I don't care how cool your friends who want you to do drugs think they are, you've got to understand that all your values and decision-making processes that you've acquired along the road of life that parents, aunts, uncles, schoolteachers have taught you – right from wrong, good from bad, smart from stupid – you're gonna throw out the fucking window on drugs. I remember being in those discotheques back in the day with a bad-ass three-piece Armani suit on, gold chains around my neck, packing a five-shot Smith & Wesson .38, my Rolex, my pinkie rings, as high as Ike Turner on coke, and that's a motherfucker who grew a moustache just so he could catch the rocks falling out of his fucking nose. I knew everybody in the place was looking at me thinking, *Man, oh, man, boy is he cool.* And the reason I knew that is 'cause the drugs told me so. It started out recreationally for me. It turned into a dependency. Let me tell you something 'cause you're getting out next year. I guarantee that you'll be right back in here if you go back to drugs. That is if you live long enough. If someone doesn't kill you. If you don't OD. Like I've told you before, there's a BD, a DD and an AD in my life. Before Drugs, During Drugs and After Drugs. The most horrendous and costly decisions I ever made in my life happened During Drugs. Many people lost their lives. I lost my decision-making processes. How the fuck can a guy like me go from living in a five-level house in a beautiful subdivision in Anchorage, Alaska, driving a gold Cadillac Eldorado and a silver Jag, with people around me who cared about me, end up on the back of a Greyhound bus at a food stop, watching people eat their fucking hamburgers 'cause I haven't got any money in my pocket?"

His advice stirs up my wolves. "Don't you think people can do a little bit of drugs and function fine?"

"Not if you're weak. It could be alcohol. It could be marijuana. One leads to others. Supposedly Cary Grant took plenty of acid after he was 60. That's OK if you're Cary Grant, and you've got a manager and motherfuckers who can protect you from your fucked-up decision-making processes. But if you're just out there, climbing the ladder, don't do it!"

"What about drug-addicted celebrities?"

"They're a bunch of fuck-ups, too. Look at Whitney Houston or Kurt Cobain. What possessed Kurt Cobain to climb up to his loft and blow his brains out when he had the number one band in the world?"

"Heroin."

"And Robert Downey Jr. How many times has he crashed and burned? And then there's motherfuckers who turn into monsters. Look at Charles Manson with the women on LSD, driving around LA, sticking turkey forks in people's bellies, cutting pregnant women open to look at their foetuses and giggling while they did it. They weren't insane. They were from Iowa and Nebraska. Their daddies were grocery store managers and shit like that. How did Charles Manson control them? With drugs. They're bad, man. Back in the seventies, when coke was chic, they lied to us. They told us we couldn't get addicted. Cocaine wasn't like that scumbag heroin that made you wanna lie around all day, puking and scratching your ass and balls. They were wrong."

"So, what's your advice for me when I get out?"

"Listen, Shaun. I like you. You're a nice guy. The cards turned on you and you wound up in this motherfucker, not because you're bad or evil, but because you made bad decisions due to taking drugs. Get out of here and just don't take them anymore. Stay the fuck away from them. It's that fucking simple. You can spend all the money in the world on shrinks, drug counsellors and thirty-grand-a-month rehab centres, but the bottom line is, 'You've just got to fucking say no!'"

After he leaves, I ponder his advice. *I know not to do drugs, but the situation is more complex. Yes, I'm off drugs now, but I fear for the future. Dramatic things tend to happen in my life. What if I get stressed out and resume drugs? By asking if drugs are OK in certain situations part of me must be stuck in that world. Two Tonys is right: the door to that world needs to be welded shut and I must take responsibility by the choices I make. I'm going to put the same question to Dr Owen, curious to compare his answer to Two Tonys'.*

CHAPTER 44

Dr Owen's listening to "The Godfather Waltz." He reads my thought journal, documenting highs – how I calmly read a long passage in SMART Recovery class and how I transferred nervous energy into writing – and lows – getting mad at Frankie for instigating wrestling when I was trying to write.

"Before we begin, is there anything you'd like to discuss?"

"Yes, there is," I say. "I'd like to get your advice about drugs. Obviously, I don't need to be running around raves doing designer drugs. But where do I draw the line? It seems everyone in the world is on drugs if you include alcohol, tobacco and prescription pills. Can I drink a glass of wine with my parents over dinner? Can I take Xanax before flying for anxiety?"

"There are two things you need to think about. Firstly, you need awareness and mindfulness to understand the situations and the premises that are drawing you to drugs. Secondly, you need an awareness of how drugs work. On the wall behind me is a diagram of the limbic system, a system of nerves and networks that, when stimulated, makes you feel good, and tells you, *Let's get higher and higher*. Then, doing more drugs gives you immediate gratification. Instead of seeking such chemically induced extremes, you must learn how to activate it at lower natural levels. Ecstasy, ketamine or whatever don't come in nature. They are refined substances that cause huge cascades of neurotransmitters. You need to think about what gives you a little euphoria without doing drugs."

"Writing. Exercise. Sex!" I say, smiling, hoping he prescribes plenty of the latter.

"But frequent sexual encounters are not a positive addiction," he says, shaking his head. "If you're having sex compulsively, you're not enjoying it."

"I never had sex I didn't enjoy," I say, hoping he laughs.

He remains serious. "If you're increasing the amount and your sexual aggression is escalating, doesn't that interfere with your ability to function normally?"

My smile fades. "I don't know. I think we're designed for sex and it's a good natural healthy thing."

"Sex is a good thing, but becoming a sex addict isn't. It may be pleasurable in the heat of the moment. Some people misappropriate Tantra for Tantric sex."

"Sex addicts?"

"Yes. The idea is mindfulness. It's part of being in a healthy relationship with a person."

"Are you saying any kind of drug is out of the question?" I ask, encouraged by the wolves. "What if I want to take a one-time trip to do peyote with North Mexican Indians or Amanita mushrooms with Siberians? I read about professional people who occasionally take these trips as consciousness-raising experiments."

"Why would Mexican Indians or indigenous Siberians want you, some Westerner, sharing their sacred rites or rituals?"

"Are you saying they'd only be doing it for commercial reasons?"

"Which leads to problems. You're assuming you can buy a cheap thrill through a mystical experience. A mystical experience is supposed to give you a profound understanding of the universe."

"Timothy Leary claimed to get that through LSD."

"Maybe he did, but my answer for you is a resounding no," he says, raising his voice. "There are no short cuts for you. Ahead is a journey down a long hard road that's going to get you where you need to be. If you do drugs once, you'll want to test yourself again and again. You'll think, *I can do this and this*. When in actuality your willpower is fucked up by drugs."

Shocked to hear him use the F word, I sit up straight. *He really cares, just like Two Tonys. It's time to tell him about the wolves.*

"Your neurotransmitters are screwed up by huge chemical loads in the brain. You'll have to become like a teetotaller who learns to appreciate tea or a highly sexual person who learns to have sex with one partner, allowing your partner to look into yourself. Yoga will help. Yoga was developed by people who sat outside, in isolated situations, and developed ideas that took place over 5,000 years of tradition. You need to find things that make sense to you and explore those to achieve unity."

"Writing and creativity make sense to me."

"There are many authors who have done drugs and done well. But on closer examination they did drugs to address inner turmoil, and when they looked back after doing drugs, they saw they had natural writing skills regardless of whether they did drugs or not."

"I've had inner turmoil." *The wolves.*

"It's something you need to figure out."

I inhale deeply. "At times of extreme stress, I heard wolves howling for me to come out and party," I say, shifting in my seat, worried I sound crazy. Clasping his fingers, he stares as if he wants me to continue. "Over time, I figured they represented my raver friends all combined into a strong force. Certain rave music also triggers the wolves. If I stayed in on a weekend, they howled so loud for me to come out that I couldn't sit still or rest and, more often than not, I'd follow their call and find a party. When I got to a party and was with my raver friends, getting high, the wolves shut up and left me alone."

"And what of the wolves now?" he asks in a low tone.

"After my arrest, I didn't have time to think about them, but talking to a friend about drugs the other day, I felt them trying to resist his advice. Even today with you, some of the questions I've asked were derived from their influence, which must mean there's still a part of me that wants to party. I feel like I've become a new person because of everything that's happened since my arrest, but another part of me is struggling to accept that, and I'm afraid of that part." Having never expressed this to anyone, I stare, tense, my breathing shallow, heart beating rapidly, hoping his guidance will make a difference.

For a few seconds, he contemplates in silence. "You need to

go back, way back, and ask yourself what were you telling yourself from the ages of 12 to 25. How old were you when you first started to hear the wolves?"

I lean back. "Early 20s." My feet shift and lock themselves around the legs of the chair. It was after I'd almost been beaten to death by some drunks. I was repeatedly kicked in the head and hit with an iron bar until pieces of my teeth were knocked out and I was left unconscious, but the incident is still too painful to tell Dr Owen yet.

"That's when your personality solidified, and you chose certain paths in life. There was something about you you were not happy with, and perhaps you filled that gap with the wolves."

"I'm not sure. I've always been happy-go-lucky. In school a lot of boys grew bigger and taller than me, and I felt inadequate until I caught up. I got mauled by some of the rugby players. As I grew, I preferred the company of girlfriends. I was always a wheeler-dealer from a young age, and that drive got stronger, much stronger into my early 20s."

"Why do you feel you were driven to acquire material things?"

"I guess I had something to prove. I set out to conquer Wall Street with a hundred-per-cent faith in my ability. I believed my destiny was to make it big in the financial markets. I equated success and material stuff with these goals. I was immature."

"So, you were mesmerised by external things, and you didn't give much attention to your inner core. There's a part of you that wanted attention and material things would generate that. You have to realise the essence of a person has nothing to do with being attracted to money and things. Look at the Dalai Lama. He looks like a regular old fella. But he's very charismatic. You need to find your internal self, and you need to ask yourself, *What person do I want to be?* Drugs aren't going to do that for you. Not peyote or mescaline or LSD. Hallucinogens may fit into certain cultures, but in our culture, they don't make sense."

"Does all the alcohol and nicotine consumption make sense?"

"Wasn't that a scene you were part of?"

"No," I say loudly. "We were counterculture. We dressed outrageously. Our music sounded like signals from outer space. We were rebellious. We sneered at mainstream, including mainstream drugs. We were out to shock."

"Is this the wolves talking?"

He's right. Wishing I could take back my words, I laugh.

"You wanted attention," he says.

"I got attention."

"But it didn't work out. Everything you did was a step on the path that brought you here."

"That's true."

"With increased mindfulness, you can learn from the previous negative things you did and determine what things are going to be beneficial to you. You're able to start afresh."

"I agree."

"Now let's discuss your thought journal. When you were in class you applied breathing at the end of each sentence, and you did well, but when your buddy instigated a play fight, you got mad. Instead of getting mad, you can train yourself to concentrate on your breathing, just like you did in class."

"You're right. But it's easier said than done."

"Absolutely. But you need to think about breathing and to be able to analyse your thoughts in uncomfortable situations. When you take a deep breath, you get a useful response, and your adrenaline doesn't pump in as much. I see progress in your thought journal throughout the month."

"Good."

"Do you realise anxiety has driven you all your life? You need to become adept and to learn to listen to your anxiety. To know when things make sense and when they stop making sense. For homework, I want you to listen to how you talk to yourself, but also to notice and to write down when anxiety causes you to cross the fence into irrational thoughts. And remember to breathe. Long deep breaths. Make Darth Vader noises if you have to."

Having discussed the wolves, I return to my cell feeling lighter, unburdened. *He's right about anxiety throughout my life. When it rises to a certain point, I get confused and make terrible decisions. I recall it from teenage shyness to adult fear of flying. My mum suffers from anxiety and depression, so perhaps I have a genetic predisposition. Instead of looking back, perhaps it would be more productive to focus on managing it. Surely prison has crushed a lot of anxiety out of me. Some of the most stress I ever had was when the SWAT team smashed my door down, and my first days in jail. Situations like that must have strengthened me for life. Having adjusted to prison, surely I'll experience outside as a much safer place, so what's to be anxious for? But circumstances can change dramatically, and anxiety can manifest for many reasons, not all of them dependent on external factors. To succeed in life, I must gain more knowledge about my inner self with the help of Dr Owen. It's giving me a sense of control over something I was clueless about before my arrest.*

CHAPTER 45

Outside the chow hall, I'm shocked to find Two Tonys fuming as if ready to kill someone, his face contorting, eyes darting. "What's the matter?" I ask, worried about my friend.

"Write my DOC number down in case I get sent to the hole," he says, unable to stand still, his jaw muscles flexing.

"Why?" I ask, dreading losing him to lockdown.

"It's nothing," he says, teeth clenched.

"It doesn't sound like nothing. Are you expecting something to jump off?"

"I'm gonna grab a shank and stab Ken," he says, eyes ablaze.

Ken. I should have known. "What's he done now?"

"I gave him batteries last week, and he said he was gonna return them today, but he never did."

Relieved the issue is small, I ask, "Is stabbing Ken and going to the hole worth batteries that cost a dollar?"

"That's not the point." He turns away from me. "It's the principle. If he feels he doesn't have to pay me, then he's disrespecting me in front of everyone. I go by the old code. I'll show this motherfucker not to fuck with me."

I take a few steps and face him. "You're emotional right now. I think you should take some time out. Sleep on it and see how you feel tomorrow."

"If the motherfucker's not gonna pay, I'm just gonna get angrier. I need to take care of it," he says, panting.

"You know he's on psych meds, heroin and crystal meth. He might not be thinking about the batteries right now. He's a little out there."

"He's definitely out in left field, but I'm out there as well."

"He's left of left field." He laughs. "Working in finance," I say,

"I learned that a loan officer has to perform a credit analysis on applicants. That means looking at the work history of the person, tax returns, debts and repayment history to see if someone's a good credit risk. Down the road, if that person defaults on the loan, the heat for that falls on the loan officer for giving the green light to someone who was a bad credit risk."

"I see what you're saying," he says, nodding, scratching his chin. "If the guy rips off the loan company, his bosses are gonna put it on him for lending to an untrustworthy motherfucker."

"Yes. The loan officer must take responsibility for misjudging the credit risk."

"So, what you're saying is, I've got to take responsibility for giving this fuck-up Ken my batteries?"

"Something like that."

He stares, his smile expanding. "You've got a good point. I can't put all the blame on Ken. I'll tell you what though, I'll never lend that motherfucker anything again."

I watch him settle in his cell. I head for my room, grab a pack of batteries that cost $1.35, and go to Ken's where I find him and his cellmate, Cannonball, lying on their bunks in their boxers, their sweaty masses – resembling two giant hairy slugs – radiating a tangy body odour.

"What the fuck do you want?" Ken turns down his Walkman.

"I'm gonna give you a pack of batteries for free," I say.

"Why the fuck would you wanna do that?" His lips harden and his huge moustache twitches inwards.

"To give to Two Tonys."

He sits up, snatches the batteries and smiles in a devious way.

I leave thinking, *It's 50-50 whether he'll pay Two Tonys or just keep the batteries.*

After breakfast, Two Tonys shows up at my cell. "Ken returned my batteries. I know never to put myself in that position again. I'm so glad I talked to you last night or I might have done something I regretted. Thanks for being my friend."

"Don't mention it. You've helped me loads. That's what friends are for." Hugging, he says I've become the son he never had.

CHAPTER 46

In July 2006, George enters my cell while I'm doing a headstand in boxers due to the heat. "Since my outburst in your cell with She-Ra, I requested new meds, and they've switched me from Prozac to Celexa."

I catch him ogling my behind, so I drop down and stand up, tickled by the sweat reversing direction on my body. "You're deeply disturbed, Jeeves, but it's good that you're doing something about it."

"I have to. I have to be the big person in our relationship because you certainly don't want to address your issues such as your closet shower exhibitionism."

"How can an exhibitionist be in the closet?"

"I'm talking about how everyone knows you take a shower after yoga, so they come and chat with you in the shower."

"It's true! That's been happening lately. Even Ken tried coming in my shower yesterday!"

"There you go!" he says, his face flushing. "You exude invitation! You should have been in the Royal Navy with little sailors soaping each other down under the façade of saving water."

"Jeeves, I thought you were trying to address your fantasy world."

"I can't help it!" he shrieks. "You scream out, 'Take me! Take me!'" He steps closer.

"Back off, Jeeves!" I yell, holding my arms out, unsettled by his predatory expression.

"I'm gonna have the psych call you to Medical, so we can explain our relationship to him at a deeper level."

"What relationship?"

"Don't give me that!" he sighs theatrically. "Your mouth says, 'No! No! No!' but your eyes say, 'Yes! Yes! Yes!'"

"I think they need to double your Celexa."

"I'm not crazy! You are! You should see yourself on the rec field doing yoga with your butt stuck in the air. You get more traffic walking by than the outdoor urinal." Trembling, he starts crying.

Worried, I step forward. "I think you're on the verge of a nervous breakdown, Jeeves."

"I think you're right," he whimpers. "Will you give me a hug?"

Before I can respond, he wraps his arms around me and won't let go. Trapped, I struggle against his sweaty hot hairy round body. He kisses my face. Squirming, but unable to break his grip, I feel his tongue enter my ear. A revolting sensation redoubles my strength. I raise my arms within his and break his grip. "Stay where you fucking are or else I'm gonna start throwing punches!" I bark, pointing at him with my left hand, my right fist cocked at shoulder level, ready to launch. He cowers near the toilet, sobbing, and then runs away. Noticing my skin is coated in grease like condom lube where we came into contact, I grab a bar of soap.

Hearing my name called for mail, I shrug off his outburst and rush to the control room, hoping for news about Jade. I rip open a letter from my sister and start reading as I walk across the yard. Karen writes that upon meeting Jade she was impressed by her intelligence and friendliness. She agrees that Jade would be a good match for me, which makes me smile, but cautions that the wedding is still proceeding, which hurts. She says that Jade apologised for not staying in touch, but she's been busy with wedding preparations as it's only months away. *I'm running out of time!* Although she feels that Jade is making a mistake marrying Theo, Karen didn't say anything when Jade described Theo's mistreatment as she didn't want to dampen her wedding excitement. Jade pledged to write soon.

The unfavourable news has at least lifted the uncertainty surrounding her situation. It seems that she is rushing blindly into a marriage that won't last. It could be one, two ... five years down the road, but maybe I'll get a second chance. Not wanting her to suffer, I feel guilty for predicting a marital disaster, but my instinct is yelling that Theo is only acting like a model fiancé.

CHAPTER 47

I'm walking to the chow hall, telling Shannon and Weird Al how much I'm looking forward to my parents' visit in two days, when Frankie grabs my wrist, his face taut, danger flashing in his eyes. "Englandman! Hammer, an old Aryan Brother on Yard 1, has put out a green light on you for blogging about people doing drugs and using real names."

I swallow hard. A green light means Hammer will reward any white inmate who attacks or even kills me; probably with drugs because he is one of the biggest dealers here, where some are willing to kill for as little as $50 worth of heroin. While my pulse soars, I swivel my head, scanning the yard for hostility. "I never used real names." *I can't believe this is happening just before my parents' visit.*

"You're not dumb enough to use real names. Hammer's full of shit. Did you write about people doing drugs?"

Frankie's gaze bores into my skull. Although I'm under interrogation, I appreciate the warning. Sex play aside, he cares about my safety. As the green light was issued to the whites, I wonder how he knows about it. "I wrote about prisoners shooting up with needles made from commissary items. I thought that was interesting." Although I never mentioned names, half of the accusation is true. *There's no easy way out.* Shook up, I stare at Frankie with a plea for help.

A prisoner scared for his life can "check in," which involves snitching out the threat in return for being locked-down and moved to a different prison. But "snitches get stitches," and having established close friendships here, I rule that out. If I'm locked-down, I won't be able to see my parents. If I'm moved to a different prison, the special visits approved here will be void. *I've brought this upon myself. I need to face it head on if I'm to stay and get visits.*

"You should never write about drugs, Englandman," Frankie says, shaking his head. "In case anyone starts any shit, I'm gonna sit with you in the chow hall. It's the whites with the problem, and I can raise a lot more homies than them. I'll have my people go to war if need be. I've got your back, Englandman. I'm ready to dig up my bone-crusher," he says, referring to a giant shank buried on the yard. Touched by his plan, I follow him to the chow hall. The convict code dictates that members of separate races stay out of each other's disputes, yet he is backing me up on an issue among the whites. He knows I'm in way above my head, and he's putting his life on the line. Because he's an "OG" – an original gangster – an army of young Mexican Americans respect him and will fight if things escalate. I'm an easy target, but his presence will make people think twice.

Indoors, I take my tray to a table. Frankie sits, covered in tattoos, a résumé of two decades of violence, showing he has killed and will kill, his body flexed as if ready to spring up, his head still, eyes roving, watching everyone. Things are so tense, I can't eat. I flinch every time someone draws near and brace to be stabbed. The urge to leave is overwhelming. "Let's go, Frankie." I give my tray to Slingblade and take Frankie to my cell to show him a printout of what I wrote:

Rig Builders

Recently, the traditional methods of procuring syringes haven't been working, so some prisoners are making their own from store items.

There are three ways prisoners obtain syringes that I know of. Firstly, stealing them from Medical, where they're commonly used for insulin injections. Secondly, "keystering" (smuggling) them in through Visitation from a visitor's body, anus or vagina to a prisoner's anus, carefully wrapped in balloons, cling wrap or condoms. Thirdly, via the mail system concealed in cardboard greeting cards delivered by the US Postal Service using envelopes with bogus return addresses.

Which store items are prisoners assembling to make syringes with? A hollow watch-band pin from a Sentry Action Watch ($2.35) sandpapered into a point. A Bic pen refill (25 cents) used as a plunger. A spray tube from Just So Curl Activator ($1.55) fitted with the point and plunger to complete the outfit.

These DIY syringes are larger than the monstrous contraption that gave Uma Thurman's character a life-saving adrenaline shot in *Pulp Fiction*. Prisoners harpooning themselves suffer considerable blood leakage. A prisoner clutching a blood-soaked arm said (allegedly), "I don't know if I'm high from the dope or the blood loss."

He reads it, and we rush to Two Tonys' cell. "Englandman never used real names," he says, handing the blog to Two Tonys.

Sat on the bottom bunk, Two Tonys appears lost in thought as he reads the printout. "He wouldn't use real names. The Brit's an intelligent motherfucker and no snitch. The problem is the dope fiends will do anything for Hammer." His eyes – just like Frankie's – communicate the gravity of the situation. I suspect they discussed the green light beforehand. Although my mistake has let them down, I'm reassured by their resolve. But with 200 prisoners on the yard, I wonder how far their help can go. "Listen, me and a few others who've got your back like Frankie here are gonna make this go away. Don't walk the yard alone for the next few days."

Terrified, I rush to my cell, my heart beating so forcefully it feels as if the left side of my body is expanding. I lock the door. With no fresh air coming in, the atmosphere boils. Unable to read, I lie on the bunk bracing for mayhem. Expecting enemies to appear at the door, I watch the window. As if my bad energy is keeping people at bay, I get no visitors. A strange quiet occurs.

Hours later, with no threat manifesting and my skin's itchiness approaching the point where I'm going to have trouble sleeping, I chance sneaking out for a shower. I stride along the balcony, enter a cubicle and close the door. Alert, I wash in record time. Feeling overexposed to danger, I barely towel dry. I peep around the door to scan the yard and emerge. Heading back to the cell along the balcony, I spot four figures rushing towards my building: Bud, Ken, his cellmate Cannonball and a big hillbilly. With my adrenaline pumping, I jog as fast as my shower sandals will allow, bumping into prisoners, almost tripping on the wonky wooden floor. My assailants speed up. While they stomp up the balcony stairs, I rush into the cell and slam the door. Seconds later, I'm staring at them through the plexiglas.

"Open your door. We need to talk to you," Ken says.

Shoving out words through my constricted throat, I ask, "About what?"

"We just need to talk to you," Ken says.

"I don't know what you heard, but I've not put any real names on the Internet."

"Come on, open your door, England," Bud says.

Ken yells to prisoners across the yard, instructing them to have a guard in the control room electronically open my door because I need a shower. My fear intensifies. Energy erupts throughout my body. I slam my side against the door and lean with all of my might. The guard hits a switch. As the mechanism grinds to unlock the door, my heart hits my chest with the force of a karate punch. They push the door. Visualising them storming in and beating me down, I strain to keep it closed, my entire body ablaze with nervous energy. The instant the door unlocks, I heave against it. The slight jolt from my push automatically locks it – *click*. I can't believe my luck. I stop shoving so hard, but keep my ears attuned to the mechanism in case it grinds, and I have to increase my force.

Ken punches the plexiglas. "We're gonna fuck you up, England!"

"You fucked up with your blog now, 007," Bud says.

"You won't be able to write by the time we're finished with you!"

Stuck to the door by my own sweat, I watch them walk away until they're out of sight. Convinced I'll be attacked when the doors open in the morning, I get on the bunk and shut my eyes. I have to rest on my right side with my body parallel to the wall as when I'm flat on my stomach or even slightly pressed down towards my left, the rapid movement of my heart feels as if a rodent is trying to burrow from my body. I stray on the edge of sleep, my mind creating violent scenarios. My fingers, crooked with tension, claw the mattress as if trying to dig a way out of the situation. To escape from the nightmarish images, I eventually open my eyes, but the threat is still so palpable, the walls seem to press in.

CHAPTER 48

Ordinarily, I view the several-hour wait in an outdoor holding cage at Medical as a waste of time, but getting called to see Dr Owen this morning is a relief. I'm off the yard and away from harm, but dreading going back. Wearing a baseball cap and shades, I'm sat on the edge of a ledge crammed with inmates, sweat stains expanding in the armpit and stomach regions of my T-shirt, listening to a discussion about the difficulties of getting the prison to treat hepatitis C – so many are infected that prescribing them all interferon would bankrupt the prison, so it's much cheaper to let them die.

When I'm finally called indoors, Dr Owen reads my homework: a journal of anxious/abnormal thoughts, including grief over my grandmother's death – which my parents disclosed on our last call – paranoia in the chow hall, and how I jumped when F-16s, jet-fighter aircraft, roared overhead so low and loud, I felt a shockwave through my body and feared getting bombed. Staring at Dr Owen, I worry my body language is betraying something is wrong. I can't mention the green light issued by Hammer as that would be snitching, and I'd lose the support of my friends. I hope to pass off my anxiety as due to what I wrote in the journal.

"The grief and guilt over your grandmother is perfectly normal," Dr Owen says, putting down the journal. "Her death is reality. But your hyper-vigilance with the F-16s is something we need to work on."

"I realise how silly such thoughts are immediately after thinking them, but it all happened so fast."

"You need to breathe normally in situations to calm the cascade of chemicals. You need to be able to appreciate and evaluate reality. There are habitual criminals who are incapable of being anxious in crowds."

"Psychopaths?"

"Yes. You need to desensitise yourself and regain control. If the F-16s catch you by surprise, breathe. I had the same reaction when someone dropped a bucket by me. Pay attention to visual clues instead of over-interpreting things."

"Also, I read about a bomb on a plane, the jet oil burning flesh, parts of the plane dismembering people before they fell to earth squished," I say, folding my arms. "I've got a thing about planes."

"With explosions at altitude you immediately lose consciousness. The shock wave knocks you senseless. It's surprising how fragile the brain is. Troops in Iraq who survive roadside bombs are torn up physically and they suffer heavy trauma to the brain. When the bomb goes off, the survivors know nothing other than waking up in Walter Reed Army Medical Center."

I pluck up the courage to tell him about almost getting beat to death. "In England, I had some head trauma. When I was twenty, I was jumped by four drunks who repeatedly kicked and hit me in the head with an iron bar. A point came when my head felt so warm I couldn't feel the blows. I thought, *This is what dying feels like*. There was absolutely nothing I could do. They left me for dead. I was passed out and woke up with pieces of teeth missing."

"Have you suffered any other head trauma?"

With my temperature still rising from describing the beating, I'm relieved that he changed the subject. "A speaker fell on my head from a third-floor window."

"Did it knock you out?"

"No, the wood broke in half."

"The break probably dissipated the force."

"I've been in about six car crashes. In one, the car knocked down a brick wall, bounced along an icy road and ended up stuck in a tree at an angle. I've also had multiple airbags smash me in the face."

"You shouldn't be too concerned about those incidents. You're not showing any signs of the subtle problems one would expect. We should be more concerned with your anxious thoughts."

"I remember anxious thoughts keeping me awake as a child. I couldn't stop them. It was usually when I was in trouble with my parents. Do I need to learn to accept anxious thoughts?"

"No. Learn to look at them: yes. Learn to build them up: no. In a dark room, the presence of objects may seem dangerous, but when you turn the light on you see the safety of chairs, lamps and small shelves. The eight-foot ogre is suddenly a small spider. When you perceive reality, breathe and push back the fear response. Comfort yourself as if you are a little kid. Calm your system down. You need to perceive reality because when you hit the streets, you'll need realistic aims of who you are, what you're doing and where you're going. In prison, it's realistic to be mentally prepared for fights, but you don't have to be hyper-vigilant."

Why's he bringing that up?

"Just be prepared to get out of the way if something's going down. There's an atmosphere you can usually pick up on when something's going to happen. I'm sure that you can interpret that by now."

Disorientated from lack of sleep, I wonder if he knows I'm in trouble. Paranoid, I squirm in the plastic chair. "You can tell if something's brewing. I just get out of the way and stay in my cell."

"And that's a realistic plan."

How realistic is that going to be when I get back to the yard?

"If you go around panicked all the time, you'll crash. With all the people on the roads in tonnes of steel going 40 to 60mph, who are just as big as idiot drivers as I am, I drive defensively. Vigilant but not hyper-vigilant. I assume the other person is going to do something. I keep my distance from the car in front of me. I check my rear-view mirror. I don't tailgate. I do whatever I can to minimise the force of impact. That's my realistic plan. Try to go about realistically."

"I will," I say, sensing the session is drawing to a close, my stomach tightening.

"For homework, I'd like you to document yourself talking to yourself in relation to how you justify or criticise your past actions.

And to compare and contrast what you're thinking and feeling with your present expectations."

I'm escorted to the outdoor cage. Stewing over the reception I'm going to receive on the yard, I can neither contemplate Dr Owen's advice nor believe the crisis is about to escalate on the eve of my parents' visit. Two hours later, a guard lets us out. Coated in sweat, I trudge across the rec field, my body coiling tighter around my sickly stomach.

CHAPTER 49

Spotting She-Ra and Frankie at the yard gate is comforting. Frankie says Two Tonys is still working on squashing the green light. Disputes have erupted between prisoners for and against smashing me. Frankie has let it be known he'll start a race riot if I get smashed. I tell him about Ken and Bud trying to get into my cell.

"Ken thinks he's all that and then some, homey," Frankie says. "He ain't shit. I'm gonna take care of his ass real good. Just wait and see."

She-Ra says *her* boyfriend announced that anyone who attacks me will have to fight him. Not only has he never lost a fight since I've been here, his opponents were all hospitalised. The last one had his face wired back together and is presently ingesting food through a straw. They offer to stay in my cell throughout the day as I shouldn't be alone.

"Who the fuck's putting our names on the Internet?" a young white prisoner yells, approaching, expanding his chest.

"No one," I say.

"Don't fucking bullshit me," he says.

She-Ra strides forward and casts a dark look I've never seen. "You've got a real pretty eyeball, youngster," *she* says, *her* eyes serpent cold. For a few seconds, the young prisoner gazes, wide-eyed, petrified. Then bolts away.

Shannon has been guarding my cell in case anyone tries to steal my property. The room turns into a command centre with people visiting to express their support and opinions on the situation. Although exhausted by the length of the crisis, I feel safe surrounded by my friends, especially T-Bone, who jokes that he was supposed to become my bodyguard *after* I became a famous author. I have no appetite or any desire to expose myself in the chow hall, but not wanting to show weakness, I attend. Other than receiving dirty looks, nothing happens as I shuffle food around on the tray. *Thank God things are calming down on the eve of my parents' visit.* Five minutes later, a pea hits my face. Surprised, I swivel my head to Ken smiling menacingly, nodding, flanked by Bud and Cannonball, jaws jutted, chewing food, gazing as if they want me dead.

"Don't think you're off the hook, England!" Ken yells, his black hair greased and gleaming like ink.

"You shouldn't have put anything about people doing drugs on the Internet," Cannonball says. "You'll be sorry, motherfucker."

With prisoners watching to see my reaction, I have no choice but to retaliate. The pea bounces off Ken's chest and lands on the tray of a massive hillbilly sat opposite with short dark hair, a broad leathery face, dark beady eyes and big pointy gnarled ears that give him the look of a hyena. Holding my breath, I brace for his response. With the folds of his downturned mouth stretching towards his chin, the hillbilly glowers. "Hey, pretty boy, I'm coming by your cell later on to take your ass," he says in country drawl.

"You ain't doing shit," T-Bone says.

"You're too spiritual to mess with me," the hillbilly says.

"Try me," T-Bone says.

I leave the chow hall with the hillbilly yelling, "I'm coming to your cell later, pretty boy!"

Outside, I keep an eye on the men in front and behind, resolved not to be taken by surprise. Sensing someone rushing closer, I turn to Ken several feet away, his head cocked so far back that his massive moustache appears to be approaching like bull's horns. She-Ra's friend, Blackheart, the almost seven-foot Lakota Indian, steps in Ken's way, blocking his path.

"You need to leave England alone, motherfucker!" Blackheart yells.

Ken tries to swerve around Blackheart, who sidesteps and

stops him. Ken stands still, perplexed. I dash back to my cell and keep the door locked until friends come over.

Nauseated with worry, I want the day to end, so I can have the first visit with my parents. From information flowing back to my cell, I learn the hillbilly is high on meth, hooch and heroin, and claiming he's going to smash T-Bone and rape me while eating my commissary. Shannon offers to lurk around outside and knock on my door if any threats approach the building.

"I saw him sneak over to A pod," T-Bone says. "Then he went into the library with something in a towel, so he's got a weapon. If he comes here, I'm gonna take care of business."

"Why don't I just keep the door locked?" I say.

"Sooner or later this guy's gonna try to punk you out. Would you rather him try that when I'm not here?"

"I'll leave the door open." Having never been threatened with a shank, I bury my face in my hands and pray that T-Bone's help prevents a stabbing. *Will the shank give him an advantage over T-Bone?*

Two Tonys arrives. "Bud and Ken are telling motherfuckers you're putting their secrets on the Internet for the guards to read. What fucking secrets? Like the guards don't know there's drugs in prison!" he says, shaking his head. "Half the time, the guards are the ones bringing the drugs in."

"What if I get what I wrote about drugs deleted off the Internet?" I ask.

"That might help," he says, nodding.

"I'll ask my parents to delete it tomorrow when I see them at Visitation."

"Say hello to Mom and Pops from me," he says. "We should find out tomorrow if the green light is squashed. I'm calling in a favour. Don't go anywhere alone until I give you the all clear."

Thirty minutes after Two Tonys leaves, Shannon knocks on the door and strides away. Panic sets in. T-Bone pushes the door open a foot and hides by the toilet. We hear low voices, people gathering below the cell. T-Bone peeps out and backs away. He says to be quiet, tucks himself against the wall and holds out a small mirror.

With my heartbeat ripping up through my chest, I climb onto the top bunk and pretend to read. A heavy-footed person approaches along the balcony. Each step closer adds to the maelstrom of fear battering my brain and rattling my nervous system. My eyes are latched onto the door, my hands shaking so much my book is moving up and down. The hillbilly charges in with a shank, blind to T-Bone springing up from the side. I barely have time to shift before a straight left and right from T-Bone – *bam-bam!* – knock the hillbilly senseless. Unconscious, he collapses as if dead. I'm speechless.

By opening his eyelids and yelling at him to get up, T-Bone rouses the hillbilly, grabs him by the back of the trousers and launches him from the cell. He hits the railing and doubles over. Disorientated, he stumbles away.

Gazing at T-Bone in awe, I drop down and thank him. "When are you going to teach me to punch like that? It was incredible."

"The knockout punch," T-Bone says calmly. "It's when you sit down on your punch and generate a lot of power or energy by rotating your hips in one motion. You can severely hurt someone, so don't try it unless I'm there to teach you how to generate the pounds per square inch. He fell fast, and a lot of it came from the fact that he was shocked by me waiting for him." T-Bone says to stay put with my door locked, picks up the shank and exits into darkness.

Alone, I worry how long the crisis will last. *How many more attempts will there be with the green light still on? I can't get injured while my parents are here and put them through the stress of seeing that.*

Frazzled, jittery, I head to Visitation the next morning resolved to shield my parents from my troubles, taking deep breaths to calm my nerves. The stress seems to have stashed itself away in my shoulders, so I rotate them, hoping to loosen up. Spotting their cheery faces, I smile naturally. I aim to bide my time before asking them to delete the "Rig Builders" blog. After hugging, we sit down at an outdoor table. "How's the plans for Karen's wedding going?" I ask, wishing I hadn't let down my sister by putting myself in here.

"She chose her dress, but what a fiasco!" Mum says. "She loved the first dress she tried on, but I told her she couldn't buy the first dress, so we went to Chester, Liverpool and Warrington. She didn't find anything she liked better than the first dress, and that's the one she ordered ..."

In the distance, on the other side of a chain-link fence, are a group of prisoners heading to Medical, including Ken. Anticipating them walking past us several feet away and within earshot, I hope Ken doesn't say anything. My body starts tightening.

"Her dress is beautiful. We're all so excited. They're getting married at St Bede's Church ..."

As Ken approaches the fence, my focus switches to him. He stops to make a throat-slitting gesture. I flick my gaze to my parents, hoping they don't see Ken.

"Keep walking!" a guard yells at Ken.

"Fuck you!" Ken yells at the guard, attracting my parents' attention.

"That's Ken," I say. My parents know my history with Ken from previous correspondence.

"I bet you don't like me," Ken says, grinning at my parents.

"Ignore him. He's crazy," I say.

"Do you want me to write you up?" a guard barks at Ken, who moves on.

"So, Karen's getting married at St Bede's, where I was going to marry Claudia," I say.

"You'll meet the right person when you're not in prison," Mum says. "You can't rationalise your feelings in here. Every emotion, every sensation is magnified."

"Karen met Jade," Dad says. "Her fiancé sounds dreadful."

"I've still not heard from her. The wedding must be real close now." The thought of Jade walking down the aisle – with someone else – hurts.

Near the end of the visit, I say, "Oh, yeah, I almost forgot. There's a blog I need you to delete because I wrote about drugs in it, and with hindsight, it's probably best I don't put anything like that on the Internet in case certain people read it." *Phew! That sounded about right.*

"Which blog?" Dad asks.

"Rig Builders."

"I'll delete it tonight."

"Thanks," I say, easing up.

After the visit, She-Ra recommends we go to Yard 1 to talk to Hammer to find out if the green light is squashed. Desperate to get things back to normal, I agree. Walking the dirt track next to a field of Bermuda grass inmates are mowing, with the sun burning my arms and the back of my neck, I'm so intimidated by Hammer, I try to prepare what to say, but my mind goes blank. *If he wants me smashed or dead, I'm probably the last person he wants to see. Even if I present my case clearly, I mean nothing to him, so why bother? Maybe the right words will come out when we get there.* As we approach the fence, I'm lightheaded with fear and hyperventilating.

She-Ra calls over a big man in his 50s with a thick moustache on a lumpy face pockmarked like the moon, grey hair short on top and shaved at the sides. His tattoos include a Swastika on the side of his neck and three teardrops below an eye. He stops at the chain-link, removes sunglasses, folds meaty tattooed arms behind his back like royalty and casts his dark cold dangerous eyes our way.

"I read the blog," She-Ra says. "England never used real names."

"Is that right," he says in a gruff voice.

"I apologise if that blog caused offence," I say. "My parents deleted it."

"We don't want the guards knowing what we're doing," he says.

"I hear you," I say. "I started the blog to expose conditions and help prisoners, not to get any prisoners in trouble. There are prisoners on Yard 4 who get pen pals and books sent to them from blog readers. She-Ra even gets fan mail."

"You get fan mail, She-Ra?" he asks.

"Yes. I now have international Cult of She-Ra members thanks to Jon's Jail Journal," She-Ra says. Briefly, he smirks.

"There's people on Yard 4 who want to kill me because they think I used real names." *He probably views the blog as a threat to his drug business.*

"If you didn't use real names, you should be all right." Someone yells Hammer and he marches away without saying goodbye.

Heading back to Yard 4, I ask She-Ra, "Do you think the green light is off?"

"He said you should be OK. He's wise enough to know that if you were gonna get run off the yard, you'd be gone by now. It doesn't reflect well on him that you've not been smashed, but it shows you've got more support on Yard 4 than he calculated."

"I'm never writing about drugs again," I say, overwhelmed by relief, aware that I'd be in hospital and my parents' trip would be ruined if it wasn't for friends like She-Ra.

"If you have a writing idea, and you're unsure what you can put on the Internet, let me read it first."

"Thanks so much, She-Ra." We hug.

In the evening, I receive a postcard from Jade. She apologises for not writing, but says I'll understand everything when she visits to disclose her "big news." I imagine she wants to relate how great her wedding was. Pretending to be happy in her presence won't be easy.

CHAPTER 50

With the library – a small dusty room with books on trolleys and no librarians or guards – gaining a reputation for being an outpost for blow jobs, I never know what to expect in there. During a previous visit, Booga asked if I wanted to see his belt buckle, yanked out his man parts, squeezed his scrotum and said, "Do you want to blow some money?" while pointing at a penis tattooed with a dollar sign above the urethral opening, freshly tattooed, leaking blood.

Approaching the library, I'm relieved it looks empty. When I walk in, someone yells, "Get out, England!" At the far end of the room is a young prisoner, Tom, on his knees, his glossy lips next to Cannonball's erection. Cannonball has one hand pressed on Tom's shoulder, the other holding his penis. I wonder whether the act is forced, consensual or Tom's prostituting himself for food like so many others.

If the act is involuntary, I want to help Tom, but he says, "Just leave, England," as if resigned to his fate. I depart with a sickly feeling.

Hours later, T-Bone enters my cell. "Have the whites stopped sweating you?" he says, stretching his fingers as if itching to hurt someone.

"It's all died down," I say, sat on the bottom bunk. "Two Tonys got the green light squashed."

"What about Ken?" he asks.

"I never know with him. He's always so high and crazy."

"I've got a problem with his celly, Cannonball." He leans against the wall and folds his arms. "He's stepped over the line. I don't care that he bulldogs quite a few guys out of dope, but he's going too far with Tom."

"How do you know about Tom?" I ask.

"'Cause I come out of my cell more often than you do," he says, smiling.

"I walked in on them in the library."

"I know," he says. "Forcing Tom to give him blow jobs makes me sick, but he's also making Tom give him store and threatening Tom's family with a bunch of lies. I just cussed Cannonball out and he went on the rampage. He threatened me with a dirty needle and he has hepatitis C. I'm gonna speak to a few people and take care of business with Cannonball." Before I can respond, T-Bone strides out. Thirty minutes later, the speakers announce a lockdown. Medical staff rushes into Ken's cell. They extract Cannonball on a stretcher, covered in blood, looking like a car-crash survivor.

To get clean clothes, I join a crowd around laundry porters grabbing net bags from trolleys, yelling DOC numbers and hurling bags at their owners.

"Ken's gonna get a surprise today," Frankie says, grinning.

"What do you mean?" I ask.

"Wait and see, homey."

"Shut up, bitch!" Mochalicious shrieks at She-Ra, attracting everyone's attention.

"Mocha likes them so big," She-Ra says in a humorous tone, *her* hands at chest height about a foot apart, "that when *her* friends are playing basketball, *she* sits upside down on the loop, so they can shoot it in *her* ass. And the great part about it is, all *she* has to do is open her mouth to let the ball out." She-Ra points at Mochalicious and winks. We laugh.

"Oh my God!" Mochalicious says, head waggling. "I really do like them big though."

"Mocha likes them so big that after *she* takes it in the ass," She-Ra says, leaning to slap Mochalicious' behind, "two points have to be deducted from *her* IQ due to *her* brain getting poked."

"I don't like them that big!" Mochalicious yells, hands on hips.

"She-Ra's a big puta. Mucha grande. Taller than DOC lamp posts. I think I should grab *her* tits now." She-Ra shields *her* chest and they play fight.

A porter extracts a laundry bag with DIE NIGGERS and a Swastika in big black writing on the white patch in the middle. Prisoners fall silent, absorbed in shock. The comedy of She-Ra and Mochalicious stops. I pray the bag isn't mine because the owner is going to have a lot of explaining to do – if given the chance. Voices erupt, the blacks demanding to know whose bag it is. A porter shouts the number.

Ken steps forward. "Give me my fucking clothes!" He snatches the bag and marches away, grinning at the words DIE NIGGERS as if proud, leaving the blacks in uproar. T-Bone and another black powerhouse follow Ken to his cell.

At Ken's door, T-Bone yells, "Which one of us do you wanna fight?"

"I didn't write it, dude!" Ken slams the door in their faces – putting the convict code into effect. Anyone called out – challenged – must fight or else get smashed by their own race for not showing heart. The whites converge on Ken's cell. A prisoner walks to the control room and asks a guard to unlock Ken's door. After the door grinds open, Ken is marched to the rec room at the far end of the yard. With so many enemies, there's no shortage of whites willing to smash Ken.

Walking back to my cell with my laundry, I hear flesh getting pounded, sneakers sliding and squeaking on the concrete as kicks are launched, moaning and groaning. After several minutes, the sounds stop. The whites march out, but not Ken.

CHAPTER 51

"Dog 11, roll your shit up! You're going to minimum!" a guard announces at 6:30 AM on August 16, 2006.

The stress of being moved to a minimum-security yard accelerates my thoughts. Although I'll get additional privileges such as food visits, I'm nervous at having to start over on Yard 1, where Hammer resides. *Most of my friends are here. I prefer having no cellmate. Who'll I end up living with? Will Hammer start trouble? Calm down. What would Dr Owen say? Take deep breaths.*

Shannon appears in the doorway, his eyes sad.

"I'm out of here. I can't believe it." I hug him.

"Say hi to Weird Al for me."

"I will. Keep the blogging up. I hope to see you on Yard 1 someday."

After Shannon leaves, T-Bone crushes me with a bear hug. "I'll come to talk to you at the fence on Yard 1. We'll keep the stories going."

"I hope so," I say. "The violence you've had puts my situation into perspective. I have nothing but respect for you. I've never met anyone risking their life for complete strangers to stop rape and for no reward whatsoever. The world needs to hear your story. No matter how long it takes, I'll try my best to get it published."

I spot She-Ra outside, *her* expression agitated. Even though it's not my fault I'm being moved, I'm overwhelmed by a feeling of letting my friends down. A tight community has formed around Jon's Jail Journal and now I won't be here for them. I step out. "We knew it was coming sooner or later."

She-Ra hugs me close, tears streaming. "I'm gonna miss you."

"I'm gonna miss you, too, but we'll stay in touch by talking through the fence." We head for breakfast.

Outside the chow hall, Two Tonys hugs me and whispers, "I've got a guy on Yard 1, Jim Hogg, that's gonna look out for you. If Hammer starts any shit or anyone else for that matter, let the Hogg know. I'm gonna miss you on this yard, little bro, but I'll come and talk to you on Yard 1."

"I'm going to miss you, too. You've taught me so much. At least we got to finish your life story."

"I want De Niro to play me when the movie comes out," he jests. "If I've got anything to add to my story, I'll just mail it to your mom and pops."

By 7:15 AM, I'm back in the cell. "Where's George?" I ask Shannon. "He said he was going to help move my stuff."

"He's probably getting a last sniff of your boxers." Shannon steps onto the balcony. "Jeeves, the governor wants you!"

"Yay, he wants me!" George yells. "The day of his departure and the governor finally wants me!"

"Not like that, Jeeves!" I smile.

"OK, governor. I'll go get a trolley to put the royal belongings in!" He disappears to the front of the yard and returns. "The other guys moving to Yard 1 already took the trolleys." Appraising the room, he says, "Good heavens, governor. You're making a mess of moving your stuff. What would Mum say?"

"Can you help wrap my clutter in sheets, then?" We shift everything onto the balcony.

"Shannon, can you check the room and make sure the governor didn't leave anything behind?" George says. While George fetches a trolley, Shannon finds toothbrushes, *Yoga Journals* and a mirror.

Outside of Building B, I ask Two Tonys, "Where's Frankie?"

"Frankie!" Two Tonys yells. "Get your fucking ass out here! England wants to say goodbye!"

Frankie struts out in white boxers with DOC printed on them. "Englandman, so they're splitting us up finally are they?"

We hug. "Yes, but I'll see you on Yard 1 when you get re-classed to minimum."

"Nah. Not with all the tickets I've had. They just gave me

another for a dirty piss test. They ain't setting Frankie loose up there."

"I'll keep in touch somehow."

"You'd better, Englandman. That's what I like about you: you're loyal. You're a trustworthy motherfucker. Let's make love one time real quick before you go," he says, waving to come inside.

"I don't think so. You're way too sexy for me."

"Let's just kiss real quick right now. I won't tell anybody."

"I'll decide," I say, imitating how Frankie says it, *deee-cide*, "who I kiss and who I don't kiss."

"No! I'll decide, Englandman." Frankie licks his lips.

"You're getting too frisky. I've got to go." I find George pushing a trolley weighed down with books. "Well done, Jeeves!" While I walk the yard shaking hands, George sings "Rule Britannia."

Bud emerges onto a balcony. "Is 007 finally leaving us?"

"Yes, good luck, Bud," I say.

"All right now," Bud says.

I pass Ken looming from Building A's balcony, scowling, his face cut and bruised around a swollen eye from the beating by the whites. "Hey, England," Ken yells. "I've already sent word to Yard 1 that the guy putting drug stories on the Internet and using real names is on his way. They're gonna smash you as soon as you touch down."

"Goodbye, Ken," I say, hoping he's joking. I exit the gate and turn back towards the chain-link. "Hey, Ken, I wish you all the luck in the world!" In two minds as to whether to risk provoking him, I do it anyway: I raise my middle finger. "By the way, you look real handsome. Did I say handsome? I mean fucking ridiculous!" Smiling, Ken nods as if to say he'll still get me one of these days.

CHAPTER 52

The blood splattered on the floor, ceiling, walls, bunks, windows, toilet, sink, door, table, shelves and corkboard in my new cell is disturbing. *What am I getting into? Can I catch hepatitis from this?* A podgy prisoner appears in the doorway. "There was a fight. The cops half-assed cleaned the blood. A dude got his cheek bitten off by a guy trying to eat his face. It ripped wide open. The other dude has skills with his fists, elbows and headbutting."

I shudder. "Holy shit!"

He laughs. "I'm a porter. I'll get you cleaning supplies."

At least I don't have a cellmate. Who'd want to live here? Shit! There's no mattress, light bulb, trashcan or chair. How can I write without a chair? I leave the cell to get a mattress. A guard says to fetch mine from Yard 4. *I just talked all that shit to Ken and now I've got to go back there. That's what you get for being a smart arse. Boomerang karma.* Dreading dealing with Ken, I trek alongside the rec field to Yard 4. I approach apprehensively and scan Building A. No sign of Ken. *Phew!* A guard opens the gate. Bracing for Ken to appear, I jog to my old cell and roll up the mattress. On my way out, I'm grabbed. While my heart jumps, I twist around to Booga.

"I'm holding my pee in until my bladder hurts," Booga says proudly. "Then when I finally pee, it's orgasmic."

"You're insane!" Flicking my elbow, I knock off his arm and rush away.

"You should try it!" Booga yells.

As I stride across the yard, people yell my name. Ken appears and charges across the balcony towards the stairs. I throw the mattress over my shoulder and run. He thuds down the stairs, failing to notice T-Bone approaching from the side. When Ken gets to the bottom, T-Bone sticks a leg out. He falls. I wait at the gate for the guard to open it. *Come on! Come on! Come on!* Ken scrambles up. Exiting, I almost collapse with relief. I take my time walking back to Yard 1, savouring the smell of the cut grass and the pinkish-orange radiance of the mountains under the sun.

Entering the cell, I spot a skeleton of a hippy vomiting blood in the toilet. I drop the mattress. "Shouldn't you be in hospital?" I ask, leaning to help him, inhaling the metallic odour of blood.

He spits. "I'm your new celly, Midnight."

"I'm England."

Rising unsteadily, he raises a chin streaked red. "Do you smoke?" he asks, his cloudy eyes lighting up.

"No." His expression sours. "That's a lot of blood," I say, furrowing my brows.

"I just spent four days at the hospital. Morphine IVs. A CAT scan. A GI tube down my throat. A cancer biopsy. They said there's a cancerous lump closing one of my intestines. After I drink fluid, it all comes up bright red."

"That's rough. Did they give you anything for it?"

"I'm on Vicodin, Elavil, Omeprazole, Acetaminophen and stomach-nausea pills."

I thought Yard 1 was supposed to be mellow. A cheek getting bitten off and now this. At least I've got plenty to write about.

A white prisoner marches in with a soldier-solid physique and dark hair in a crew cut, German words tattooed on the base of his neck. "England."

"That's me," I say, meeting his eyes.

"I need to speak to you outside."

Probably one of Hammer's thugs. I stride out, blood pumping faster and hands fisting. "What's the matter?" I ask, facing him, scrutinising his body language.

He points at me. "Look, your new celly just got smashed. I've been asked to tell you not to get involved. He owes money. Stay out of it. He might have to move off this yard."

"If he owes money, I'm not getting involved." *Cellmates should protect each other, but I've only just met him and I won't back anyone up over drug debts.*

"Who's England?" yells a tank of a man – twice the size of the prisoner I'm with – motoring closer with no neck, wild eyes and a scar from mouth to ear.

Shit's getting out of control. Bracing to shift as he closes in, I say, "I'm England."

"I'm Jim Hogg, Two Tonys' buddy," he says, shaking my hand, almost ripping off my arm.

Thanks, Two Tonys!

He barks at the prisoner with me, "Is there a fucking problem here?" The creases in his sunburnt forehead deepen into ravines.

"Nope." The prisoner disappears.

"If anyone starts any shit with you, they'll have to answer to me. Me and Two Tonys go way back." After telling a story about being Two Tonys' cellmate, Jim Hogg roams the yard asking people if they have a problem with me, swinging his arms like a gorilla.

I go inside. "Did someone beat you up?" I ask Midnight.

"Yeah. I've had two fights today. One on Yard 2 before I left and another one just now."

"In this cell?"

"Yeah, some dude just came in, asked for the time and sucker punched me."

"That's a lot of drama. Will there be more problems coming to this cell?"

"I think it's squashed now. I've got to tell you something upfront, celly," Midnight says.

"What's that?" I ask.

"'Cause of my medical problems, I have to pee through the night. Would you rather I flush the toilet and make noise or just leave the pee in the can?"

"It'll wake me up. Just leave it in the can." We spend hours scrubbing blood, but keep finding more.

Chow is announced. I brace to see if Hammer still has a problem with me. *Best approach him and say hello. Better deal with it than avoid him and risk looking weak.* Outside the chow hall, I spot him standing in line. I walk over and wait for him to finish talking. As I ponder what to say, my jaw tightens, mouth dries and throat constricts. When he looks my way, my words fly out: "Hi, Hammer. I finally made it to Yard 1." I offer my hand.

He grips my hand and tugs my arm. "Your accent sounds like it's changed. Are you sure you're really from England?" He cocks his head from side to side as if reading words on my face.

I search for a response. My breath pauses, my heartbeat accelerates and pressure rises in my chest. With dozens of prisoners watching, waiting to judge my reaction, I take a chance on trying to diffuse the situation with humour. In a slow southern drawl, I say, "No. I'm really from Alabama." Everyone laughs. "Can't wait to have a food visit," I say, breathing easier. "When's the next one?" He responds and the prisoners reminisce about food their loved ones brought to previous visits. While the conversation slows down, I walk away. *Hammer can't be trusted. Stay out of his way. If he wanted me smashed, it would have happened.*

I sit with Weird Al, who joined Yard 1 a few months ago. "So how are you and your celly getting along?" he asks.

"He's a smoker," I say, picking through potatoes soaked in orange oil in the hope of finding some that aren't rotten. "Even with the best-matched celly in the world, nothing beats your own cell."

"Yes, even if Mother Teresa were my celly, after three months of living together, I'd probably gut-punch her. But there's an especially dark cloud hanging over your blood-infested cell, the scene of a violent encounter between two men who, despite repeated attempts, failed to kill one another. It's a karmic part of your black aura. As is being assigned a cellmate who smokes like an eighteenth-century wood-burning train, transmitting his cancerous tumours to your body while you sleep by his simple exhalations. Now that you've finally made it to Yard 1, I'll set about working up anti-British sentiment with the locals into a frenzy of further bloodletting. Let's add some British blood to your cell."

Laughing, I realise how much I've missed his sense of humour.

The narrow window at the back of the cell opens at ground level – an invitation to insects. A dragonfly whizzes in and zigzags from wall to wall like a pinball with wings. While I read John Updike on the top bunk, its elongated maggoty body rams my face. Flinching, I slap it away. It descends and buzzes into Midnight's ear. Cackling insanely, he grabs a shower sandal, leaps around and beats the dragonfly beyond death. Darkness brings mosquitoes. They drill into my skin and whine by my ears, startling me awake. I wrap myself in a sheet, but sweat severely in the trapped monsoon heat. The next morning, I wake up itching pink lumps on my head and neck, shocked to see the wall splattered with blood and mosquitoes mangled from the fan blades sucking in bloated insects during the night and blasting them back out. I take a washcloth to the wall.

I scrounge a chair and sit to fill out a form requesting a cell change on the grounds the blood is hazardous. Harvester ants spill through the window and crawl on the paper. A harvester ant under threat will pinch with its jaws, while curling its stinger over to pierce skin and inject painful venom. I flick them out, but they return in larger numbers.

After going to Medical, Midnight sits on the bottom bunk and tells his story:

"In '93, a semi hit my Olds Cutlass 442 and broke my back. I was paralysed from the waist down, so they did a laminectomy. They took out part of a disc and moved the sciatic nerve a little bit, so it wasn't being pinched by the L4 and L5 vertebrae. In '95, I had a fusion: they put in two stainless steel screws and removed the disc. In '97, they removed the two screws and put a plate in there, and drilled four screws into it. In 2003, at Sheriff Joe Arpaio's Durango jail, I was smashed for standing up for an old-timer, and my L4 and L5 vertebrae were cracked. I thought I was gonna be killed. They broke my eye socket and cheekbone and fractured my skull. Four ribs were cracked. They had to screw a plate and pins in to hold my eyeball in its socket. Feel here."

I press the metal at the top of Midnight's left cheek. "That's enough injuries and illnesses for one lifetime. I hope there's nothing else wrong with you."

"I've got no gall bladder, appendix or tonsils," he says proudly.

"Do you mind if I ask what you're in prison for?"

"Theft of means. I stole a truck to finance a $250-a-day crack addiction and a $100-a-day meth habit."

"What started you on drugs?"

"Before the accident, I was straight. I was a heavy-machine operator driving backhoes, graders and bobcats, making $23 an hour. Me, my old lady and son had money in the bank. We didn't want for nothing. After the accident, I couldn't work. I didn't feel like a man no more. I took an overdose of Demerol and Valium on my first suicide attempt. I became addicted to painkillers: Valiums, Somas, Vicodin 750s, Demerols and morphine. When the doctor cut me off because he didn't want me to kill myself on his drugs, I started self-medicating with street drugs and lost every damn thing. My family, home, vehicle, my freedom. I've been in and out of prison five times as I have no one to help me. Last time I got out of prison with the $50 gate money, I was picked up by Mesa Police who reinstated a fine for a shoplifting case and released me with no money, wearing blue dungarees and sandals. I had to shoplift shoes from Wal-Mart. I ended up sleeping next to railway tracks, eating out of a dumpster by Papa John's Pizzas."

After lockdown, Midnight says he witnessed his father's suicide, and shows me his Office of the Public Defender Presentence Report:

M's father committed suicide just four days before M's 18th birthday. M's father put a 12-gauge shotgun in his mouth and pulled the trigger ... it blew most of his face and the top of his head off. M was reaching for his father's arm to stop him when he witnessed this horrible tragedy. He was never the same after that.

In 2004, after consuming a large amount of crack cocaine, M tried to commit suicide. He wanted to die like his father. He took a 9mm gun and pulled the trigger, but the gun jammed. He was prescribed several medications, but did not have the money to get his prescription filled, therefore he didn't get the necessary medication to help stabilize his condition.

M's mother passed away in 2001. She was involved in a serious automobile accident and haemorrhaged to death.

Deeply moved and horrified, I count my blessings and wonder how I can help him. The next day, he returns from Medical. "I've got three stomach ulcers and the biopsy shows cancer in my upper intestine. The nurse said I need to quit smoking. And the doctor wants me to look at my stool, at my bowel movements. If they're real dark, then there's blood in it, and he wants a sample. I'm supposed to pick my shit out of the commode and bring it to Medical."

"You'd better do what they say," I say from my bunk.

"Nope. I ain't doing it. I drop one, flush one. I ain't looking at my shit. To be honest, I don't wanna know if I'm bleeding from my ass. I've got enough problems."

"But you could die."

"OK. I've got a deal for you," he says, smiling. "Tomorrow, I'll take a peak, and if there's blood in there, if you want, you can fish some out and take it down to them."

"If I'd just been diagnosed with cancer, I'd be fishing my own bloody shit out in a heartbeat."

The next morning, he refuses to examine his stool. He's more concerned about the doctor telling him to stop smoking than his cancer.

CHAPTER 53

Two weeks later, I swap cells with a friend of Midnight's who smokes. Upstairs, alone,

I start to unwind. With fewer mosquitoes, I sleep better. The next morning at 6 AM, I hear the mechanical sound of the teeth in the doors grinding open, followed by a chorus of sneezing, coughing, farting, noses blowing, urine splashing, toilets flushing, water running and razors tapping against sinks.

I laugh as my new neighbour, a massive African American with frizzy hair, yells in a sexy voice, "I'm *sooo* very gay," and begins a song, "Jack-jack-jack me off ..."

Smokers emerge on the balcony, yelling. To block the commotion, I put my Walkman on and surf the radio: "Call 1-800-Progressive. Progressive Direct Insurance Company ... Krispy Kreme Donuts ... Do you suffer from heavy or long-lasting or frequent menstrual cycles? Call 886-800-9060 ... When you're a hardcore biker like me, it's nice to know that Geico ... This week on ABC it's Extreme Makeover ... XM Satellite Radio ... Do you have what it takes to be a successful rapper? ... Zero per cent interest for sixty months. Jim Click Dodge in the Auto Mall ... Zicam Cold Remedy Swabs ... There is a massive shortage of helicopter pilots ... M&M Reese's Pieces ... Arizona women's basketball is taking off ... Circuit City, HD radio ... Vegetable oil has an extremely high lubricity factor ... How do you not have a celebrity shredding service?"

Announcements come in a gravelly female voice: "Yard 1, last call for chow ... Visitation porters turn out for work ..."

A man with rotten teeth and insane eyes peeping from long dark tangled hair resembling seaweed launches into my cell. "I'm your neighbour! I'm a dope fiend! C'mon, you bloody bloke! The chow hall's open!" I join the stragglers heading for breakfast and banter with Weird Al.

After chow, a tall young Native American walks into my cell – slightly overweight, baby-faced, wearing rectangular glasses – and introduces himself as Max, a friend of She-Ra's. Aware of my blogging, he's keen to share a story.

"What's it about?" I ask, sat on the chair.

"Selling my jizz to a prisoner."

"Are you kidding?" I ask, studying his expression.

"No."

"This blows my mind. Before we start, how'd you end up in prison?"

"I got nine years for kidnapping. It was a carjacking. I took the guy in the car with me. I was only 16 at the time. I'd just finished Carson High in California."

"Did you have a weapon or any priors?"

"No."

"How old are you?"

"Twenty-five."

"So, you've never had an adult life on the streets?"

"No."

"What do your tats mean?"

"On my chest is a medicine wheel. On my left arm is the Chukchansi tribal seal: a basket, and the word Hil-le which is a greeting. I had to earn this tat, AIM, which stands for American Indian Movement."

"How did you earn it?"

"I took off a piece of scalp with a hunting knife."

"Ouch!"

"It's not like I peeled it down to the cranium. That earned me respect on the streets of California."

"When you getting out?"

"I've got six months left. I also have a tat on my cock."

"What is it?"

"It's kind of funny, dude. It's a dicky bird. Do you want to see it?"

"No, thanks. So how did you hook up with the jizz buyer?"

"My buddy told me about him."

"I hope he pays well."

"It depends, dude, on your looks factor, age and shit. I figured, I'm young, I'm not bad looking, maybe I can get something from the motherfucker."

"How much did you charge?"

"A $40 sack of commissary."

"For how much?"

"I dunno. A couple of teaspoons every week and a half or so. Whenever my commissary ran out. I only did it five or six times."

"How did you get it to him?"

"He told me to put it in a little baggie. And the crazy thing is, if you've ever studied your own jizz, it stays solid for a while. It has a gelatine-like consistency, but after it's been in the open air in a warm environment, it turns runny. Do you know what I'm talking about?"

"No. I've gone my whole life without jizz lying around the house." We laugh. "But I'll take your word. You delivered it in a baggie?"

"Yeah. I'd walk across the pod with the warm jizz in a baggie in my hand with all eyes on me. I was trying to keep it a secret, so the dude would keep buying me commissary. What could I have said if someone had stopped me, and asked what I was doing? How do you say to someone, 'I sold my nut, dude, to an old perv who uses it as skin lotion, finger fucks himself with it and eats it'?"

"Jesus, Max! I thought I'd heard it all. That's insane! Did he demand a certain consistency or freshness?"

"Yes. He wanted it as fresh as possible."

"How do you feel about it now?"

"You compromise a lot of morals to survive in prison. I imagine a lot of people would have done the same in my situation, needing soap, shampoo and food. Forty-dollars' worth of commissary is a lifesaver sometimes."

An announcement: "Lockdown! Everybody lockdown!"

Max returns to his cell. I shut the door and watch the yard empty. Medical staff emerge from downstairs with Midnight on a stretcher. When he doesn't return, rumours of his death circulate, but he shows up days later. I check on him. "What the hell happened?"

"I'd just finished taking a piss and my left leg went completely dead," he says, sat on his bunk, smoking. "I fell against the counter and cut my eye. They did an MRI and said my sciatic nerve's being pinched. Then they sent me to House 9 and I demanded to leave there. They brought me back here, but a captain said, 'We were told your life's in danger on Yard 1. How much money do you owe for drugs?' I said, 'I don't owe nothing for drugs. I just owe two honey buns.' He wanted to send me to lockdown, but I told him I wasn't in any danger, so he had me sign a waiver saying DOC isn't responsible if I get killed."

"Did you check your stool for blood?"

"It's full of blood every day. I'm seeing clots on the toilet paper now."

"Did you tell Medical?"

"Yeah. They told me to submit a request. I ain't doing that so they can charge me $3. Fuck them."

"But it's your life on the line."

"I don't care. I'm 42 years old. I've lived a good life. I'll be out of here if I die, and I'll never have to worry about coming back. I believe there's another life as well as this one. As long as I don't wake up in hell, I'll be OK."

"When are you getting out?"

"January 19, 2008 is my TR," he says, referring to a ninety-day-early temporary release. "April 5 is my ERC," he says, referring to an early release credit date, usually 85 per cent of a sentence. "But to get my TR, I've got to have a residence approved and I don't have one. I have no family or friends on the streets."

"Can you go to a shelter for the homeless?"

"Not on a TR. I'd have to wait till April for my ERC."

"Hopefully this time, the cops won't steal your $50 gate money."

"What's fifty bucks gonna get me? You can't make it on $50. I have to buy socks and underwear as soon as I get out. Then I'll have to go to McDonald's or Burger King and then I'll be broke."

"And then what?"

"I dunno. My social security disability will start, but it'll be a month or two before I can receive a cheque, and I can't get a cheque unless I have an address, and I can't afford to pay rent until I get a cheque. I can get a PO Box with my cheque, but that'll cost almost half of my $50 gate fee."

"What if someone had a place for you to stay at on the basis you would pay them rent when your cheques come in?"

"That would work for my TR, but I won't get a cheque till March."

"Where would the residence need to be?"

"I'd like to try and stay here in Tucson if possible. I'd like to give it a fresh start. But I can go anywhere that'll have me within the State of Arizona as long as the person whose house it is isn't a felon. They would have to agree that there would be no alcohol, drugs or firearms in the residence."

"So, if I put something on the Internet in the hope of finding you a place in Arizona—"

"I'd get out in January instead of April," he says, smiling. "The person would have to send a letter saying I could stay there and I'll give it to CO3 Rose and he'll give it to the parole people and they'd verify it with the person. Then they'd go to the residence, make sure there's a room I could sleep in and that they agree to the conditions of parole."

"So, any person in Arizona could do this?"

"Yes."

"How much rent could you afford?"

"I'll pay five or six hundred monthly out of my disability check. I'll be getting $917 a month. But I'll need some for clothes, food and eventually a car 'cause I wanna be able to return to work. That's my goal. If I have a phone number to be contacted at, I'll be able to find a job. If I leave in April, I'll be homeless. The parole officer will give me a listing of shelters, but it won't be easy getting my life together from a homeless shelter."

Hoping to help, I put his story online with a request for someone to house him. My parents Google other options in Tucson and mail printouts of places that take prisoners. Barry, Claudia's father, offers to house him, but wanting to stay closer to Tucson, Midnight contacts and is accepted by a place my parents googled. I'm inspired by the success to keep blogging pleas for help for Slingblade. Getting him released would make me happier than all of the money I made in the stock market.

CHAPTER 54

Walking to Visitation, I brace to hear Jade describe her wedding. Even though it's going to hurt, I'll muster enthusiasm. She's done so much for me, I must be the best friend possible. Entering the room, I spot her at a table, staring anxiously, a peculiar sadness in her eyes. We hug. "What's the big news?" I ask, sitting down.

"I don't know where to begin," she says.

"What's the matter?"

She scans the surrounding tables to see if anyone's listening and says in a low mournful tone, "I called the wedding off at the last minute."

"Holy shit! Why?" I ask, shocked, surprised, wondering about the implications.

Sniffing, she rubs below an eye. "I guess I was more in love with the idea of getting married than actually getting married to Theo. Not that I didn't love him. I did with all my heart. It's sad because I never thought that he truly loved me. Maybe he did in his own way, but he was such a …" She breaks down sobbing. I fight the urge to reach out and hold her as I don't want the visit to be ended by the guards. "He wanted the best of both worlds. It felt like he wanted his whore in the bedroom and his house-cleaning, cooking Stepford wife. We got our marriage licences. We did our Catholic-church requirements. I thought it brought us close together. In the back of his head, he obviously wasn't thinking that. We got into a really big argument before we met the priest. It had to do with the selection of prayers. Out of all of the really nice prayers –" her voice cracks "–he wanted me to include: 'So Sarah called Abraham her master and it was a reflection upon him how she conducted herself and dressed herself. She dressed humbly in front of her master and the Lord,' and it went on for

235

two paragraphs, Shaun, about how I was to be subservient to him. I said, 'Over my dead body is that going into my wedding!' He said that it was a traditional prayer read at weddings in his church. I said, 'I don't know if you've noticed, but I'm not from the Dark Ages. It's the twenty-first century. I'm not having that read at my wedding.' We had a huge fight. I have to wonder what was truly going on in the back of his head because a month before the wedding there was only me and my family who had tickets. That's why I kept the wedding ring. I told him my family and I had incurred all this cost, which equated to the cost of the ring."

Stunned, I try to imagine her disappointment. "You poor thing. I can't believe the bastard put you through that. How did it actually end?" I ask, gripped by the saga.

"He called me at two o'clock in the morning and told me to get the fuck up. I said, 'Hey, I'm sleeping. Can we wait a few hours?' He said, 'No! We're talking now!' He said it wasn't right for me to put a stipulation over his head that we were going to move to the US. He changed the length of time we'd need to stay in the UK from three years to five years to seven years. I said, 'I love you and if you feel you need that much time, then OK, but I do want to move back eventually. You pick somewhere in the US, and I will follow you, but not here. I'm not happy in England.' Theo said I was wrong to say that, and I should trust that he would do what was right for his family. He made it abundantly clear in our relationship that because my parents were divorced they were the lesser part of the family, the part that he didn't like to talk about. I said, 'If you're backing out of the one promise you've ever made, I don't see how this can go forward.' I told him I needed some space. I was gutted. I had to go and return wedding presents on the verge of tears. The saleswoman didn't even look at my face. She said, 'What's wrong with them?' I said, 'Nothing's wrong with them.' 'Then why are you returning them?' I looked at her and said, 'Because there is no wedding.' She really looked at my face at that point and said, 'Oh. OK. No problem.' I had to explain to 200 people – between work and family and friends – what had happened. Look, Shaun, I'm so sorry that I haven't written or visited you more."

"Don't worry about that. You've had a lot to deal with. I'm just glad you're here."

Jade sniffs on a napkin and stops crying. I console her. She says she's going to keep visiting. I return to my cell with my suppressed feelings reigniting. Later on, I write:

I just awoke from a nap. After seeing you, I got back to my cell and tried to read but the words weren't registering because my mind kept reverting to your visit. I became overwhelmed by an urge to sleep, so I locked the door, buried myself under a blanket, hugged a pillow (the closest substitute to you), and fell into a spacey pre-sleep with the kind of relaxed feeling Xanax gives you before you nod off. The tension of prison went away. I slipped into the happiest of naps. The last thing I was thinking about was the magic you brought me today. I'd almost forgotten how beautiful you are. Those big eyes. Those full lips. The heart-shaped face dappled with freckles. And your wit and good nature and whatever it is that is so relaxing about you. When we hugged and I filled my lungs with the scent of your neck I felt so at home.

I'm still half-asleep writing this, but I wanted to get it down to capture my emotions.

Thanks for another lovely visit. You looked as striking as ever. I shall be thinking about you often. I hope the sadness you're experiencing due to recent events quickly lifts.

CHAPTER 55

In a blue-and-white-striped Polo shirt and tan trousers, Dr Owen looks more like a stockbroker about to play golf than a therapist. He has two books: *The Human Mind Explained* and *The Executive Brain*. He examines my homework:

What I was thinking when I was high on drugs at raves, and how I presently think about these actions.

On drugs at a rave: I'm having the time of my life. Everyone is having fun. My friends are behaving as bizarre as can be. There are thousands dancing to electronic beats, European style. I'm getting hugged and thanked for organising the party and supplying Ecstasy. I'm excited about the after-party I'm throwing, and the extremes of human behaviour and drug taking that will happen. My wife is kissing a girlfriend, turning me on. I'm high on GHB, Special K and Xanax. I'm starting to feel the hit of Ecstasy. I'm rushing. My skin feels warm and fuzzy. I can't stop smiling. Life is divine. The music and my heartbeat are moving in sync. Gooseflesh is rippling across my skin. Just breathing, tasting air, I feel so alive. I never want it to end.

How I think now: At the rate I partied, I'm lucky to be alive. That lifestyle starts out as fun, but leads to trouble and incarceration. I was emotionally immature. I've developed other interests I enjoy such as writing. I hope to use my knowledge in positive ways and to help prisoners. No more drugs and wild partying. Incarceration was meant to happen to force me to grow up, educate me, and to show me the error of my ways. To accomplish positive things, I can't screw up my decision-making processes, otherwise I won't succeed in life or as a writer.

"It seems," he says, staring up from the paper, "you've compared and contrasted your present thoughts with your past actions. You've realised if you go back to partying, it's not going to do you any good. You'll also have to look more closely at the decisions that led you to the substance-abuse lifestyle."

"Earlier in my life when I felt shy, drugs enabled me to socialise. I figured I'd do them for fun, mostly on the weekends and quit whenever I wanted."

"Do you consider yourself a drug addict?"

"No," I say, insulted. "I'm not a heroin addict who wakes up and sticks a needle in his arm, who has to get high every day or else feels ill. I was a functional recreational drug user. I'd party all weekend and work on the weekdays."

He shakes his head. "Addiction is when doing drugs interferes with your ability to function and interferes with your life. Take a look around you. Where are you right now?"

"Prison."

"What brought you here?"

"Choosing to do drugs." For the first time my denial is lifted. I realise I have been an addict for over a decade. I blush with embarrassment, yet feel empowered: identification of a problem is the first step towards a solution.

"If you weren't addicted to drugs, you wouldn't be here. You have a narrow view. Acknowledging your addiction exists is difficult for you. You must look at it in terms of how you would introduce yourself at an AA meeting: 'I'm Shaun. I'm a drug addict. I've been clean and sober for so many years. Have you read any Patañjali?"

"I've read Patañjali's aphorisms. There was a commentary about them in the Siddha Yoga lesson I did. It mentioned stilling the thought waves or tendencies of the mind. I can learn that stuff for the rest of my life, but it doesn't stop the thoughts flooding my mind when I get emotional or anxious."

"Such as?"

"An example would be a recent visit I had from a female. I was so happy, I was thinking about her for hours. Is that manicness?"

"Actually, it's normal. When you're deprived of female contact, you're going to have a tremendous physiological response. It feels good. It's a great thing. *Yadda–yadda.* In the emotional context, neurotransmitters are being released. It can feel quite intrusive. It's not necessary to get rid of those thoughts. You just need to be aware. To be able to observe them run from fantasy to fantasy. What the prisoner deprived of female contact experiences is similar to how teenagers react. How you reacted in your earlier lifestyle led you to being in here. You've got to learn how to analyse data in every situation. If you don't factor in your previous mistakes, you'll repeat those mistakes. How did you analyse stocks?"

"I'd analyse data: moving-averages of price, volume, that kind of stuff," I say excitedly. "I'd review thousands of charts, read annual reports, especially the notes, look at various financial ratios, and come up with a short list of stocks I felt had a high probability of success."

"When you were running the math, how did you feel?"

"I had tunnel vision. Nothing else existed. That worked well. I got rich, but I self-destructed."

"Did you read about Warren Buffett giving all that money to Bill Gates?"

"Yes."

"Why do you think Buffett has done so well?"

"He's a natural. He had an excellent mentor, Benjamin Graham. He must be an expert in forensic accountancy, but more importantly, he must be a master of his own psychology."

"Are you familiar with where he lives? Omaha, Nebraska?"

"It's folksy."

"There's corn fields. It's rural, agricultural, a small-town environment. Buffett eats at the same places and he's approachable. He hasn't succumbed to the trappings of power. He said it's easy to make money, but hard to give it away responsibly."

"For me, it was easy to make money, but then I'd go nuts."

"That's why you have to look at the reasons, understand the

road map, watch for the danger signals, blinking lights, cabarets, dancing girls, whatever."

"So, was my happiness over the visit a danger signal?"

"Most guys think with their little head. Do you have a penchant for that?"

"I did in the past. But the visit wasn't about that. We're intellectual equals. I was engrossed in conversation, electrified by her personality. It was reassuring to feel that good sober around her."

"Then in situations like that you just need to be aware of your chattering little monkey mind. In relationships in general, you need to apply the analytical discipline you apply to stock selection. Here's what I'm seeing: with yoga, you're doing well with your spiritual side; with stocks, your pragmatic side seems fine. It's the emotional side you're having problems with."

"I do have a deficit there. My mum and sister want to put their seal of approval on future girlfriends. In the past, I've chosen the wrong partners, and my depressions and increased drug taking came about during break-ups. I never realised I should step back and analyse potential partners with the discipline I analyse stocks. That's an important point you've made."

"When it comes to relationships, you've got your ratios all wrong. For homework, I'd like you to write down your awareness of who you were, who you are and who you're going to be."

In my cell, I struggle with the addict label. Some of the books I've read compare addiction to a lifelong disease with the addict at constant risk of relapse. *When I'm 60 years old will I be fighting the urge to take Ecstasy and go raving with glow sticks? That's ridiculous. Am I really going to have to be on guard for the rest of my life? Will people cross the road because they see me, the drug addict, walking towards them?* The more I dwell, the more the word addict puts a bad taste in my mouth. But I can't dismiss it either. I'm surrounded by its reality. Over 90 per cent of my neighbours are injecting drugs. The cycle of addiction is too hard for most to break. Even with hepatitis C shrinking their livers and lifespans, addiction rules their lives. I constantly see prisoners get released with high hopes, only to relapse and return – almost by design to keep the prison industries in business. *If the end of the road for addicts is prison and death, it's a road I'm not going any further down.* Having dealt drugs, I'm ashamed for sending people down a road of misery and devastation. *I can't reverse my past, but I'll never deal or do drugs again. Perhaps I can use my experience to steer others away from it.*

How can I analyse my relationship with Jade through the cold lens of stock-market discipline? She's a woman, not a set of numbers on a computer screen. Even though I agreed with Dr Owen, my emotional side loses rationality when it comes to her. I hate to see her suffering, but the split with Theo is my lucky break. If I play it cool, I might lose her again. I can't allow that. Maintaining a relationship from prison is hard. I need to do everything possible to keep her close in this final year before my release.

CHAPTER 56

Wielding a stick, Two Tonys – in sunglasses, an orange smock and a baseball cap – strides through Yard 1's gate and heads for the basketball court, where inmates surround him. Excited, I join the crowd. "Two Tonys! What the fuck are you doing here?" Max yells.

"I'm down here to run this yard, motherfucker." Two Tonys canes his left palm. "Don't start no shit and there won't be no shit. My schoolteacher, Sister Teresa – God rest her soul – used to whack me in the head with a stick like this."

"He's got the stick 'cause he's turned kinky in his old age," a Native-American transsexual says.

Two Tonys shakes his head. "It looks to me like you've got some of the kinkiest motherfuckers in captivity down here on Yard 1."

"Shit!" Jim Hogg yells. "Just 'cause you're a killer and Yard 4's the killers' yard, you think you can come here and talk shit."

"So what if I killed a few motherfuckers?" Two Tonys says light-heartedly. "So what if I left a few bodies along the highway? All those punk-ass bitches had it coming." A paint crew from Yard 3 arrives to work on the court. "I'm happy to see you motherfuckers," he says. "Now who's gonna fix me up a sandwich or get me a honey bun or some shit?" Jim Hogg fetches bagels smeared with peanut butter. "I salute you," Two Tonys says, raising his hand to his forehead. "You are my ace cool spoon, my pride and joy, my dog, a big-headed motherfucker, but still my road dog."

"How come they're all painting the basketball court and you're walking around with your hands full of bagels?" Midnight yells, pointing at Two Tonys.

"Put your finger down, motherfucker," Two Tonys says. "You

ain't on the fucking witness stand. And I sure as hell ain't your crime partner. I'm the supervisor of the paint crew and it's about time someone brought the boss a cup of coffee."

"Why've you got a stick?" Max yells.

"To bust a motherfucker in the jaw with," Two Tonys says.

"Why don't you lick my cock?" someone yells.

"I'd rather," Two Tonys says, "put a bullet in your head."

Delighted to see Two Tonys in action, and eager to chat with him, I wait for an opportunity to steer him aside. "I miss you on Yard 4, little bro," he says.

"I feel the same," I say, wishing I was back on Yard 4 with my friends.

"How's Mom and Pops doing?" he asks.

"Great," I say. "They're visiting soon. They told me you broke your blog-comments record with 'Two Tonys on Drugs.' It got ten comments. That's the one with your advice for me about staying off drugs, where you're driving down the freeway, all high, after whacking someone and your decision-making is messed up."

"Yeah. That's the time I had my .357 ready. If the cops had stopped me, I was gonna shoot it out with the motherfuckers."

"My mum said a guy who was going down the same path as you read that blog and emailed to say it's changed his life. Maybe sharing your experience saved him."

"I often wonder late at night – after whacking some flies, lying on my bunk and staring at the motherfuckers on the ceiling – if I was put on earth to whack motherfuckers or save someone's life. I wonder why I'm going through all this suffering and bullshit. Maybe this guy is saved. Maybe he's gonna have a son or a grandson who discovers the cure for AIDS or West Nile virus. It might have been my calling in life to save that guy."

"My parents just mailed a stack of blogs with comments. I can't wait to read them."

"You can't wait! How the fuck do you think I feel?" he says, beaming.

We chat until an announcement comes: "Yard 1! Lockdown! It's count time."

"Take care, little bro." Patting a fist against his chest, he says, "L&R," for Love and Respect. Watching him leave, I despair over the limited time I get to see him.

CHAPTER 57

Stood in the outdoor Visitation area, Auntie Lily – my mum's sister by adoption, a short round woman with silver hair who I haven't seen in fifteen years – appears to be rubbing tears from her eyes. I hurry to give her a hug, but slow down when I see she's pretending to shield herself from the glow of my clothes and the sun blazing off my head. "You look like a bloody Buddha in that orange!"

We laugh and hug. Mum and Dad seem happy, their faces more relaxed than at previous visits, which I credit to the chance of my immediate release if the clemency hearing they've flown to speak at goes well. I've applied for a reduction in my sentence on the grounds that I'm a first-time non-violent drug offender with a good track record, extensive accomplishments, positive post-release goals and strong family support. The hearing has put us on a high. To avoid the sun, we sit indoors, away from the windows. The smell of microwaved Mexican food provokes hunger. Distressed by the absence of burritos, I settle for peanuts.

Auntie Lily points at the prisoners by the restroom. "That one's waiting for a wee. The other'll be wanting a number two."

"How do you know?" Mum asks.

"Because he's letting people go ahead of him," Auntie Lily says.

"They don't do number twos in here, do they?" Dad asks.

"It's got to be bloody urgent to do a number two in here," Auntie Lily says.

"I couldn't come here to visit and do a number two," Dad says.

Having paid $10 for five photographs, I flag down the inmate photographer. We gather at a wall designated for snapshots. A sign reads:

PHOTO RULES FOR POSES:

ALLOWED:
  SIDE BY SIDE
  ONE ARM AROUND SHOULDERS OR WAIST
  HOLDING HANDS

ABSOLUTELY NO:
  HUGGING
  KISSING
  KNEELING
  SIGNING
  FAILURE TO COMPLY MAY RESULT
  IN DISCIPLINARY ACTION

A prisoner takes the photos. Outdoors, I buy Mum and Auntie Lily flowers so rich in pink and magenta the colours look spray-painted. For vases, empty water bottles are used. We chat for hours, mostly about the clemency hearing, my sister's wedding and the return of Jade. At 2:30 PM, we hug and say goodbye.

Heading back to my cell, I see Weird Al walking laps. "Did you have a good visit?" he asks.

"Yes. Very good," I say.

"Did you ask Auntie Lily to marry me, so I can obtain British citizenship?"

"Certainly did. She said yes, so long as you're rich and she's handsomely rewarded."

"I'll make sure she's handsomely rewarded."

I laugh. "Mum warned that Auntie Lily would be crying when I first saw her, but instead she called me a bloody orange Buddha."

"I'm starting to like the sound of this Auntie Lily. Does she have a hairy back?"

"I can't confirm it, but I'd bet money that she doesn't. She does have silver hair like you though."

Caressing his, he says, "Is hers as dignified as mine?"

"Yes, every bit as dignified."

"Oh. I have a message for you from Yard 4." He grins. "Frankie asked me to tell you that at 6:05 PM you are to touch yourself and think of him, and he'll do likewise."

"Oh dear," I say, shaking my head. "What's he mean, he'll do likewise? Is he going to touch himself and think of himself?"

"I'd rather not think about what you guys have got going on. Anyway, he said to tell you that you'll be receiving a letter from him and not to think just because you're on Yard 1 that the gay marriage is off. Perhaps Auntie Lily and me, and you and Frankie can get hitched at a double wedding."

"That would be real nice, Al," I say, punching his bicep.

Outdoors at the next visit, we sit at a picnic table under a wooden roof. Weekdays show the prison at its busiest. Things I take for granted – prisoner work-crews, medical call-outs and prisoners flocking to pick up commissary – are a source of fascination for Mum, Dad and Auntie Lily. A short Hispanic wearing a hairnet brings two chow trays to the Visitation porters.

"That's Mochalicious," I say.

"*She* looks bloody funny in the headgear and the plastic gloves," Dad says.

"Chow servers have to wear them for hygiene purposes."

"*She* looks like a surgeon," Auntie Lily says.

After putting down the trays, Mochalicious spins theatrically, pivoting on a heel. Swinging and swaying *her* hips, *she* waves in a feminine way.

"Good grief!" Dad says. "Did you see that?"

She-Ra appears in the garden, tending sunflowers and zinnias, *her* presence exciting my visitors who've read so much about *her*.

"Do you think we could see She-Ra's butterfly tattoo?" Auntie Lily says.

"No," I say, grinning. "*She'll* get into trouble if *she* shows you that. And they might end our visits."

A dozen Yard 4 prisoners heading for Medical spot us from the other side of the chain-link. "Englandman!" Frankie yells.

We turn our heads.

"Oh my God! It's Frankie," I say.

"What have you been suggesting to my son?" Mum asks.

"He left me," he says, pouting.

"You have to ask my permission for this gay-marriage thing," Mum says.

"Mum, I'll decide who I marry and it won't be no bloody man!"

"He's got it all wrong," Frankie says. "I'll decide. I'm the man in this relationship. Did you get my message, Englandman?"

"Yes, and I was thinking of J-Lo, not you."

A hundred prisoners weighed down by net bags march across the recreation field towards Yard 1.

"What are all those orange Santas doing?" Dad asks.

"They're coming back from the store with the week's commissary."

"It's an amazing sight," Mum says.

"The yard comes alive when they get back," I say. "People run around with commissary, paying off debts. Some pool food and have cookouts, making tamales, enchiladas, burritos."

"Is commissary the highlight of the week?" Auntie Lily asks.

"Other than visits and mail call, yes," I say.

Parting, Mum promises she'll do her best at the clemency hearing tomorrow – October 19, 2006 – that I'm not allowed to attend.

"Don't worry, once they see us, they'll let you out," Dad says.

"More likely double your sentence," Mum says.

"I don't know if I'll be able to speak up for you," Auntie Lily says. "I'll probably be crying too much."

"Do what you can. You'll be there for me. That's all that matters."

Walking back from Visitation, pumped up by the possibility of an early release, I spot my counsellor, CO3 Hepworth, a lanky man, well-spoken with thin grey hair.

"I've got a fax for you," he says, his expression grave. "From the Arizona Board of Executive Clemency."

"What's it say?" I ask, afraid the date has been rescheduled beyond my parents' visit.

"The result of your hearing is you were not approved."

"That doesn't make any sense. The hearing's tomorrow."

"Your hearing's tomorrow?" CO3 Hepworth frowns.

"Yes. My parents have flown all the way from England for it."

"Are you sure it's tomorrow?"

"Absolutely sure."

"That's strange."

"How does that work? Could they have made a decision before the hearing?"

"I don't know. I'm just the messenger." He hands me the fax at arm's length as if the paper is poisoned and strides away.

Breathing shallow, I read, disappointed, frustrated, angry, shaking:

It was the decision of this board at your hearing on: 10/02/06 to take the following action: not passed to phase 2 commutation.

The bastards must have decided before the hearing and accidentally faxed the result a day early, exposing their own corruption. My poor bloody parents are just going through the motions. Surely this is illegal and my attorney can do something with the fax.

The next day at Visitation, my family look shell-shocked, their eyes downcast. "It didn't go well, did it?" I ask.

"How did you know?" Mum says.

"I got a fax from CO3 Hepworth just after you left yesterday saying I'd been denied clemency."

They gape, perplexed, as if the notion is preposterous. "You've got to be joking," Mum says, frowning.

"The whole thing's a farce," Dad says, slapping the table.

"How can they treat people like that?" Mum says.

"We've been treated like bloody morons," Dad says, shaking his head.

"It's unbelievable," Auntie Lily says. "But you could sense it. They didn't have to think when the vote was called for. There was no discussion. It was cut and dried."

Upset, I'm speechless. "I thought the sentencing was bad," Dad says, "but this was one of the most humiliating experiences of my life. It soon became pretty obvious that the decision was already made before we could make our beggings and pleadings."

"I was crying the whole time," Auntie Lily says. "The atmosphere felt awful as soon as I walked into the room."

"What made it worse is that we were quite optimistic," Mum says. "We were told it would be informal and relaxed, just sat around a table. But it certainly wasn't like that at all. The board were on a raised platform looking down on us like judges. I felt there was something wrong. They were antagonistic. One of the first things the chairman said was, 'We know you love your son, but we are here to address the harshness and suitability of the sentence. Anything else you say will be disregarded and I will stop you if you repeat yourself or if any one of you repeats the same thing as a previous speaker.' I felt intimidated. The tone of his voice made it sound like he was reading the Riot Act."

"It was as if we were on trial," Dad says.

"I felt panicky, and my mind was racing." Mum spills coffee on her blouse.

"You all right, Mum?" I ask, riddled with guilt because my situation continues to hurt them.

"Yes. But I cried when I spoke to the board."

"Alan Simpson did a great job," Dad says, referring to my attorney, "and he did it free of charge. He answered the questions raised by the board, but it didn't seem to matter. There wasn't a lot of eye contact from them. It was a strange business, as if an iron curtain had been slammed down on us."

Hours later, a guard announces visits are over. Mum's eyes water when we say goodbye. "No need to be upset, Mum. The next time you see me, I'll be a free man." Sad, ashamed, I watch them exit through the set of security doors.

CHAPTER 58

"Standby for chow, Yard 1. You're getting breakfast first."

On a cold crisp Christmas morning, below a pink and blue sky, I join the prisoners drifting towards the chow hall, mostly depressed as if suffering a virus. A few swap gang handshakes.

"Merry Christmas, homey!"

"Happy Hanukkah, you sarcastic motherfucker."

"Happy Kwanzaa, dog!"

"Feliz Navidad, ese."

Breakfast is pancakes, scrambled eggs, cinnamon rolls, cereal and an apple. A guard with a clipboard checks off names and boasts how hungover he is, antagonising us. The din is lower than usual, our expressions rueful. The rising sun floods the room with light, illuminating dust motes dancing over our food. After fifteen minutes, the guards order everyone out. The prisoners rise from tables strewn with spilt milk, cornflakes and apples stabbed to prevent hooch brewing.

We retire to our cells. While I reflect on being absent from my loved ones, a sad silence spreads across the yard. No basketball. No pull-ups or dips at the workout stations. No squabbling. No "motherfucker" this and "dog" that. No announcements.

At least it's my last Christmas here. I read to take my mind off the mistakes I made that cost almost six years of my life.

At Building B, a guard starts a security walk. "Put away your hypodermic needles! Don't let me catch anyone drinking hooch!"

By the time the swing shift arrives, the sun is shining through a sky mottled with clouds like a cow's hide. In a slow sarcastic voice an announcement comes: "We would like to take this opportunity to wish you all a very merry Christmas and to thank you for providing us with such a wonderful 2006!" The yard animates:

"Merry fucking Christmas to you, too!"

"Shank you very much, motherfucker!"

"Come and say that to our faces, bastards!"

The guard continues: "And you'll all be pleased to know that we fully intend to keep up the time-honoured Christmas tradition of shaking your houses down."

Two guards – a female and a Mexican we call the "Fruit Nazi" for overzealously confiscating apples and oranges from inmates exiting the chow hall – raid cells, scattering property, confiscating food, thwarting hooch operations and handing out disciplinary tickets.

Late afternoon, we emerge for a surprise. The Gatekeepers – a young and high-spirited choir – sing carols from the other side of the fence. Briefly, I'm not a prisoner anymore. I'm someone's son, brother. I'm human again.

At dinnertime, skimpy portions of roast beef, broccoli and watery mashed potato that reeks of bleach provoke outbursts that unsettle the guards. Tension remains high. After eating, I join a queue for phones that barely work. Written on the faces of the prisoners are the usual concerns. *Will our loved ones be home? Will they accept the expensive call charges?* Unable to get through, some prisoners hang up, cursing life. Nearby, a demolition team of pigeons is pecking the plastic film off chow trays abandoned by the guards. From a gust that deposits sand in my mouth, Chihuahuan ravens descend – a vortex of big black birds with a purple and blue iridescence – scattering the pigeons and ravaging the spoils. A final announcement at 7:55 PM: "Yard 1, rec is over. Take it in and lockdown." The atmosphere is so heavy, I'm thankful that Christmas Day is nearly over.

On Boxing Day, I meet Two Tonys at the fence. "How the fuck was your Christmas?" he asks.

"Not too bad. The day before I got a visit from Jade, which gave me a boost. We got a little kissing action in, and she said she's coming back soon. How was your Christmas?"

"Good 'cause I ain't got no beefs," he says. "Let me ask you something, Shaun. You ever heard of Chad or Somalia or Sudan?"

"Yes."

"Well how nice a fucking Christmas do you think those poor motherfuckers had?" he says, raising his chin.

"I see what you're saying," I say, nodding.

"Do you know how many pieces of apple pie I got?"

"No."

"Three and two issues of roast beef. It might have looked like shoe leather and tasted like shoe leather, but that's OK 'cause guess what? Ivan Denisovich would have snorted those motherfuckers up with his left nostril and been as happy as if he were having supper with Mikhail fucking Gorbachev." We laugh. "That's my barometer now: how rough Ivan had it. Imagine being happy to lick some carrot gruel off a spoon. Or having to ride the cook's leg to come up on some extra gills and tails in your fish-eyeball soup. Or Slingblade grabbing your bowl of oat mush, and you've got to go toe to toe with the fucking Neanderthal or starve to fucking death. My point is this: how the fuck can I complain when there's always someone worse off? Of course, I'd like to be chowing down on a Caesar salad, some escargot, a little bowl of scungilli and some ravioli stuffed with spinach, but I ain't gonna let those thoughts get me down."

"What did you do on Christmas Day?" I smile.

"Played a little casino card game with Frankie. Watched a little TV. Sang some fucking Christmas carols to myself: 'Silent Night,' 'Jingle Bells,' and all that shit. How the fuck can I get depressed in here? This is my retirement home. Not just any motherfucker qualifies to be in here, you know. You don't just hop on a bus and say, 'Driver, take me to the big house.' This is an exclusive club. You've got to put in some serious work to get here. And what's good about it is they can't ever kick me out, 'cause I'm doing life. If things get shitty in here, I just tell myself, *Get a grip, man. What would Ivan Denisovich be thinking? Would he be raising hell about his waffles being cold in the morning? Would he fuck!* Like I've said before, that's PMA, bro. That's my positive mental attitude."

CHAPTER 59

The visits from Jade and a heightened sense of my release bring worries about incarceration affecting my sexual ability – a common fear stoked by older prisoners circulating myths of men freed after long sentences who suffer erectile dysfunction and premature ejaculation. They say, "If you don't use it, you lose it."

Making matters worse, Max drops off *How to Give Her Absolute Pleasure: Totally Explicit Techniques Every Woman Wants Her Man to Know* by Lou Paget. Reading that masturbation establishes nerve pathways that condition men to ejaculate quickly, a hard habit to break when making love, I almost choke on a cheese cracker. Later in the book, Lou offers hope. She quotes Barbara Keesling: "Once you take control of your [pubococcygeal] muscle, however, you can voluntarily delay or prevent ejaculation." I learn the "love muscle" runs from the front to the back of the pelvic girdle in both sexes, and men have two holes through it: the anus and the urethra. It can be strengthened by stopping and starting the flow of urine. According to Lou, "A good male exercise is placing a washcloth on your erect penis and doing penis lift-ups." *Ah ha. There it is! Dick-lifts. I can try them in the shower. A lot worse than dick-lifts goes on in there. Maybe I ought to speak to someone about this first. Someone wise and worldly.* Setting myself up to be the target of Weird Al's irresistible wit, I insist he read the book and return a week later.

Sat on his chair, he furrows his brow as if gearing up to impart lofty knowledge. "Given your proclivity for masturbation and in light of the thesis put forth in this book, it's highly unlikely you'll ever get past hello the first time you meet a woman, let alone get your zipper down. Simply put: your sex life is over. I'd get myself a good chin dildo if I were you."

"Forget about the chapter on chin dildos," I say, leaning against his bunk. "Did you read how dick-lifts increase your stamina and control?"

"I take it you're unfamiliar with the love muscle?" His brows lift.

"I've just never thought about it before. Have you?"

"Unlike you, I don't need dick-lifts. At my age, I'm lucky if I masturbate sixteen times a year. These days, I only get my rocks off on major holidays such as Christmas and Easter, and I'm even contemplating skipping those. I know this though: you'd look awfully cute in a chin dildo."

"Al! Can we please stick to dick-lifts?"

"OK. All right. The thing about flexing that muscle has been known since ancient times. Socrates flexed his dick, for God's sake. It's the same exercise as trying to stop peeing in the middle of peeing. It was described to me when I was young."

"Any advice on it?"

"My advice to you is to never give advice to an insane person as it's like pissing in the wind."

"Not that kind of advice! On dick-lifts!"

"My advice is this: do them when I'm not around. You're here. You're queer. Get used to it. Come out of the closet and move on."

"Thanks, Al. That's just great."

"Knowing your tendency to broadcast your sexual perversions through the known universe—"

"It's called the blogosphere."

"I find it highly unlikely that any woman who reads about your distasteful proclivities will come within a nautical mile of you. You probably will get laid, but not by someone of the opposite sex or in any way you presently imagine. I see chin dildos in your future. Dick-lifts will lose all relevance. It's my humble opinion that even mentally ill women who have no access to electricity – provided they're not too ill to read – will shun you like the devil avoids holy water. You should forget about dick-lifts and become more proficient at masturbation, if humanly possible. Take pride in the fact that if quantity supersedes quality, you'll be one of the Top Ten Jack-off Artists in the Northern Hemisphere. You should hook up with a woman who shares your masturbatory skills. It'll save you time and money and can be done in the comfort of your own home or by phone. Besides, attempting to do dick-lifts with that pencil-like penis of yours would be the equivalent of a piss-ant getting into a body-building contest. And while you're at it, why don't you write a book titled *Spanking Your Monkey: Memoirs of a Masturbator*. If you like, I'll pay to have a chin dildo put together as long as you agree to at least wear it in the chow hall. We have a saying here in Arizona that I suggest you apply to your dilemma: You dance with the girl who brought you here."

Bent over, I laugh so hard I snort. I gasp until I can speak. "So, basically, you hold out no hope for me with or without dick-lifts?"

"Your only hope is that somewhere in the world there's a female masturbating in a cell at the same twisted frequency as you. If you're lucky, she'll have developed the same demented need to manipulate her body parts. Perhaps one of your readers will commence a Google search to locate said woman, otherwise all hope is lost."

"Great, Al. You leave me no choice but to consult She-Ra." I snatch the book and leave.

Figuring I need to try dick-lifts before consulting She-Ra, I grab soap, a towel and a washcloth. I avoid the lengthy queue for the most popular showers because the prisoners are harassing those inside for staying too long – not conducive to what I have in mind. I enter a damp mouldy shower, disused because the water runs hot and cold. When prisoners abandon a shower, insects move in. Big black shiny beetles like globs of oil are plodding across the walls. I turn the water on, hoping to avoid its tempera-ture extremes by angling my body to one side. Feeling my back touch a beetle, I shiver and adjust myself slightly forward.

Soaping my man parts, I close my eyes and replay previous sexual encounters. When my penis is hard, I grab and soak the washcloth. Feeling pleasant against my skin, the hot wet material weighs down the angle of my erection. Drawing on weight lifting, I try sets of ten. *One, two … ten. That was easy. Keep going. Eleven, twelve … twenty. Keep going. Twenty-one, twenty-two …* Every so often, usually when I'm absorbed in a sexual highlight from my past, and my prostate is pulsing with a ticklish sensation, water scalds my penis, breaking my concentration. At sixty reps, my erection wilts, but I still feel my love muscle contracting and expanding. I keep counting, but the contribution from my penis dwindles. I call it quits, satisfied with sixty reps.

A few days later, Weird Al and I greet She-Ra at the fence. I tell *her* about Lou's book, dick-lifts and Weird Al's fixation on chin dildos. "Hey, Al," She-Ra says, staring through the chain-link. "If you take one of those little balls they use as gags that vibrate and strap it on a chin dildo, you can make love to your old lady with the chin dildo while the ball vibrates in her ass."

"Thank you for the useful information. If I ever—" Weird Al says.

"Or," She-Ra says, "you can flip your old lady over, work her poontang with the chin dildo, stick your tongue in her ass, sing a little tune and it's almost the same as a vibrator except it's your tongue."

"What tune do you recommend?" I smile.

"'Yankee Doodle Dandy,'" She-Ra says.

"I have the libido of an 80-year-old eunuch," Weird Al says, "so I'm going to file your advice under the category of useless."

"Or," She-Ra says, "if she has hems, you can hold onto the hems with your lips and hum."

"You guys are sick! I'm leaving you to it." Weird Al puckers and jogs off.

"Al!" She-Ra yells, attracting attention from inmates and guards. "It doesn't have to be your old lady! It could be your boyfriend if you ever get one! I could find a good man for you if you want! One that will want to use a chin dildo!" Two young guards approach She-Ra, Officer Rivero and a stern-faced cowboy. "I'm gonna explain dick-lifts to these COs as it's important to get a full spectrum of opinion on the subject, not just what prisoners think."

"Let's not do that, She-Ra," I say, reluctant to provoke the guards.

"Guards jack off, too, silly." As *she* explains dick-lifts, the guards stare incredulously. When it dawns *she's* serious, they contribute in good faith.

"If it works, I'll try that," Officer Rivero says, smiling encouragingly.

"That's so not true, dude," the cowboy says, shaking his head.

"Before dick-lifts," *she* says, "I could only go a couple of hours. Now I can go all day!" She-Ra throws *her* hands up.

"Without Viagra?" Officer Rivero asks.

"Without Viagra," She-Ra says, "but *with* dick-lifts. And I could never last that long when I was doing oestrogen. Now it's all day long!" *Her* hands shoot up again.

"It sounds to me like bull crap," the cowboy says.

I'm reluctant to get entangled in the conversation with the guards, but compelled to back up She-Ra. "It may be true. We have a, er, health book on the yard that says dick-lifts give you better control of your love muscle, which enables you to postpone your orgasms."

"There's a lot of bull crap in health books," the cowboy says.

"I do tongue lifts!" *she* yells so loud that dozens of prisoners stop what they're doing – working out, walking laps, sweeping, mopping – and turn around.

"So, you have stamina when you go down on people?" Officer Rivero asks, his smile expanding.

"It works," She-Ra says. "You ought to try it."

"I'm gonna try dick-lifts," Officer Rivero says.

"What about you?" She-Ra asks the cowboy.

"It's bull crap. 'Cause to make it stronger down there, you'd have to tear that muscle."

"The book never mentioned tearing it," I say. "It says reps strengthen it, give you more control, and eventually you can become a multi-orgasmic man."

When the prisoners have resumed their activity, She-Ra yells at full volume, "I'm so homosexual!" freezing all movement on the yard. The guards hurry away. *She* yells at them, "Now you know why us convicts can stay up longer! 'Cause we practise dick-lifts! Does anyone want to apply to join the Cult of She-Ra?" In a quiet voice, *she* asks me, "If I cut my nuts off, do you think that'll send inspiration to the rest of me? Do you know anyone who knows the best methods to remove the testicles?"

"Have you talked to Gina about it?"

"I really don't want anybody else knowing. I really must do it on my own. But I'd like to get some info on it, so I can learn about it."

CHAPTER 60

Dr Owen reads my homework: my awareness of who I was and who I'm going to be.

Who I was.

Immature. Hedonistic. Materialistic. Spiritually devoid. A thrill seeker. Sometimes selfish. Sometimes naïve. I worked and played hard. Overgenerous to the wrong people. Experienced mood swings from depression to euphoria. Goal orientated, albeit grandiose. Sometimes extremely focussed, other times devil-may-care. A sexaholic party animal. Mellow and reserved when sober, and generally happy-go-lucky.

Who I'm going to be.

Mature. A sober reasoner. Goal and success orientated without ostentation. Spiritually fulfilled via yoga, philosophy, healthy relationships, music, etc. Less naïve and more knowledgeable. Generous to the right people. Able to cope with and manage mood extremes. Stoic like Epictetus. Highly motivated and driven, but not in an unhealthy fashion. Hard-working. Optimistic. More skilful and more able to apply myself without messing up.

"From what you've written, you've identified the vast fluctuations between your emotional extremes. A hard worker versus devil-may-care. Depression versus euphoria. The way you over-respond into grandiosity. The way you under-respond into depression. You need to remain mindful of your polar opposites. As you tend towards one pole, pressure builds and you explode. Towards the other pole, pressure builds and you get depressed. Consider a water bottle at 5,000 feet. You empty the bottle and seal the cap.

At 14,000 feet pressure on the inside will expand the bottle and make a violent explosion. At sea level, with atmospheric pressure of 101,325 pascals, the bottle is fine, but plunge the bottle deep into the ocean and it is crushed flat."

"Good analogy," I say. "But when I get excited about something, it's hard to rein me in."

"You need a constant awareness of how you interact with the environment. It's the same as what you do during yoga. There's an expansion into your environment, into the universe. If your alignment and breathing are right, you're having a good experience that's not for the glory of you. Don't get caught up in ambition. Constantly remind yourself of this. Don't be too front-focussed. In yoga, the front is you and your back is the universal. That's what the back-orientated Friend of the Universe Pose is about. Lean back into things and your universe will open and expand."

"Are ambition and success compatible with yoga?"

"Yes. When awareness goes with it. Look at B.K.S. Iyengar, author of *Light on Life*."

"The smiley yoga master with the massive eyebrows?"

"Yes. When he goes on tour, he's expansive. He has a happy presence, but it's not him."

"What do you mean, it's not him? Who is it then?"

"It represents energy. Compare Iyengar's behaviour to the actions of a politician. A politician's actions are about ego. If you don't recognise the politician, he or she ceases to exist. Compare a politician with the Dalai Lama, a person who represents universal consciousness. What's contained within the Dalai Lama isn't ego and the individual. It's energy much larger than the person. It dwarfs the average politician."

"The politician's aura is sleazy and shallow."

"Yes, but other people project something real. Cultivate that."

"Isn't that a goal in itself?"

"I don't know," he says. "Should there be a goal on the path you are designating for yourself? The only thing that matters is to keep doing it. A goal implies potential failure. It's better to break the task into little pieces. Alignment. Breathing. Awareness of now. Sense of contentment. Think in terms of what's going on here and now, right at this moment. Not in terms of, *In four hours, I'm hosting a meeting where VIP's are going to recognise me and pat me on the back.* Don't be seduced by thinking you are bigger than you are."

"What if I have big goals to make positive changes in the world?" I ask, hoping my writing contributes to ending the human rights violations in Sheriff Joe Arpaio's jail.

"Mother Teresa had to be hard-nosed to help the poor of Calcutta. She didn't do it to win the Nobel Peace Prize. Her goal was to help others. Having big goals to help others is a good way to direct your energy. By all means keep working towards that form of dedication. For your homework, I'd like you to select some quotes from your studies of philosophy and describe them in the context of your character development and aspirations."

Reviewing my life, I realise how much I've changed. When I was first arrested, I pined for my old lifestyle – but I no longer identify with that person. Having rushed through life without a care in the world, I never considered the consequences of my actions. I'm grateful to Dr Owen for breaking down my personality and providing the tools to deal with the parts that lead to excess. After each session, I feel better prepared to face the world.

A week later, I'm called to Medical, which is strange as I haven't submitted a request to see Dr Owen. I present my homework:

"There is no wealth but life" – John Ruskin
Previously I believed, 'There is no wealth but wealth,' 'Greed is good,' etc. Ruskin's quote crushes shallow materialism.

"A man can surely do what he wills to do" – Arthur Schopenhauer
To succeed, I have to think bigger than before. To think, to will, to implement my plans are the necessary steps.

"Make haste slowly" – Gaius Suetonius Tranquillus

On my life journey, I need to take breaks, restore energy, and relax in order not to deviate too far from mental equilibrium.

"Misspending a man's time is a kind of self-homicide" – George Saville

Realizing how little I know and how much there is to learn, I shall devote a big portion of my life to pursuing knowledge.

"He who hates vice hates mankind" – Publius Clodius Thrasea Paetus

I'm learning to live with my vices, and determined not to become a slave to their cause.

"We cannot learn without pain" – Aristotle

There are no shortcuts in life without consequences. Input determines output. The discomfort of exertion is the price of postponed happiness.

"We will either find a way or make one" – Hannibal

My dreams will remain unrealised without action.

"Knowledge alone effects emancipation" – Shankara

Learning loosens the shackles of conditioning.

"Rule your desires lest your desires rule you" – Publilius Syrus

If I had heeded Publilius Syrus, I wouldn't be in prison. Implementing this maxim may be the main ingredient in the recipe for my future health and happiness. This may be the most important quote I have presented here.

"An excellent array of quotes," Dr Owen says, smiling broadly.

"I had fun doing it," I say, enjoying our bond.

"Ruskin is talking about being dedicated to having a healthy life. Last time we met we discussed how being dedicated to help others is a good way to channel energy versus channelling energy into destructive egocentric goals. The third quote implies making rapid movement slowly. Take breaks. When driving down the road take time to avoid wrong turns. You have a good interpretation of Saville's quote. You show a dedication to effort. The quest for knowledge is good, but don't forget experience and work have roles to play as well. Again, with Hannibal you show dedication to a way. It's for you to decide whether it's a way to Beverly Hills glitz or a way to understanding yourself and your life. Some say ascetics acquire wealth of character. Others, such as the Kashmiri Yoga traditions around 700 AD, say you do not have to become ascetic to achieve enlightenment. You can be a householder with a job, family, responsibilities and still be dedicated and achieve enlightenment. Folks do it in different ways. There is no one spiritual path. Now, I've got something to tell you." His face turns serious. I brace. "I'm being moved to Rincon Unit, so this will be our last session."

"Oh no!" I yell, shocked, hurt, disappointed. "I thought this was too good to be true. We're making real progress, and now I have to start all over again with someone else."

"Yes. Dr Pedder will be taking over. She's a little older than me and she's had plenty of experience."

"I can't believe this! I feel like I'm building a house and it keeps getting knocked down."

"But you're learning to build a stronger house. You're becoming more skilled with plaster, nails and floorboards."

"That's not the point. Now I've got to build rapport all over again. You've influenced my life more than any other prison staff."

"How so?" His gaze intensifies.

"You've enabled me to build a mental framework to deal with my anxieties. I laugh things off because of what you've taught me. If I get stressed out, I think of your advice and breathe deeply. You've enabled me to bundle my studies, my yoga and your words of wisdom into a solid foundation to deal with whatever life throws my way. You've increased my understanding of myself immensely. It seems everything I've been working at has come together under your tutelage. I was afraid this would happen: that you would eventually leave."

"Is there anything you'd like to ask me before we part?"

I pause. "What's the single most important piece of advice you can give me?"

"You need to be willing to accept who you are. Don't always want to be better or new and improved. You contain a lot of good inside you. You're doing a good job of sorting yourself out. You're putting tremendous effort into it. Make haste slowly. Don't let your abundant energy distract you. Don't destroy yourself. Don't rush down the path. You'll do exceptionally well if you don't get confused and if you realise what's going on around you and how it could affect you. Be cognizant of the pluses and minuses – the consequences of your actions. Learn about yourself from yoga. Over the next year, focus on several poses, the alignment, the breathing, the micro-adjustments, the fluency of the poses themselves. A foundation will develop, not just muscle on bone, but a strong foundation from which you'll know yourself better and be able to expand in all directions. From your physical practice, you'll develop a mental foundation. Developing into quite a nice person is the goal."

"A final thing: what about the wolves?"

"You have to decide where to channel that energy. If you channel it into your previous negative addictions, you'll end up back in here. If you channel it into the positive ones you've cultivated such as yoga and writing, you'll thrive. I wish you the best of luck in life."

"Good luck to you, too," I say, shaking his hand, my eyes glazing over. When I turn to leave, I fight back tears.

In my cell, I write up the session from notes I took. Devastated by the loss of Dr Owen, I pour over every session I documented, treasuring his words. Charged up with emotion, I hope to better absorb his advice. What he said about the wolves rings true.

Towards every weekend, the wolves used to raise my excitement to the point where all I could think about was partying. But in prison, days are indistinguishable. The sun rises. I pee, eat, drink, shit, exercise, read and write. The sun falls. Even Christmas Day, New Year's Eve and birthdays are meaningless. How can the howl of the wolves entice me now that I've broken a lifetime of being conditioned to view the weekend as special? I've just got to be strong enough to prevent that scene from luring me back. It wasn't just the drugs I was addicted to, it was the lifestyle. It dawns that the wolves – whom I viewed as my friends – were a manifestation of the strength of both addictions. Thanks to psychotherapy, the wolves are weak, whereas I've grown strong and Dr Owen has armed me against them.

CHAPTER 61

Shaped like a brick, Iron Man is sat next to me in the chow hall, talking about exercise, suffusing the area with adrenaline, endorphins and testosterone. Striving to be in shape in case I need to fight, I'm nervously wondering if I can work out with him. "How come you're always so jacked up?" I ask.

"'Cause I just did twelve-hundred push-ups and one-and-a-half hours of burpees."

"What's a burpee?"

"If you really wanna know, show up at the rec room when our doors open and I'll give you a crash course. By the time you walk out – if you can still stand – you won't have any doubts in your mind what burpees are."

"I'm looking to increase definition and put on some muscle mass," I say.

"Look, I know how to do it. If you learn my routines and put 100 per cent fucking effort into them, I'll have you in the best fucking shape of your life – guaranteed."

"I heard you have knowledge of martial arts," I say quietly as martial arts are banned.

"Yeah. I've had some training."

"Which types?"

"Look," Iron Man says, his neck, shoulder and jaw muscles rippling, "this is the deal: I don't like talking about this shit 'cause it tips my hand. When people know what skills you have, it's possible for them to come up with a defence against them. But if you're gonna be working out with me, I'll tell you what's up."

"I'm definitely going to work out with you."

"OK, then. All through high school, I trained in judo and karate, and then I did years of kung fu. My kung fu master was a class-four special-forces bad-ass whose job in Nam was to go out the night before the Marines and kill every sentry within a mile-wide area using only silent killing techniques: garrottes and edged weapons. He was a fourth-degree black belt in a style that was a combination of the tiger, horse and mantis."

"Can you show me some of that?" I ask.

"We'll see," Iron Man says.

"Do you mind if I ask how long you've been down?"

"Nine years. My first time I did four and now I'm doing eight flat for collecting a drug debt. I smashed someone's door down. I didn't hurt anyone. I just wanted my fucking money."

The next day, groggy from waking up, I trudge to the rec room. "I can't believe we're working out at 6 AM."

"It's the coolest time of the day and your stomach's empty," Iron Man says, a sadistic gleam in his eyes. "Anyway, this isn't social hour. Let's do fifty jumping jacks to get the blood flowing." With the rising sun heating up the building and no ventilation in the room, I'm soon wide awake and shedding drops of sweat. I remove my soggy T-shirt. Iron Man fetches a fan. "On to burpees," he says. "Stand with your legs shoulder-width apart. Jump your legs out behind you while dropping into a press-up position without planting your face into the concrete! Do five push-ups and then in one swift motion draw both legs forward, planting your feet in the original shoulder-width position and stand up. Congratulations, you have just done one burpee. Run in place between repetitions. While I do my burpee, you run in place and vice versa."

Thirty minutes in, I'm fighting the urge to quit. *What the hell have I got myself into?* Every muscle is in shock. After an hour, I'm out of breath, seeing stars and barely able to stand. I finish, satisfied with myself for persevering, but almost fall down the stairs. "Thanks, Iron Man. You destroyed me." We laugh. "When can we do this again?"

"Tomorrow. If you're committed, I'll introduce you to more routines. We'll do pull-ups, free-squats, push-ups, lunges, dips, inverted shoulder presses and a wide variety of other exercises for triceps, biceps and every other body part."

"Why are there no weights we can use?" I ask.

"During a major riot they were used to smash skulls in. Prisoners and guards ended up dead, so they were taken from all of Arizona's prisons."

The next day, I exercise on the yard for ninety minutes, with muscle soreness, dozens of prisoners watching, and Iron Man yelling, "Embrace the pain!" My heart beats so fast for the rest of the day, I have difficulty falling asleep. But as the weeks pass, my soreness and resistance towards his regime fade. I crave the workouts, which release, along with yoga, the tension accumulated from lying on my bunk for most of the day reading at an accelerated rate to hit my 1,000-book target.

My appetite soars. I purchase cheese stolen by a Mexican cartel worker from the kitchen that I store in the swamp-cooler vent to keep it from melting and away from the guards. Iron Man plies me with powdered-milk drinks. The only thing that halts exercise is the occasional pulled muscle or when the prison is locked-down, which happens a few times due to fights and the extraction of corpses, usually from illness, suicide or murder. In torrential rain, we run outside, watched by astounded inmates pressed against cell-door windows.

Iron Man implements a week of "Torture Olympics" – various timed strength and fitness events, during which I manage 200 push-ups in five minutes. We jog laps and sprint, monitored by guards who keep advising us over the speakers to drink water and not stay out too long. Pull-ups become my favourite exercise: I delight in cranking myself up on a bar, feeling the heat penetrate my skull even though I'm wearing a baseball cap and shades, tasting the salt in the sweat running over my eyeballs and down my face. I'm complimented by a few prisoners on "getting cut." One says, "You're not getting big, but you're looking sexy." Appreciating his remark means I've been in prison for too long. I happily remind myself that I've only got six months left. Working out on the rec field with Iron Man, away from the noise and hassle of the yard, admiring the view of the mountains where I used to live, discussing self-help and psychology books we've read, I occasionally forget where I am.

My spirits are raised by a letter from Jade offering to come to the next food visit. I respond:

I just finished reading Falling in Love for All the Right Reasons by Dr Neil Clark Warren. The book advocates marriage and cites twenty-nine areas couples need to score highly in if they are to sustain a relationship in the long run. We scored so high it was frightening. It was also sad because you've made it clear that due to my past, you'd never have such a relationship with me. More than anyone I've dated, you have the characteristics I believe would sustain a long-term relationship.

The homies have been asking if you were coming to the food visit. I told them you'd run off with an Australian as you'd grown tired of the British accent. You should have seen their disappointment. You have quite a following in here! Also, now that I work out with Iron Man, my appetite is like that of a wild beast.

Iron Man asks about yoga. In the rec room, I warm him up with sun salutations and administer a strenuous routine catered to his personality out of fear he'll lose interest if insufficiently challenged, including lots of warrior poses – holding lunges for up to two minutes with arms outstretched – inversions such as headstand, handstand and scorpion, similar to a handstand but with the forearms on the floor and the legs curled towards the head. I throw in some one-legged balance postures. We wind down with corpse on the floor. He enjoys it so much it becomes a regular thing. Other prisoners start taking notice and ask to participate. Before I know it, I've got my own little yoga class. To keep them motivated, I attach the relevance of yoga to prison

– such as pointing out that a benefit of doing the splits includes the flexibility to kick someone in the head – while aware they'll leave relaxed and less likely to pick a fight.

Reading in my cell, I spot guards clustering outside and brace to be raided and ticketed if they find the cheese hidden in the vent. "Attwood, we have a question for you," one yells.

Wondering why they've not barged in yet, I jump up, heart rapid and stand in the doorway. "What is it?"

"If we can get a yoga class going, would you be willing to teach it?"

Relieved, delighted, I smile. "Absolutely, I've already been teaching yoga to some guys, and more are asking to join."

"We're gonna put in a proposal for a yoga class and there'd be a turn out for you to teach it in a room off Yard 1."

"Great! The rec room we're using has no air con."

"And you're not supposed to be using that room anyway."

"Oh. OK. Some guards say it's OK and some boot us out."

"Well, we're gonna put this proposal in 'cause we feel yoga will do the guys some good."

"It's a positive thing. I'd love to teach it. I just hope it gets approved."

CHAPTER 62

At the food visit, Jade's wearing black, her hair in a ponytail, lips dark pink, nails silvery pink, toenails gold and mauve. "Thanks for coming," I say, my eyes pinned to the plastic boxes on the table.

"I went to The Cuisine of India," she says, removing a lid from a container, releasing a curry aroma that causes my nose to twitch and mouth to salivate. "I've brought chana masala, aloo gobi, garlic naan and rice pilau."

"Perfect! Please help yourself before I devour it. I skipped breakfast. I'm hungry enough to gnaw on your arm right now."

"I thought you were a vegetarian! You can save that kind of behaviour for when you get out."

I laugh. "With you?" I ask, smiling.

"We'll see," she says, raising her brows.

"*Grrrrrr.*" The food disappears fast. Bloated, I sink into my seat, rub my belly and take deep breaths. The world slows down. "I ate so much, I feel as if I'm going to die."

"I'm behind on reading your blog," she says.

"I know She-Ra's your favourite."

"Have you given in yet?" Her eyes narrow.

"What do you mean?"

She tilts forward, eyes wide. As I lean, my eyes drift to her lips. "You know ... with the transsexuals," she whispers.

"No!" I say, pulling away.

"*Mm-hm,*" she says, eyes sparkling with accusation.

"And I never will! I'm almost out of here!"

"My friend said, 'I bet you he has.'" I gape. "She read about you in the *Phoenix New Times*. She said you're sexually deviant and too adventurous."

"Huh!" I say, blushing.

"And I think you are, too."

"Are what: sexually deviant and adventurous or going with transsexuals?"

"Sexually deviant and adventurous."

"I thought you were on my side."

"Yes, but I still have to ask."

"Indeed," I say, nodding. "Frankie said that after five years, I'd be so frustrated, I'd start getting oral from transsexuals, but, I'm sorry to report, my dear, it hasn't happened."

"I'm just checking."

"It's not such a bad thing to check on actually. The longer I've been down, the more I've found out what goes on. According to She-Ra, the majority are getting it on, including some of the biggest, baddest-looking prisoners. I almost broke down once when I first met Gina." I tell her about Gina. "The prisoners abstaining worry they'll be incapable of sex when they get out."

"What do you mean?"

"They fear it's been so long, they'll ejaculate prematurely or be so anxious, they can't get erections. Hopefully, I've kept my apparatus in working order in other ways ... with ... er ... magazines, photos."

"Oh, yeah," she says, her cheeks reddening.

"I'll find out soon enough if a certain someone follows through on her idea of deflowering my re-virginity."

"My idea!" she shrieks.

"OK. Maybe it's a joint idea of ours."

"Huh!" she says, shaking her head, rolling her eyes. "But I will be in England for certain other reasons when you are due to be released."

"I like the sound of that."

"So, are you nervous about getting out?"

"I can't wait. I'm so excited. There are all kinds of books and stories I've drafted that I want to re-write and start submitting. I've spent months working with Two Tonys and T-Bone on their autobiographies. I think it would really make a difference in their lives if I can get them published. I'm less nervous than most about getting out because I have such strong family support. Most of the guys get released with next to nothing, $50 gate money, and are expected to make their way in the world. They end up taking the easiest route to get food and clothing: committing crimes. Nearly everyone I've blogged about who has been released has come right back. The prison gets almost $50,000 a year to house each person. That's why they give them no rehabilitation or education. They want them to come right back to keep the money rolling. The politicians and legislators are in on it, too, receiving massive contributions from guards' unions and private prisons and all of the other contractors cashing in." Noticing how loud I'm speaking, I say, "OK. I'm getting off my soapbox now."

"Are you coming back?"

"Hell no! I'm going to focus on becoming a writer. And if I make money, I'll use it to repay my parents, help my prison friends and maybe eventually get back to trading stocks online. That way I'll be able to stay home with the good woman who helps me settle down."

"You're too wild to settle down. You'd grow bored with someone like me."

"That was the old me. The kind of stuff I used to laugh at – watching plays, listening to concerts, reading books other than stock-market ones – that's all stuff I wouldn't mind doing now. I still want to have fun, but I've realised fun is a state of mind. When you've had your life taken away, you learn to enjoy simple things. And there's nothing wrong with the funnest most natural thing in the world: making love. Wouldn't you agree?" I lean forward.

Jade folds her arms. "We'll see about that."

"Shall we have a stroll in Lovers' Lane?" I ask.

"OK." We stand.

Outdoors, Frankie and a gang of Mexican Americans at recreation spot us. He cups his hands. "I'm giving you a thumbs up, Englandman. But I still want a bathing-suit shot. No, let's make that a G-string shot. I'm also gonna need a letter from her asking for permission for any more kisses."

"That's Frankie," I say to Jade. "But I can't yell to him because the guards will cancel the visit. I think he approves of you." She chuckles.

"Did Englandman tell you," Frankie says, "that we've been doing tongue exercises together? I showed him how to kiss you behind the neck with my magic tongue. Ask him how Frankie tastes?"

"I worry about you and Frankie." She shakes her head.

"He's bonkers. But he's got a good heart. He was the first to protect me when all hell broke loose over a blog I wrote."

"*Mmmm-mmmm-mmmmmm!* Englandman knows what time it is!" Frankie yells.

"What time it is!" Her brows leap. "What does that mean?"

"That I've got it going on because I'm with you."

"How funny." She smiles. "Why do I feel like I'm being paraded around prison?"

"I can't deny there's an element of that to Lovers' Lane. Do you mind?"

"No. It just feels strange."

"There's She-Ra," I say, pointing. "The blonde giantess playing volleyball with tattoos all over *her* body."

We eavesdrop on the players. "Come on, Miss Priss," a prisoner yells at She-Ra. "Hit the ball! Don't you like playing with balls?"

"That's fucking queer stuff!" She-Ra yells.

"You're a fucking queer!"

She yanks up *her* shorts and wiggles *her* hips. Revealing the butterfly to the players, She-Ra yells, "Queer this!"

"Are they the balls you practise on?"

"Come to a cell with me," She-Ra says, "and I'll show you how to hold balls. The only difference is mine are hot and sweaty."

Jade's hand that I'm holding is moist and my scalp sizzling, so we go indoors. At the visit's end, our parting kiss is prolonged and passionate, leaving me hungry for more. After she leaves, I join the prisoners awaiting strip searches in an outdoor cage known as the Arizona room, some clutching bellies expanded as if pregnant.

"We saw you macking, England," Max says, referring to kissing.

"Englandman's not lost his touch," says Frankie's massive compadre with gold teeth and a bald tattooed head.

Max points at me. "Homey's got G-A-M-E. England's a pimp. A mad pimp."

When I get back to my cell, I write to Jade:

You brought just the right amount of food. It was delicious. I'd like to express how you made me feel with a quote from Tolstoy's love story Anna Karenina:

"But what struck him like something always new and unexpected was the look in her sweet eyes, her calm and sincere face, and her smile, which transported him to a world of enchantment, where he felt at peace and at rest, as he remembered occasionally feeling in the days of his early childhood."

Jade responds:

... I find your affection for me endearing and it is mutual to a certain point. My affection for you, however, is more rooted in a deep friendship than a future relationship. I know you know this, but I don't think that you listen very well. We will just have to continue as we are. I should feel guilty for that and I do, but not enough to have not said it. I will be at the next visit that is on a weekend day.

PS sprayed with Victoria's Secret Perfume

Her insistence on friendship increases my determination to forge a relationship. With T-Bone insisting that she wouldn't be wasting her time visiting unless she has strong feelings, I'm convinced a relationship will happen. *She probably just needs more time to sort her emotions out after the cancelled wedding.*

CHAPTER 63

Amid paperwork and personal effects on Dr Pedder's cluttered desk are *Power Plays* by Tom Clancy and an *Arizona Highways Magazine*. Dressed in a brown blouse and skirt, she has big slate-grey eyes like a cat. Her long light brown hair is parted and pulled back. Her sceptical gaze is intimidating. After discussing my ups and downs, and the progress I made with Dr Owen, she asks about my level of self-understanding.

I wish Dr Owen was here. "Before my arrest, I was oblivious to my flaws," I say, shifting in my seat. "I never thought about the reasons behind my behaviour. Since then, thanks to psychotherapy and my psychology and philosophy studies, I've come a long way in understanding myself. I realise we all have dual natures: good and bad. I've tried to analyse what triggers my bad side, and how to channel that energy into positive things like yoga and writing. Throwing parties satisfied my rebellious nature, but so does writing. My goal is to become a better person, instead of being a sex-and-drug addict, and having my life crash again."

"Out of the disorders you mentioned, bipolar and anxiety problems are classified as Axis I major mental disorders. Bipolar is thought to be genetic, and although I'm against meds, 99.9 per cent of psychiatrists would recommend treatment with meds such as lithium and Depakote."

Not another pill pusher! "I prefer the holistic approach," I say in a hostile tone. "By changing the way I think, I'm trying to address the root causes of my problems instead of just masking the symptoms."

"In the past were you impulsive?" she asks.

"Yes."

"Self-damaging?"

"Yes."

"Did you drive recklessly?"

"Yes."

"You already mentioned sex and drug abuse. Did you have intense relationships that went bad?"

"Yes."

"Did you feel devastated afterwards?"

"Yes."

"Did you feel totally alone?"

"Sometimes I liked being alone. Other times I threw parties, so I'd be surrounded by thousands."

"Do you experience emotional ups and downs on the yard?"

"Not as much as before Dr Owen. It's tapered off."

"Were you abused as a child?"

"No. I had a normal upbringing."

"Does anyone visit you?"

"Yes. My parents usually come at least once a year, my sister has been three times and a female friend comes."

We discuss my post-release goals: writing and further education. "It sounds like you have good plans," she says, "and you've come a long way in understanding yourself. It's obvious that Dr Owen had a big impact on you. Is anything really stressing you out?" she asks brusquely.

"My release," I say. "I keep thinking that I'm not going to get released come November."

"Anxiety is normal in this situation. I would expect your symptoms to increase as you get closer to the date. Have you been using cognitive techniques?"

"Yes. I've been reading more Aurelius and Epictetus, and last night I taped to my wall a quote from a Siddha Yoga lesson: concentrating on any problem only intensifies it. I even laugh at how ridiculous I am for worrying, but then later I convince myself I'm not getting out again. Do I have gate fever [short-timer madness]?"

"That's not how I'd describe it. This anxiety is a normal thing."

"Even if it keeps me awake at night with racing thoughts? So many strange things have happened with my legal case that the law of averages suggests my release will get botched somehow."

"Staying up at nights isn't a good thing. You need to sleep. Concentrate on breathing. Are you aware of how rapidly you're breathing now?"

"I wasn't, but now I am. I felt so excited when this year began, but now my thoughts have shifted in another direction."

"Freedom equals the realisation of your hopes and fears. You must use cognitive techniques or else your symptoms will get worse. Is there anything else bothering you?"

"No. That's my main concern."

"Then put in a request if you need to see me again."

Disappointed, I leave longing to decorate the house built by Dr Owen, not having to rebuild with Dr Pedder, whom I feel zero rapport with. *Don't give up on psychotherapy. Try to make the most of it.*

Early in my incarceration, survival was paramount. Getting released seemed so far away I never really thought about it. But when this year began, I became more forward focussed. Increasingly, I'm dwelling on freedom. Sometimes, I think about my goals and get manic joy. Other times, I worry about how I'll cope, but reassure myself that prison has enabled me to deal with anything. I'm concerned about being a burden to my parents. All of my assets were confiscated by the State of Arizona, and I still owe my parents almost $100,000 in legal fees. I don't want to cost them any more money. I'm a natural money-maker, but sometimes doubts arise. I worry about the effects of my behaviour on my parents' mental health. My sister sent printouts of my mum's blog: barbarabarnes.blogspot. Reading them, I felt ill – and deservedly so – as I was reminded of how my situation continues to affect my mum. Since my arrest, she's been on and off medication and is in therapy. Recently, she sent a letter describing reoccurring nightmares she had about me with drugged-up eyes. Shocked and riddled with guilt, I replied that incarceration has increased my common sense and maturity, and focussed my mind on a path that I won't divert from by behaving idiotically. I'm driven to do well for their sakes and my own. What do I do for fun when I get out that isn't illegal? Spending time with family and friends. Reading and writing. I've finished with drugs. My future will be wasted if I repeat the same mistakes.

Whatever is driving my writing is coming from deep inside. I'm convinced I was given a platform not just to share my experiences, but also to bring attention to the plight of others like Slingblade. To improve, I'm making a final push by reading everything about writing I can get my hands on and forcing myself to read more classical literature. I read 268 books in 2006. I'm on track to achieve my goal of over 1,000 by my release. Thanks to literary journals, I've become a short-story junkie. I believe that style is inherent, but it's important for a novice to learn what not to do. Visualising myself sat tapping away at a computer, I smile. Being this close to the gate feels like I'm on the verge of a brand-new existence full of the joy only known to those who have lost and regained their lives.

A month later, I request to see Dr Pedder. "How're you doing?" she asks.

"Much better," I say. "I realise how silly I must have sounded worrying that I'll never get out. I think what happened was this year began, and I spent months in a state of euphoria telling myself that this is the year I get out. Then there was a backlash, and I spent several weeks convinced I was never getting out. I'm over that. I can feel the euphoria building again. I'm eligible to be released to ICE [US Immigration and Customs Enforcement] in November."

"But it usually takes a few weeks for ICE to pick you up."

"Yes. And then I'll be processed at ICE. According to the British Consulate, if I have a passport, that should only take a few weeks, so I'm hoping to be home by Christmas. If you get a request from me in January, you'll know we've got problems."

"So, are you ticking things off a list of things you need to do?"

"I'm beyond ticking. The things have been ticked and worked to death. I think my stressed-out-about-never-getting-released phase was productive in that I kicked and screamed to my parents, my attorney and CO3 Hepworth so much that everyone is now doing everything they can to ensure my release is processed. We're getting regular emails from my attorney updating the status of the proceedings for my deportation order."

"So, if you expect to be home by Christmas, where will you live?"

I smile. "It's become a joke among my family and friends that I'm going to live in my parents' garage, and they're going to feed me orange trays through the cat flap."

She laughs. "What are you going to do when you get out?"

"My goal is to go back to university some time in 2008 to do a creative-writing master's. A senior academic in England asked me to consider going to his college. He pointed out that if I did, a certain best-selling author would confer my degree."

"So, you wouldn't be living with your parents then?"

"No. That university has quarters for mature students."

"How are you going to afford this?"

"That's the main barrier. The State seized my assets, so—"

"Why did they do that?"

"They said to offset the costs of the case. Anyway, I can't fall back on my parents because I owe them a lot, so I'm making inquiries about scholarships and loans. Prisoners Abroad provided useful info and I've sent them more questions."

"How are things on the yard?"

"Everything's going great. I'm doing correspondence college courses. I just finished a philosophy one, and really hit it off with my teacher. My heart and soul are demanding that I take a shot at a career as a writer, and as I've only got a few months to go, I'm putting all of my energy into that. I've submitted some stories to magazines. I can feel changes coming on in my prose. I believe that all this effort now will help me succeed when I get out. I have manic energy that I'm focussing. I think that being bipolar can be an asset for a writer."

"Not if you're suffering delusions of grandeur of being the next Shakespeare, and all you're writing is gibberish."

"Believe me, I've written my fair share of gibberish, and gone through some peculiar phases which I'm embarrassed about, but there are some gems among the rubble. It's a question of culling them. Look at all of the legendary bipolar writers and poets, ranging from Virginia Woolf to Lord Byron. I'm not so delusional I'd place myself in their league, but if I didn't have this manic energy, I couldn't sit and write for twelve hours feeling on top of the world, not wanting to take a break for a shower or to go to chow."

"So, you are familiar with the diagnostic criteria for bipolar."

"I've read books on it."

"You do get talking very fast and loud. Do you have racing thoughts?"

"Yes."

"How often do they prevent sleep?"

"Only sometimes. They can keep me up for hours at nights, but I do eventually get to sleep."

"You've mentioned times during your life when you contemplated suicide, and you've mentioned times when you're on top of the world. So, you do seem to experience the bipolar extremes."

"I spend most of the time happy hypomanic though."

"And doesn't it feel great?"

"Yes!"

"That's why a lot of people with bipolar disorder don't want to take meds. They want that high."

"And I'm certainly one of them. My dad asked if I had a choice not to be bipolar would I take it. I told him I'd stay as I am even though it may have contributed to my propensity for doing drugs and partying. Being bipolar gave the energy to succeed at many things, including stockbroking."

"Do you think stockbroking contributed to you breaking the law?"

"I was attracted to investments due to my risk-taking nature, which contributed to my demise."

"What about the office environment you worked in?"

"I went from being a university graduate in England to working in an office full of feisty New York Italians, some of whom liked their coke, crystal meth and strippers."

"It may be a stereotype, but when I imagine stockbrokers, I see coke-snorting macho guys."

"You're right, but that was nothing compared to the levels of drug consumption among my friends in the rave scene. That's what pushed me over the edge. And I'm not going back to that. I'm determined to succeed in literature and to get back to trading my own account, neither of which I'll accomplish if I cloud my mind. Prison was necessary to mature. I can't imagine who I would be without all of this personal development. It's been such a good thing. The main downside has been the effect on my family, and that pain has motivated me to make amends. My sister asked if I'd just intellectualised to pacify my parents – which hurt my feelings – and I tried to explain the ongoing development of my new self and the continuous shedding of skin that's occurred as I've attempted to transcend incarceration."

"How's your sister?"

"She's doing phenomenally well. In the eyes of my parents, I see her compensating for my misbehaviour. She's doing us proud."

"It's great that you seem so happy today."

"Thanks. I've a lot to look forward to."

"Are you sad about leaving America?"

"There are people here who I'm sad to leave. But I broke the law and it's part of my punishment. America was good to me. I prospered, thought I was invincible and overstepped myself. Maybe I can arrange to come back legally someday. If not – oh well – there's plenty of the world I haven't seen. I enjoy the challenge of fighting the odds, of building things up. If I can do well in prison, I can thrive anywhere. As funny as living in my parents' garage sounds, being reduced to rock bottom puts me in my element. I can't wait to work on my comeback. That seems to be the way I'm hard-wired."

"So, no more worrying about not getting out, eh?"

"Definitely not. In my most recent Siddha Yoga lesson, Guru-mayi pointed out that if we were to view a videotape of our lives and see how much time we spend worrying over things that don't materialise, we'd be slapping our heads and wishing we could do it all over again." I leave, pleased with the session, wondering if Dr Pedder was just having a bad day the last time.

CHAPTER 64

"You're showing a positive reaction for TB," says a nurse, examining a red mark on my arm from an injection of five tuberculin units two days ago.

"Are you sure?" My forehead scrunches.

"A reaction of that size is positive."

Devastated, I return to my cell, where I find a slip of paper attached to the door, instructing me to report for duty as a dishwasher for thirty cents an hour, considered the worst job on the yard. Shannon arrives. I tell him that I have TB. He says it took six years of litigation after DOC diagnosed him with hepatitis C to force the prison to treat him, and wishes me good luck. He fetches a medical book. Reading about the deaths caused by TB and the difficulty of treatment raises my blood pressure. He points out that a positive TB test precludes kitchen duty as it's a food-preparation area.

I notify the counsellor in charge of work assignments. The next day, I receive a response: he contacted the nurse, my TB reaction is no longer positive, and I must report to work or risk disciplinary sanctions and the possibility of losing my release. Shocked, I consult Shannon, who also has a kitchen assignment. He says my result was switched to negative because the kitchen is desperate for workers. He takes his top off to show his back – a landscape of bleeding sores from cystic acne. The same counsellor refused to give him a work waiver even though he has open sores, hepatitis C and will be around food.   •

Confused, disturbed, I consult Weird Al. He shows the criteria for a positive TB test set by DOC in Department Order: 1102 Communicable Disease and Infection Control: A reaction greater than 10mm is considered positive for inmates and corrections staff. With a ruler, I measure mine: 15mm x 18mm. "Fuck!" I storm out, angry enough to strangle the counsellor.

Prisoners – aware of my TB reaction, and not wanting me near their food – make it clear I'll be smashed if I report for work. I request to see the nurse again. The next day, I join the line of inmates displaying their arms to the nurse. As I'm not on her list, she tries to ignore me, but I persist. "It's not a positive reaction," she says without examining my arm. "It has to be 12mm." She turns away.

"It's 15 by 18," I say to the back of her head.

"That's your opinion," she says, walking away.

"Shall I get my ruler?" I yell.

"That's not necessary."

"Then have someone measure it at Medical!"

"I'll schedule you for this afternoon."

At Medical, a plump man puts a ruler to my arm and removes it with a magician's sleight of hand before I can show him the size of the reaction. "It's not 10mm."

"It is. I measured it myself."

"You're not from this country, right?"

"Yes."

"That explains the reaction. You've had a shot that causes this reaction." For five minutes, he insists it's negative.

"Untreated TB can kill someone within five years!" I yell. "To be on the safe side, I'd like to be referred to the next test."

"I can do that, but if you're positive, I'm going to put you on drugs that'll really mess your liver up." His lips tighten.

"According to DOC policy, you can't do that until an X-ray confirms it. Before that, you have seven to ten days to test my other arm."

Taken aback, he says, "Let me look at it again. To be honest, I just can't tell. It could be TB. The nurse did it in the wrong spot. I'm gonna do it over here." He pens an X on my arm.

"So right now, is it possible that I have TB?"

"It is possible, but we don't know for sure, so let's keep it quiet."

Uproar spreads on the yard. I fend off dozens of irate prisoners by promising to refer the matter back to the counsellor. In my note, I state I may have TB, and quote Department Order 1102: *For the safety of staff and prisoners, suspected cases can be placed in isolation, can have their movement restricted, can be made to wear surgical/paper masks when out of their rooms.* My heart sinks when I read his reply: *Kitchen workers are not removed until the X-ray is taken, and the disease confirmed to be infectious.* I appeal to a sergeant. His reply threatens disciplinary sanctions and the loss of my release if I don't go to work.

In the kitchen, I show the white shirt – a worker in white clothes, neither a guard nor inmate – the reaction and state I may have TB. The white shirt – a lanky Nigerian nicknamed Apple Sauce for defying the menu and upsetting inmates by serving apple sauce instead of fruit – shrugs and walks away. I might as well have told him I collect stamps. The prisoners, disturbed by my presence, bring the supervisor, Mrs Hannah, a kind-faced wizened woman wearing circular spectacles, her long grey hair in a ponytail.

"You're TB positive," she says, staring at my arm.

"Yes, but I've been told I'll get a ticket if I don't work. I'm getting another test next week."

"That'll be positive, too. You need to go home until we know for sure from the X-ray."

"But all the staff I've told said it doesn't matter. I must work."

"People have different ways of viewing things." She sticks a Band-Aid on my arm and I'm banished to my cell, where I fret about having a disease, but decide not to tell my parents until I know for sure.

A week later: "I'm giving you another test because you had a positive reaction to the first. Hold out your arm," the nurse says.

"You're doing it in the same place again. The other nurse said you shouldn't do it there. He has a different spot."

"What the hell does he know?" she yells. "He ain't no doctor! I've done fifty-two of these recently!"

"I'm just telling you what he said."

"I don't care what he said. Hold out your arm!" She stabs the needle in. While she wriggles the point below my skin, I wince. "Sorry, your skin is funny." She pushes the plunger. "I'll see you in two days."

Later on that day, I receive a note from the counsellor stating I need to report to work or else receive a disciplinary ticket.

At the kitchen, I'm greeted by Mrs Hannah. "You've been called to work today because an inmate told me you made the mark on your arm yourself by scratching it with a comb."

"I don't own a comb," I say, pointing at my shaved head. "Are inmate rumours overriding DOC policy now?"

"After he told me that, I called Medical and the nurse said the same."

"That I scratched it with a comb?" I ask, flabbergasted.

"Yes."

"Don't you think it would be best to get the test result before putting people at risk?"

"You're in the kitchen, so if you've got it, the kitchen's already contaminated."

She's enforcing orders from above, but her heart's not in it. "Prisoners are telling me not to work. They don't want their food contaminated. I get the results in two days."

"OK. Go home then. If I need you, you'll be called back."

In the evening, Iron Man – newly assigned to kitchen duty – warns that the inmate who started the rumour that I scratched my arm with a comb is Magpie, whose promotion in the kitchen from dishwasher to food server hinges on my occupation of his former position. He is a stocky Mexican with a squashed nose, and numerous scars on scaly skin like elephant hide, who has served over thirty years for shanking two prisoners to death in separate incidents. He was mouthing off about stabbing me for avoiding work and hindering his career prospects.

Recommending I take no chances with Magpie – who has institutionalised mental illness and is unpredictable – Iron Man insists on giving me a crash course in martial arts. Terrified, I follow him to the rec room. He demonstrates chokeholds, pressure points like below the Adam's apple, and methods to disarm someone with a knife. He recommends I kick Magpie in the thigh, where he was shot by a guard, and gouge his eyeballs. Whenever a guard does a security walk, we switch to yoga to avoid getting caught practising martial arts. I go to bed wondering why this is happening just before my release, praying that a disaster doesn't unfold that upsets my parents.

Two days later, I'm called to the male nurse. "Let's see your arm."

"OK."

"It's only a 5mm reaction. That's negative."

"Great," I say, leaning back, inhaling with relief.

"But I'll put you in for an X-ray just to be on the safe side."

"Welcome to hell's kitchen, son," says a withered Mexican American with sincere eyes. "You're gonna be in the clipper room, washing off pots and pans and hundreds of trays. It's more than a workout. It's the hardest job on the yard."

"It'll be good for my soul," I say, trying to accept my karma cheerfully, appraising the men in hairnets and aprons bustling around stainless-steel tables, wielding sharp instruments, cursing and throwing objects at each other, making animal noises and play-fighting. Feeling a long hard object ram into the back of my trousers, partially into my anus, I jump forward and bite the tip of my tongue so hard it bleeds. With my buttocks clenched, I spin around, ready to punch someone.

"I broomed him first!" announces a bodybuilder with big light-blue eyes and no hair or eyebrows. From doing hundreds of pull-ups daily, his lats fan out as if he has wings tucked under his clothes. Before working in the kitchen, he threatened to kill me over a discarded apple that I picked up seconds before he got to it. Everyone starts laughing.

"You motherfucker!" I yell, blushing.

A young white prisoner walks over with a cucumber. "My dick's this size! Can I stick it up your ass?" I laugh along.

"Don't let the kitchen get to you, dog," Iron Man says. "We get to eat all the left-over pizza."

"I like the sound of that." A serving of pizza is such a thin slice it just whets the appetite.

Iron Man whispers, "Magpie's not working today or tomorrow. You'll run into him soon enough though."

In the clipper room, condensation is dripping off the ceiling. I have to be fully dressed to be in compliance for work, so within minutes, my damp clothes are stuck to my skin. Before attempting anything, I observe inmates working. In the middle of the room is a dishwasher the size of an automatic car wash. A prisoner inserts crates of trays in one end. They emerge from the other, conveyor-belt style. "Here come the trays!" A young white prisoner hands me a hosepipe. "Wash them off with this." Caked in food, trays cascade through a slot in the wall and fall into the first of a row of giant sinks. I grab a tray, turn it upside-down over a bin, bang it against the rim to knock the food off and spray it, with water ricocheting all over me. "C'mon faster," he yells, watching trays pile up quicker than we can shift them to the other sinks. Twenty minutes later, I jump to increasingly loud gas explosions inside the dishwasher: *bam-bam-bam* ... A two-foot flame fires towards us. We're so wet, we don't catch alight. We leap out of the way. *Bam-bam-bam* ... "It's gonna fucking explode! Someone press the fucking panic button!" Iron Man slaps a red button on the dishwasher, turning it off. I wince and cough at the smell of gas.

"Get back to work!" Apple Sauce yells rapidly in a Nigerian dialect. "The trays are jamming the slot!" We turn to see trays piled so high prisoners can't deposit anymore. Prisoners are yelling threats through the slot.

Technicians from Ecolab examine the dishwasher. One tells Apple Sauce, "Those gas explosions are really dangerous."

"There it is!" Iron Man yells. "Did everyone hear that? The

exploding dishwasher is really dangerous. I've been saying that since they put me in this motherfucker. Now we just heard it from an engineer's mouth." Scared for our safety, we insist Apple Sauce radio a lieutenant.

A lieutenant arrives, listens to Iron Man and says, "The dishwasher's been exploding for a long time and nothing seems to have happened yet."

"The engineer just said it's unsafe," Iron Man says. "Look at the flames shooting out of the burner. It's exploding every day and the clipper room fills with natural gas. How can that be safe?"

"OK," the lieutenant says. "Turn it off. Don't use it. I'm gonna call the captain."

While he radios the captain, Apple Sauce says, "Listen, guys, it's been exploding like this for years. You've got to use it. It don't matter."

"Why we gotta use it?" Iron Man asks.

"'Cause we're not spending extra money on switching to Styrofoam trays. And if you guys wanna leave the dishwasher off and switch to Styrofoam trays, it's not happening. I'm gonna make you hand wash every single one of them orange trays instead. That's just how it is."

"That's bullshit!" Iron Man says.

"I'm just telling you how it is."

"You ain't telling me how it is!" Iron Man punches the dishwasher. "You ain't telling me fucking nothing! I'm not washing these trays by hand!"

Still on the phone, the lieutenant says, "The captain wants to know whether these technicians are from the company maintaining the dishwasher."

"No," Apple Sauce says. "They're just technicians from the company that supplies the chemicals for the dishwasher."

"The captain wants to know if these guys have any authority to tell us to stop using the dishwasher?"

"No. They only have authority over the chemicals."

"Well, then, the captain says it doesn't matter what these technicians say, we're running the dishwasher."

An hour later, the explosions begin, followed by flames that set fire to a chow-server's hairnet. Protected by our wet clothes, we spray water on him, putting the flames out. Choking on natural gas, I accidentally snap the top off a tap. Helplessly, I gape as a fountain soaks the room. Water and threats rain down until I'm rescued by Iron Man, who rigs the top back on. During break, I wander into a short white inmate with both of his hands in a bucket of bleach and water. "What are you doing?" I ask.

He extracts his hands to show skin bleeding and peeling off. "Fuck the kitchen! If they won't fix the dishwasher or give me protective gear to wear, I ain't working here no more. I'm gonna show my hands to the doctor and get a waiver."

Towards the end of an eight-hour shift, my clothes are soaked with sweat, water and cleaning chemicals. The insanity of the prisoners running around, cackling and brooming each other is rubbing off on me. *The ceiling's raining anyway. Why not?* I aim the hosepipe at the ceiling and pull the trigger, but soon get threatened by everyone I'm wetting. After scrubbing giant pots and pans and cleaning and mopping the entire kitchen, we strip naked and stretch our behinds open to be inspected for stolen food – much earlier, the stolen food was passed to prisoners in the chow hall through various means. With barely any energy left, I trudge across the yard, take a shower and collapse on my bunk, where I pick loose skin from my hands. Dreading returning to the kitchen and having to deal with Magpie, I search for inspiration in *The Myth of Sisyphus* by Camus.

Iron Man stops by. "Your eyes are all red!" he says.

"Check my hands out," I say, displaying layers of shedding skin. "I asked for gloves, but Apple Sauce just blew me off."

"Have you read the label on the dishwashing fluid you're working with?"

"No."

"It's a toxic chemical. If it gets on your skin, it says you must call poison control. The label says wear goggles or a face shield, protective clothing and rubber gloves."

I fill out a medical form, stating I'm having an allergic reaction to the chemicals as no protective gear is being provided. The next day, I march to the dishwashing fluid, read the label and confront Apple Sauce. "It says on the label I'm not supposed to work with this chemical with bare hands. Where's my rubber gloves?"

"Don't talk to me," Apple Sauce says. "Talk to the guy in plain clothes. He's my supervisor." He points to another lanky Nigerian we call Blood Diamonds, who responds in an even faster Nigerian voice than Apple Sauce: "You don't need gloves."

"How about we go and read the label." I take him to the chemical bottle.

"The stores are closed," he says. "I can't get you gloves. Maybe I can get you latex ones."

"Little latex ones will fill with water. I need up-to-the-elbow rubber gloves."

"And you need a face shield and an apron!" Clapping, he laughs so hard he bends forward.

"Look, I practise yoga. I'm trying to stay as healthy as I can under the circumstances."

"You look, Yoga Man!" he barks. "I'm a Buddhist. You and me are enemies. Can you teach me to fly, Yoga Man?" He bends over laughing.

Everyone working in here is insane. Staff and prisoners.

In a theatrical voice, Blood Diamonds says, "*Oohwee!* Yoga Man's gonna sue me. So, sue me, sue me. I just love being sued." He scarpers.

On my third day, I put two crates at the foot of a wall in the clipper room, sit down and start writing a description of the kitchen for Jon's Jail Journal, while awaiting the avalanche of trays.

Magpie swaggers in, pointing at me. "That's my fucking seat! Get the fuck off it!" The prisoners turn to watch my reaction.

If I get off the seat, I'll look weak and get preyed on by everyone. If I stay put, things will escalate with Magpie. Simmering inside, I keep writing, ignoring Magpie, my pulse skyrocketing.

Magpie turns to the Mexican American who welcomed me

to hell's kitchen. "Tell him whose fucking seat that is." Silence. "I put those crates there," he says, scowling. "I always sit there in the corner. Look, England, I can see we're gonna bump heads already." Mustering willpower, I ignore him and keep writing. "You can't be writing shit down in here. And if I find out you're using my name, I'm gonna fuck you up."

"I'll write whatever I want," I say. "Everyone knows I never use real names."

"Well get off your ass, man. That's my fucking seat."

"I put the crates here," I say, staring at his eyes. Bloodshot. Worn out. Crazy.

"I'm telling you now that's my corner. That's where I sit. I can see it now, I'm gonna have a problem with you. I'm not bullshitting you, I'll put you in the garbage disposal head-fucking-first." He grabs a scraper with a long blade, and comes at me. "Now talk some fucking shit, England!"

Fear constricts my throat. Blood surges to my temples. My stress and frustration rise. Aware the security camera is on us, I suspect he's tempting me to throw a blow, so he can stab me in self-defence. *Unless I act first, I doubt he's willing to risk another sentence or the death penalty. On the other hand, he's insane.* Watching him closely, I remain seated. He throws the scraper in a sink and storms out.

Minutes later, the bodybuilder who broomed me appears and we go outside. "Look, Magpie just came and complained to me about you. But you know what?"

"What?" I ask.

"He's full of shit. He tried the same tricks with me when I was in the clipper room. Look, man, you're about to get out, so don't let him get to you. Whatever he says, let it slide off your back."

"OK. I'll try. Thanks."

I return to Magpie sat on the crates, radiating triumph. "England, people are complaining about you. That you're not a team player. That you work too slow. The head white shirt's here today. He's gonna get you." He points at Blood Diamonds.

"I already had it out with him over the gloves." I turn to Blood Diamonds. "Where's my gloves?"

"I'm gonna get you them. I'll go order them right now. Teach me to fly, Yoga Man!" He laughs and joins Apple Sauce.

Maintenance workers start dismantling the dishwasher. "I don't know why it's doing this exploding stuff," one says.

"It introduces the gas before it ignites it."

Spraying trays, working side by side with Magpie, is surreal and frightening. I keep an eye on his hands and their distance from sharp instruments. After the maintenance crew leaves, Magpie says, "You ain't getting gloves. You ain't getting shit." I ignore him. During break, I write. "I'd better not find out you're putting shit on the Internet about me, dude. I'll scalp your head off. You think you're crazy! You've got two crazies in here, motherfucker. I'll show you some shit you ain't never seen."

My anxiety's so high, I'm ready to fight to let off steam. *If I don't get stabbed, I don't mind spending my last few months locked-down. It'll get me out of the kitchen. I won't start a fight, but if he lays hands, I'm going to unload blow after blow.*

He positions himself a few feet away. We lock gazes for what seems like forever. I'm waiting for him to make a move and vice versa. He backs off a few feet. I pace, approaching him and backing away, my mouth drying up, my mind starting to crackle, conscious of the blood swelling my veins, my heartbeat roaring louder. I work myself up until I'm on the verge of attacking him.

"Look at England," he says. "He's tensing himself up to come and beat me down."

I visualise kicking his injured leg and sticking a cleaning tool into the space below his Adam's apple and through his windpipe. *All on camera. I'll get an additional sentence. My family will be devastated. Walk away. But he'll have won. The smart thing to do is to walk away. Can't let him win. Walk away.*

Throwing off my hairnet and apron, I march out. I tell the guard, "I've got to go. My mental-health problems are kicking in. I don't want to snap and end up with more time."

"Mental-health problems?" he asks. "That doesn't mean much to me. If you go, I'm gonna have to write you up for refusing to work."

"That's fine. It's the least of two evils right now."

"You're on report then, Attwood."

Back in the cell, I do strenuous yoga to reduce my tension, while watching the door for Magpie. In the evening, Iron Man dashes in. "That motherfucker Magpie's over on A run saying he's gonna stick you over that shit in the kitchen."

"He never stops running his mouth," I say.

"This shit's serious. He's already stuck two people in the joint and they're both dead."

"If he comes, I'll fight him like you taught me." I hurriedly put on my sneakers.

"As soon as he walks in, you've got to feint with a left jab, and do a front snap kick to his left thigh as hard as you can right where he's got the steel rod."

"You think I'll lose my half-time release if we get busted fighting?"

"Fuck all that! Would you rather get out in a pine box? What the fuck's wrong with you, man? Your life's in danger!"

"I totally see what you're saying. Don't get me wrong: if he does come into my cell and attacks me, I will be forced to defend myself. What worries me though is if he's got a shank."

"Listen, you're not understanding what I'm saying! All this about him coming in your house and you being forced to defend yourself, get that shit out of your mind! OK? Are you hearing me? If he comes in your cell, you attack him the minute he walks through that door. He may well be carrying a shank. It's not like he's coming over for high tea, England. I already taught you this. If someone comes at you with a shank, you get a hold of their arm and break their fucking wrist. Let me show you again. Stand up and come at me like you've got a knife."

I go at him. He grabs my arm and twists it until I feel my bone about to snap. "OK! OK!"

"See how I gained control of the situation?"

"Yes."

"But like I said: go for the left leg, the steel rod. If he can't stand, he can't fight."

"I've got a feeling this might escalate and mess up my release."

"If this guy comes to your cell with murder in his heart then whatever happens, happens. You've gotta let the chips fall where they may. It's survival, man."

After he leaves, I read in the cell, keeping an eye on the door, not absorbing much as I'm dreading things escalating. Magpie doesn't show up. After lockdown, I remove my sneakers. Worrying about what might happen next prevents sleep.

CHAPTER 65

A visit from Jade earns a day's reprieve from the kitchen. "How's your release and deportation arrangements going?" she asks.

"Immigration have to pick me up and take me to a holding centre. I just hope they process the paperwork fast and put me on a plane," I say excitedly.

"Are you prepared for freedom?"

"Yes. But my mum's worrying about how I'll adjust. I can't wait to embrace the world. The prospect of freedom makes me so happy."

"But are you prepared for both sides?"

"What do you mean?"

"The positive and negative."

"Like what?"

"Like how people are going to respond to you."

"I'm not the type to hide who I am. People can respond however they want."

"People may be wary of you coming from prison."

"That's up to them. Prison's made me who I am today. I'm happy with who I've become."

"I think prison has made you a better person."

"Thanks."

"Attwood! Come here!" a guard yells from his desk.

Oh shit! What trouble am I in now? Kitchen related? "I'll be right back." Agitated, I rise.

"Did you know you have another visitor?" he asks.

"No," I say, surprised.

"Well," he says, nodding at Jade, "I can stop the person from coming in if you'd like?"

"No. Let's not do that. Let's find out who it is."

"OK." The guard picks up a phone and asks for my visitor's name. "Do you know a Barry from Quartzite?"

Claudia's dad. "Oh, yes! Let him in," I say, smiling.

Barry arrives through the set of security doors and we hug. Due to weight loss from illness, he looks like a different person, but his big kind eyes have the same sparkle. "Thanks for coming, Barry," I say, touched by him travelling over 200 miles. "I didn't expect this. I have a visitor right now, so come and join us."

"You have a visitor?" he asks, his voice rising an octave.

"Yes."

"I just wanted to surprise you before you go back to England," he says. "Where's the visitor at?" I point at Jade. "Then maybe I shouldn't stay."

"Don't be silly. It's great to see you. But a few minutes before visits end, I'd like to get some kissing action in."

"With me?" He smiles.

I laugh. "Not today, Barry. We'll save that for another occasion."

"In that case, I'll leave before the end." I introduce him to Jade. "Have you still not gone with a transsexual?" he asks, smiling.

"No. Although She-Ra is demanding a parting kiss before I leave."

"I've got a good gimp mask for you when you get out," he says. We laugh. Watching us chat, Barry says, "You two would be perfect for each other." We both blush. I feel more happy than embarrassed, then proud.

"He's too wild," Jade says.

"But you're the perfect calming influence," I say.

"I think she'd be a good influence," Barry says.

Turning to Barry, Jade says, "He needs to focus on himself."

"I'd rather focus on you."

Flustered, she says, "He sometimes acts like I'm being mean or something."

"I like it when you put me in check. I'd thrive if I were with someone like you. Don't be fooled, Barry, she has a wild side, too. She has a tattoo on her tailbone."

"They call them tramp stamps these days," she says.

"Check Barry's out," I say, pointing at the ink on his arms. A tribal barbed-wire band. Hot-rod flames scorching skulls. A green dragon below a cloudy moon.

Near the end of the visit, Barry stands. We hug, teary-eyed, and say goodbye. I remember all of his support over the years: accepting expensive phone calls, showing up in court after having a seizure, visiting at the lowest moments of my life …

"Did you put Barry up to that?" Jade asks. "To saying we would be perfect for each other?"

"I didn't even know he was coming. He must have quickly formed his own opinion. Do you disagree with what he said?"

"I'm not sure."

"I feel there's something between us," I say. "Something I can't put into words."

"You put it into words on the blog."

"Last time I really let my feelings for you flow, you backed off. You don't want a soppy man. You want a tough one."

"But not too tough. Did you really say those things to T-Bone you blogged?"

"Yes. T-Bone knows how I feel for you. He's encouraged me all along; even when you backed off, he said you were coming to see me because you love me and we'd end up together somehow."

"And how do you feel about me now?"

"I remember laying my cards on the table. I'm not going to act like that again. I just hope we meet in England."

"We'll just have to see what happens."

"Visitation is over!" a guard yells.

We stand and embrace tightly. I relish the scent of her soft skin. Her lips join mine with unexpected passion, seeming to confirm her feelings. Holding her close, I break the kiss off – but not for long. The second kiss is even more passionate.

Returning from Visitation, I run into Slingblade working on the recreation field. "How are you doing?" I ask, offering my hand.

He stares at my arm. "Shaun?"

"Yes."

"Are you from England?"

"Yes. Why?"

He yanks my hand and I'm almost pulled over. "Is that where Buckingham Palace is?"

"Yes. Why?" He concentrates, eyelids flickering, no words emerging. "I'm getting out soon," I say. "I'd like to see you get out, too. What's going on with your release?"

"I'd like to go to Florida. They've moved the Hope Diamond there for me. It was in California." He reels off the names of famous people he's going to live with.

Feeling sad, I try to snap him out of it: "Look, you've served almost twenty-eight years! You were eligible for release three years ago! It's time you were out of here! You've more than paid your debt to society. You're stuck in here because you need help getting your release package filed and processed correctly."

"But John McCain—"

"Forget about John McCain! I don't think he's going to help you. He's taking massive political contributions from the private prisons."

"I wrote to the President and the Queen of England."

"The Queen of England!"

"Yeah. She was here two weeks ago. I saw her on TV, so I wrote to her."

"To help you get out?"

"Yeah."

"You need an organisation that has legal expertise in getting prisoners released. We need to establish a place that will take you. Look, when I post stories about you on the Internet, I'm going to mention that you're stuck in here, and see if we can get you help. Would you like that?"

"Yeah. Do you know my name and number?"

"Yes. I know who you are. And if nobody steps up, when I get out, I'll contact organisations myself."

"Gee, thanks." He turns and walks away.

Contemplating how to get him released, I return to my cell, but my thoughts soon revert to Magpie.

CHAPTER 66

Expecting the slip on my door to be instructions to return to work, I'm relieved it's a Master Pass for rape class. Having never been to rape class before, unsure what it entails, I join dozens of prisoners in a room, facing a beat-up TV and CO3 Dunn, his massive barrel body expanding with each inhale. Prisoners discuss the class:

"What's this motherfucking shit?"

"It's a rape pageant, motherfucker!"

"How many times have you been raped in the past month, motherfucker?"

"You can't rape the willing, dog! We're gonna get all the fucking details about getting raped. They're gonna show us a video and give us free rape kits."

"Stun guns."

"Tasers."

"Knockout drops."

"Chloroform."

"Condoms."

"Everyone shut the fuck up!" CO3 Dunn yells. "This class will prevent you from getting a ticket for not showing up because I'm giving motherfuckers tickets. This program is truly mandatory. They handed me the son-of-a-bitch video and said, 'Do it for everyone.' PREA stands for the Prison Rape Elimination Act. It covers inmates and staff, for whom there is zero tolerance for sexual assaults. The law was signed into effect by President Bush on September 4, 2003."

"2003!" Weird Al says. "It's 2007. Where the fuck have you been the past four years?"

"What do you mean?" CO3 Dunn asks.

"Has the law slipped your minds until now or were you waiting for the anniversary of the 40,000th prisoner to be raped?" We laugh.

"What the fuck do you care?" CO3 Dunn growls.

"Nothing," Weird Al says. "I was just touched by your concern."

"Well, I don't give a fuck!" CO3 Dunn says. "Let's get onto the video."

The out-of-focus TV shows a round table of prisoners, a guard and a female warden. The first inmate describes moving from a juvenile to an adult facility at 17, serving a sentence for a minor crime. In prison, he was encouraged to get drunk on spud juice and pruno laced with Thorazine. As he details getting gang-raped, I fold my arms. He says his assailants tossed a coin to decide who owned him. The winner protected him in return for sex. The second inmate describes how his neighbour hanged himself after being raped. The next section is "What to watch for."

"It's the guy with the sweets!"

"Not the sweets!"

Anticipation sweeps the room. The video shows sweets left in a cell by rapists sat in a day room. A young inmate picks up the sweets, leaves the cell and puts them on a table. He says, "I'm not interested." The rapists look defeated. The classroom erupts with laughter.

"It's the kind of people that laugh at this video that are most likely to commit sexual assaults!" CO3 Dunn thunders.

The video warns not to take stuff from predators. Stamps. Coffee. Writing supplies. New prisoners should stay at the back of the chow line to avoid sitting in the wrong seat. They should avoid gambling, drug debts, isolated areas, and have friends watch their backs.

CO3 Dunn presses pause. "If you don't have the heart to help someone out, you're an animal not a man, including staff. If it was your sister or brother, you'd help. Do you have any idea what happens to an inmate who stops a rape on staff?"

A freckled bespectacled redhead raises a hand. "You get

locked-down, lose your job, get moved to another yard and generally screwed over by the prison."

"How do you know?" CO3 Dunn asks.

"I rescued a kidnapped female about to get raped." I make a mental note to get that prisoner's story.

"Welcome to the fucking real world!" CO3 Dunn says. "I remember a fish, scared as hell, fresh out of juvie. The fellas were wrestling with him. I told him, 'You need to stop those guys putting the body bump to you.' He said, 'They're just playing.' He was a bitch within two days. They turned him out. It doesn't matter how big or bad you think you are, four or five guys can hold anybody down. No one is immune. In DOC, any sex is now classed as rape, willing or unwilling, with prisoners or staff. Prisoners will be prosecuted, and staff will be fired and prosecuted for rape."

Iron Man raises his hand. "What if you get caught having sex with yourself? Is that rape?"

Ignoring the question, CO3 Dunn restarts the video. A prisoner states he was hungry coming to prison, so he took commissary to eat. He ended up repaying the debt with oral sex. The class laugh and howl. The recipient of the oral told him he was preventing others from hurting him, and would stop taking care of him if the oral stopped. The new prisoner continued the oral sex. Laughter.

"Listen to the movie!" CO3 Dunn yells. "Keep your fucking voices down!"

"We want popcorn!"

In the final scene, a guard orders an inmate to clean an isolated area, and rapes him. At the round table, an inmate urges rape to be reported and concern forms filled out. The female warden urges victims to preserve evidence. "Don't shower, brush your teeth or use the bathroom." A prisoner states that rape can turn a five-year sentence into the death penalty by diseases such as AIDS.

"What are you gonna do if sexually assaulted?" CO3 Dunn asks.

"Shank the rapist!"

"Then you're gonna go to the hole. Predators need to be off the yard. Personally, I think they should be hung by their dicks until dead, but that's not the way to go in here. Report it!" Everyone mocks the ridiculousness of reporting anything.

"Report it to who?" Iron Man asks.

"Me," CO3 Dunn says.

"And suffer the consequences. Getting shanked for being a snitch? It's a no-win situation."

"I understand there's pressure on snitches, but reporting is the only way to get rapists prosecuted. This isn't a trivial matter. Would you like it if a fish came in today and got raped here?"

"He'd better become a motherfucking man overnight."

"You guys need to back him up. Someone needs to talk to me. It's the only way to create a safe environment for all of us. OK. Class dismissed."

Sadly, after the class, a young mentally ill inmate on Yard 4 is gang-raped and put in lockdown for his own protection. No one reports anything.

CHAPTER 67

Just two weeks until my release and everything is accelerating. Time. My thoughts. My excitement. My feelings for Jade. My problems revolving around the kitchen.

Due to my ticket for walking off the job, I'm summoned to a disciplinary hearing. In a tiny room, I sit facing a panel of guards and counsellors eager to make an example out of anyone weaselling out of kitchen duty. One asks why I walked out. If I say to avoid violence with Magpie, I'd be violating the no-snitching code, and end up smashed. Anticipating them ruling negatively regardless of what I say, I tell them it was anxiety and I'm in psychotherapy. Their impassive expressions morph into distaste. Rattled by their negative energy, I sense what's coming next. I'm told they've already contacted Dr Pedder, who said I'm fit for work. I'm ordered to return to the kitchen or else receive more disciplinary sanctions, and something I've never heard of – Parole Class 3 status – which means the loss of my half-time release and two more years to serve. Agitated thoughts batter my skull, twisting my ability to reason. I pledge to return to work, but yell that my attorney will individually sue them if they try to pull my release. I storm out ready to punch a wall.

At all costs, I must come up with a plan to save my release.

In the evening, Magpie bursts into Weird Al's cell, threatening to shank me if I don't resume work. The next morning, I receive a slip ordering kitchen duty. After sighing, ripping it into little pieces, dropping them into the toilet and urinating on them, I get dressed and put as much effort into work as I can. Fortunately, Magpie isn't there. I spray trays and scrub pans with no protective gear and lots of cleaning chemicals. At the end of the shift, a guard admits he's under pressure from his superiors to give me tickets for the last few days I didn't show up, but so far he refused as he considers it unfair. *Those bastards are really going after my release.* I return to my cell exhausted, shower, put sneakers on and watch the door for Magpie, only removing my footwear after lockdown.

The next morning, I submit a request to see a doctor: I woke up with bleeding pus-filled sores on both middle fingers. Have repeatedly requested gloves from the kitchen manager, but none have been forthcoming even though I showed him my deteriorating hands. At work, I lavishly use cleaning chemicals, aware Magpie will be in tomorrow, we'll probably end up fighting and even my attorney won't be able to salvage my release. By the time I finish, my eyes are vampire red, my tonsils as hard as golf balls and my fingers have bleeding sores. In the morning, I rush for the slip on my door, hoping it's not a kitchen assignment. *It's for Medical. Yes!* I join twenty inmates walking to Medical, half of them hoping for work waivers, others just glad to get a day's reprieve from the kitchen.

"There's two doctors," Iron Man says, hoping a knee injury qualifies him for a waiver as kitchen duty involves standing all day. "If it's Dr Miller, we're fucked! He never gives waivers. We've got a chance if it's Dr Wentworth."

For hours, we stew in an outdoor cage, obsessing over which doctor it'll be. The first inmate to emerge from Medical announces it's Dr Wentworth. Elated, we smile and nod, wide-eyed, aware the battle's not over, bracing to perform in front of the doctor. Iron Man goes in and returns ten minutes later, grinning, staring at a waiver, entranced, as if detaching his eyes might make it vanish. After high-fiving him, I go next. Doddering old Dr Wentworth asks questions, squeezes my tonsils and examines my eyes and hands. I tell him about my requests for protective gear, and Apple Sauce's mockery. He says I'm having an allergic reaction and issues a waiver. I walk out of Medical and kiss the paper in front of Iron Man.

Twenty minutes later, a female guard appears at my door. "Attwood, step outside of your cell in your shower shoes. You have been chosen to have your cell searched."

Retaliation for dodging kitchen work. "OK." I walk onto the balcony, open a book and read while two guards toss my property.

"Oh!" she says, nose in the air, sniffing like a rabbit. "You've been smoking in your cell."

"I don't think so," I say.

"Like I can't smell the smoke," she says.

"Like the smoke doesn't come through the vents," I say.

"Yeah, right," she says.

I flush with irritation. *No matter what I say, I'm just another lying inmate, so I'd better keep my mouth shut. Won't have to deal with this bullshit for much longer.*

"When did they move you from D run?" she asks.

"The last time I was on D run was on Yard 4."

"I'm talking about Yard 1. You're the one always hanging out on D run."

Here she goes again. "I think you've got me confused with someone else. I'm in my cell mostly reading and writing."

"No. I remember seeing you always hanging out on D run. You were over there all the time," she says, radiating deviousness.

"I just told you, I stay in my cell all day long."

I stay silent. *She's looking for trouble, trying to provoke me. Another test before freedom. She wants to give me a ticket to jeopardise my release.*

"Where's your TV at?"

"I don't have one."

"You don't have one?"

"No. Like I said, I read and write all day. By not having a TV, I've managed to read over 1,000 books in just under six years." She scowls.

"Aren't you getting out soon?" the male asks.

"Next week," I say.

Their shared expression says, *He's getting out, so he sold his TV.* "So, you don't watch TV, eh?" she asks, smirking knowingly.

"No, I don't. I try not to waste any time," I say.

"You've been down long enough to get a TV."

"I don't have one by choice."

"Hmm," she says. "It must be inconvenient to have us come along and disrupt your day."

My blood stirs. *Stay quiet. Don't let her suck you into her game.*

"What, are you tongue-tied now, Attwood?" she asks.

Straining to contain my resentment, I ignore her. They eventually leave, but return with reinforcements. Every cell on the yard is searched for the TV she thinks I sold, causing uproar among the prisoners and antagonising the guards who've worked here long enough to know I'm the only prisoner without a TV.

Hoping to reduce my tension, I join Iron Man for martial arts. "Magpie's pissed 'cause you got your waiver. He's mouthing off about smashing you."

"I'm sick of waiting for him to show up at my cell," I say. "I'd rather just go to his cell, fight and get it over with." Most disputes are settled by in-cell fighting, which I'm prepared for.

"Don't do that. They'll see it on camera. You'll be the aggressor and you'll lose your release. The fellas are sick of him running his mouth. They told him, 'Go handle your business and squash it.' He has to make his move now, or else they'll run him off the yard."

"Show me those chokeholds again …" After the session, I'm rearing to fight Magpie.

Hours later, I'm reading with my sneakers on when the door opens. "England, we need to talk," Magpie says, walking in.

I bounce up, adrenaline soaring. "What's up?" Our eyes lock, but my peripheral vision takes in his hands in case he has a knife. Intensely focussed, I feel energy coursing up from my solar plexus, activating the strength accumulated from working out daily for months with Iron Man. *Punch the shit out of him now. No. Wait. See what he does.*

Maintaining a safe distance, he holds his hands out, palms up. I can see in his eyes that he knows I'm ready. "Look, England. I didn't mean anything running my mouth the other day. I'm like that with everyone."

He's full of shit. Why would he run around saying he's going to smash me? He's setting me up for a sucker punch or a shanking. Maybe he has a knife tucked in the back of his trousers. I stare, ready to pounce.

"Look, England, I like you. That's why I fucked with you. I know it made you mad, so I apologise." He offers a hand.

He seems sincere, but I'm wary of entering the range of being struck by a knife. I step forward, slowly, approaching at a 45-degree angle, so my vital organs are harder to stab. I offer my hand – bracing to retract it and snap-kick him in the thigh – but he makes no sudden moves. "All right, I accept your apology." We shake hands. "When someone like you who's killed two guys in prison fucks with someone like me it's a major concern to me and my friends. You've got a reputation."

"But that was years ago. I came in the system a youngster, a short-timer. Killing them dudes was something I had to do. It was either me or them. I'm getting out next month. I don't want to cop no more time."

That makes perfect sense. He's getting out. He's not going to risk his release. I ease up a bit. "I never knew you were getting out. I know you've been down a long time. Are you going to make it out there, man?"

"How am I gonna make it?" He shakes his head. "I'm a junkie. Someone from parole came to see me, and they told me I'm institutionalised. I've got money. My father owned a business. But I'm a junkie, man. What am I gonna do?" He gazes with despair as if I should know the answer.

For the first time, I see how vulnerable he is. My ill will and perception of him as a maniac disappear. Saddened by his prediction of getting released only to come right back, I view him as human and try to imagine what three decades in here have done to him. "You've just got to try to stay off the shit, Magpie."

"I've been doing heroin my whole life."

"It's going to be hard, but try to find other things to do. Travel the country. Go places you've always wanted to see."

"If I come to England, will you show me around? I'm serious. I've got the money."

"If you get around to it, you can find me online."

"Cool." He turns and leaves.

With the kitchen and Magpie problems resolved, all I can think about is being *free-free-free!*

CHAPTER 68

"You look happy," Dr Pedder says.

"Yes," I reply, beaming. "My release was finally processed. I should be leaving here next week. Do you have any advice for when I get out?"

"Get some therapy set up."

"We have the National Health Service in the UK. I'll see if I can continue with them."

"And look how revved up you are right now." Her spooky grey eyes widen as if seeing a ghost. "Your enthusiasm is worrying. You need to slow down, pull yourself back. Don't allow yourself to ascend into the clouds."

"But I'm so close to getting out. I'm so happy to be alive and in one piece after everything I've been through."

"But when you get overwrought like this, you're apt to making stupid decisions. There's enthusiasm, and there's giddiness, and you're almost giddy."

"Being happy hypomanic is one of the best feelings in the world!"

"I have two dogs at home, and one of them nearly got herself euthanised."

"Why?"

"Because she was bounding around with overexcitement, jumping on people and grabbing their arms with her forelegs. That's how your excitement is coming across right now. Your emotional side has taken over. The rational side needs to be running the show. If the rational part is in control then you'll stop and think before you make decisions. You'll ask yourself: does this make sense? Does this lead to trouble? What is the downside?"

"As far as the bigger picture is concerned, I feel that prison has enabled me to do that."

"Then you should be able to stay out of trouble."

"I've got a post-release plan and I'm determined to apply the discipline it requires. When I came to the US, I worked long hours on the phone as a stockbroker. I aim to put equal effort into becoming an author. To write daily and not to be swayed by past pleasures. I recently read a Solzhenitsyn biography. He wrote for so many hours a day, not allowing any interruptions. The odds against him were overwhelming. If he could get out of the Gulag with nothing, and go from living in some old lady's kitchen to accomplishing so much through discipline, then I'm ready to take on the world."

"Take on the world! There you go again. Why do you feel the need to take on the world?"

"That's just the way I am."

"But isn't that what got you into trouble in the past?"

"I have manic energy. I got arrested because I used it neg- atively, but if I use it in a positive way, I can avoid trouble and achieve great things. That's my goal. I was way too immature before. I feel that my experience has tempered me somewhat, although I recognise I'm still immature in certain ways. I've tried to eliminate the immaturity that led to prison, while maintaining a spontaneous spirit in the way Jung recommended we harness the energy of our inner child."

"But when you're too spontaneous, consequences suddenly arise that you hadn't thought about."

"That's been the story of my life and the hardest lesson to learn. When I say I'm ready to take on the world, I mean I'm excited to pursue the plan I've formulated to achieve my long- term goals. When I think how close I am to employing everything I've learned in prison to the purpose of succeeding outside, I'm thrilled."

"Well don't get so thrilled that you're like my dog jumping up on a visitor with a look that says, 'Let me chew on your arm, please.'" She lifts a hand and presses the tip of a forefinger to a thumb. "I'm telling you, she was this close to getting euthanised."

"I'm not averse to chewing on someone's arm."

She laughs. "Well, I truly wish you luck out there."

"And thank you for the sessions. I'm going to be all right on the outside."

"As you're pursuing these grand plans, don't forget to pull yourself back from time to time, and to ask yourself whether what you're doing is going to lead to trouble."

"Believe me, I will."

CHAPTER 69

"Guess what happened to your friend, Bud?" T-Bone asks at the fence.

"He talked some shit about you, so you smashed him," I say, smiling.

"Nope. He got strung out on heroin and passed out. To wake him up before the guards busted him, his associates shoved ice cubes in his asshole."

"No shit!" I pucker. "It couldn't have happened to a nicer guy."

"Frankie got busted sending heroin through laundry bags and trying to incite a riot in the chow hall, so they've shipped him off to supermax."

"Oh no! I hope they don't give him more time."

"She-Ra sends *her* love from lockdown. *She* got in trouble for talking shit to a guard."

I'm never going to see her *again.* Being unable to say goodbye to She-Ra hurts.

"I'm so glad you're getting out," he says. "I can see you are, too. It's written all over your face. But listen, something you really need to do is sit down with Mom and Pop and learn who they really are as human beings. How long have they been married?"

"Nearly forty years."

"Can you imagine all the ups and downs they've been through? Yet they're still together. They're successful people. Learn how they did it, so you can grow and obtain wisdom and knowledge and understanding. You've been through some things in the States, and you didn't connect with your family in the right way. I'm telling you as a man, you need to sit down with them over a cup of tea. Do you have the guts to do it?"

"Yes."

"And when you're talking with them, if your heart doesn't jump with pride, honour and astonishment, then you're empty inside 'cause what they've done takes strength. You also need to stay away from party girls and to focus on one woman. What are you gonna do if you meet some chick in a flimsy little outfit, a fishnet dress maybe, and she's five-seven, nicely built, up on heels, with plenty of make-up, and she has a bunch of X, and she comes to you, and says, 'Bring your pretty little butt over here, Shauny?' You have to make a choice. She's mesmerising. She's tantalising. She's sexy. Her breath smells like cinnamon and jasmine. Her bed is perfumed with myrrh and aloes like the harlot in Proverbs 7. Are you gonna go for the temptation that leads you down the path of destruction?"

"No!" I shake my head.

"Are you gonna allow her perfume and drugs to seduce you, to take you to the demonic realm?"

"I'm out of that lifestyle. I'm more likely to be hanging out at the library than at a club with women like that."

"You think people don't do drugs at libraries! At the Phoenix library, two guys started talking to me about Civil War history. We went to a coffee shop. We were having an intense enlightening conversation. The next thing you know one of the guys goes, 'I wanna do a line of meth to wake up.' So, I leave them to it. I get in my truck and keep going. They weren't my type of people. They were brainiacs like you. And if you're going back to university, so many people do drugs there, it's unreal. It's part of college life now to do meth to stay up."

"I know."

"You need to understand some simple things. All kinds of challenges are gonna come at you," – *bam!* T-Bone punches his palm – "'cause you're back out there again."

"I'm not gonna worry about it. My mum's more worried than I am."

"That's 'cause she loves you. You're getting out, the weather's gonna hit you, your mom's face, your father's face, your sister, the smell of the house, memories, some good, some bad, and you'll think about stuff that happened here – the American women – and you're gonna miss that. There's gonna be times when you feel bored, incomplete, and those are the moments when you've got to make the right choices. In your little town, there's not gonna be a whole lot of things going on."

"I know, but I intend to go back to university."

"For what?"

"Creative writing."

"You're an intelligent man. You don't need a professor to teach you something you already know."

"I need refinement."

"And practise will bring that. Find some interesting characters to write about. You'll be like Dickens. I've come to realise, patience is the key when you first get out. You have to develop things, build things slowly. There's people who are positive and negative that are gonna come into your life – some will be sneaky, others outright. If they catch you in certain moods and situations, and you make a bad choice, you'll fall. It doesn't matter if they're in a stretch limo or a compact car, you have to be able to size them up and make the right choices in every situation you're in. When I first got out, I thought I'd changed from my old ways, but I went back to it in a different way. There's levels of stupidity. You think, *Well, I've changed. I'll do it this way now. I'll go to the clubs, but not get in the mix. I'll just get a drink, say hello to a few people and leave.* But then you fall."

"My focus is on writing, not clubbing."

"So, you've made a conscious decision that that's what you're gonna focus on in your life?"

"Yes."

"If you're set with that then you can't deviate if things go south."

"I won't. I'll persevere."

"You never know what tomorrow will throw at you. There are levels of intensity you've got to go through, like being a Royal

Marine set on defending England. Or the guys with the bearskin caps that stand there without blinking. It takes a special man to be able to do that – English focus – and you have that in your blood. You have ability, just apply it. Apply the positive you've learned; the negative, get rid of it. Stay focussed on your objective. Don't allow small-minded people to bring you down. With a mind like yours, you're gonna make money, but challenges will arise. And don't forget to sit down with Mom and Pop."

"OK."

"I know you won't go back to your old ways, because if you do then you're gonna have to deal with me." He punches his palm.

"Yikes!"

"I'm gonna miss you, man," he says.

"I'm gonna miss you, too. L&R, my friend."

"L&R, and God bless you."

Through Yard 1's perimeter fence, I shake the biggest hand I've ever seen.

Later on, I meet Two Tonys at the fence. The sadness in his eyes weighs on my heart. "I can't believe I'm never going to see you again," I say.

"Me, too, little bro. But I'm sure glad we crossed paths on the road of life. Out of all the motherfuckers I've ever met, you've changed my way of thinking the most."

"I really appreciate that coming from you. But ultimately, you've changed your way of thinking," I say, drawing on Dr Owen.

"You need to take some fucking credit!" he says, smiling. "And stop being so fucking humble."

"All right, I'm glad I've helped you."

"That's more fucking like it! I'm not good at saying goodbyes, so I'm gonna head back," he says, his voice quavering as if he's breaking down.

"Wait!" My ability to remain composed crumbles. Fighting tears, I gulp. Pressure streaks down my jaw and rises up my face. "I love you, Two Tonys. I'm never going to forget you. I'm going to keep writing to you."

"I love you, too, my little bro." He stares, saying nothing, gazing intently, as if etching my image onto his brain screen to take back to Yard 4. The emotion on his face is warm but devastating. He raises his hand and pats his heart. "L&R, little bro. L&R." Behind his glasses, tears glisten.

Tears stream down my face, clinging to my cheeks like memories of everything I've been through with him. "I'll always remember your PMA and what Ivan Denisovich went through. L&R, Two Tonys." He turns and walks away. The more he shrinks in the distance, the more my heartache intensifies and the louder I sniff and sob. I imagine he feels the same.

Back in my cell, I reflect on the intensity of my feelings for my prison friends. *All my life, I've gone on missions, from conquering the stock market to throwing raves. My new mission revolves around my friends. I'll help them however I can. Getting their stories out to the world will make a difference in their lives. It's my destiny.*

CHAPTER 70

Monday 12 Nov 07

To Mum,

I appreciate the motherly and protective concerns that you expressed in your last letter. I know that you worry because you care for me, but I think you are worrying a bit too much, and this is what is making you ill.

My former neighbour Max wrote from Las Vegas saying how well he is doing there, and how the things he had worried about before getting released didn't even come to pass. You are concerned over how I'll cope with freedom, but, like Max, I have a family and a home to go to, all of which make coping easier. For me coping applies to being in prison and dealing with daily hazards, such as striving to maintain health and sanity. I'm leaving all that behind and the coping skills I've learned in here will help.

You are worried about my intention to isolate myself and concentrate on writing. You interpreted this to mean that if I'm around certain people, I'll be tempted to get involved in the kind of things that led to me wearing pink boxers, and so to avoid temptation, I'm going to cut myself off from everyone. I know you want the best for me, but your interpretation is wrong. I don't intend to cut myself off from everyone. I need to talk and meet people. The "shutting myself off" you mentioned refers to my commitment to a disciplined routine, which I'll need to further my writing.

Your concerns apply to the former me. My immature self had his wild-partying-oats-sowing days. Those days are long gone, and I've been forced to change and mature in prison. Such former wild behaviour is over. I'm driving myself forward and all the temptations in the world will not stop me. You claim I'm unbalanced – ah! – you've got me there. Unbalanced, I am. But bipolarity can provide the energy needed to excel at things many people would give up on. Don't worry, I intend to take breaks and have some fun, but I have no desire to re-visit the excesses of my former life. And nothing or no one could ever influence me to do so.

You are also trying to soften the blow of my former behaviour by rationalising it away as the influence of my friends. But the truth is I chose those friends and chose to behave in that way, so I take full responsibility for what happened. I want very different things when I'm released.

My heart is in the right place, so stop worrying because the former me no longer exists. Try to be happy for the new me who has so much to look forward to when he gets home.

Love you loads,

Shaun

From letters to my parents:

Tuesday 13 Nov 07

... I read a Solzhenitsyn bio that I couldn't put down. It's as if fate stepped in just before my release and strengthened my commitment to making a go of writing.

My suffering can't compare with what Solzhenitsyn had to endure, yet he rose from prison to spearhead the literary elite of Russia. Death called on him so many times: on the front fighting the Nazis, in Russian prisons and then in the form of cancer. Reading about the odds he overcame has inspired me. From prison he was exiled to Kazakhstan where he knew no one, and he ended up lodging in a corner of a kitchen in an old couple's house. As for me, I have your loving home to go to. He set strict limits on his social life and gave writing his all. He funnelled his prison experiences into fiction in such an honest and compelling way that his book about Ivan Deniso- vich caused a revolution in Russian writing. This quote really touched me:

"The writer's tasks concern more general and eternal ques- tions – the secrets of the human heart and conscience, the clash between life and death, and the overcoming of inner sorrow."

These Russian literary geniuses (including Tolstoy and Chekhov) seem to have a knack for penetrating the soul and portraying it in an uplifting way in their prose. Not that I could come anywhere near their genius, but I've tried to go some way in that direction, and as I continue my writing should mature.

Anyway, I learned a lot more from this bio than I can convey in this letter – especially how I need to have a disciplined work ethic, like I had when I began stockbroking. I'm used to a monastic life, so you locking me in the garage and feeding me meagre meals won't be a problem.

I'd like to use the knowledge I've gained to help with prison reform, or speak to young people about my involvement with drugs and how I ended up celled up.

I've certainly undergone the "impoverishment and dev- astation" that, according to Thomas Mann, constitute the preliminary conditions to serious writing. And Solzhenitsyn claimed: "Good literature arises out of pain." I'd be happy to accomplish a fraction of what Solzhenitsyn accomplished.

With your help, I just need to follow through on the oppor- tunities that continue to be provided, and to keep myself emo- tionally stable …

Wednesday 14 Nov 07

Today has been a day of conflicting emotions. Thanks for putting in the calls necessary to get the wheels of bureaucracy turning. I am insanely happy that my release was finally confirmed this afternoon, and I have been scheduled to be picked up by ICE this Friday. This morning the counsellor said, "Your release is confirmed," at which point my heart leapt, and he added, "but you're not down as being scheduled for release," at which point my heart sank. Getting released isn't easy.

The prisoners, who knew I wasn't scheduled for release (because word came back from the prisoner clerks privy to these things), have been placing bets on whether or not my release would go through and what day they expected me to get out or whether I'd be stuck here until my next release date. Some still doubt I'll get out on Friday. Others have been shaking my hand offering congratulations and asking for my mailing address in England. A few who have barely ever talked to me before, have come to my cell, struck up a conversation, and then at the end of the conversation have asked me something like, "By the way, have you decided who you are going to give your sunglasses to when you leave?"

Departing prisoners shower their friends and neighbours with gifts, in the form of personal property before they leave.

Thursday 15 Nov 07

I said goodbye to Shannon. How rough he had it in his formative years, and how well he's turned out. I hope he sticks with blogging. He has a following now, and it's great that he's experiencing the feedback and fun of blogging that I've experienced. He'll be out in a few years.

Slingblade trundled across the rec field. I yelled, but he didn't respond. I wanted to say goodbye, and to assure him I'd

325

try to get some organisation or other interested in helping him get out. He should have been released two or three years ago.

Friday 16 Nov 07

10:45 AM (Lockdown for count)

… Prisoners and guards are asking why I'm still here, aware that ICE should have picked me up today. I have to explain that due to a clerical error they're coming on the 20th. Only four more days.

Most days, I read and write in-between eating, showering, teaching yoga and working out. This morning I spent two hours taking notes as Fat Boy dictated the rest of the short story 'A Homey Who Finds Jesus.' Fat Boy was involved in the kidnapping and murder of another youngster. The victim was shot point blank with a shotgun before being set on fire.

Being able to write uninterrupted in your garage is one of the things I'm most excited about – not to mention the roast potatoes and chocolate oranges you'll feed me to boost my brainpower.

Prisoners are saying I'm the luckiest man here because the whole yard is going to be moved to dorms in two weeks' time. I'm just getting out in time. Prisoners are mad at the prospect of being warehoused. The deputy warden has warned, "Any vandalism will not be tolerated." The heads of each race and their lackeys are spreading the word that anyone who makes noise in the dorms between 9 PM and 9 AM will be smashed and rolled up. It's uncanny that I'm getting released just before the coming disruption. There's a rumour that the hardcore at Yard 4 are going to go off and refuse to move. Apparently, some of the dorm cubicles have double bunks. Ouch! Iron Man said the last time he was dormed he would get up and see the spectacle of Slingblade giggling to himself and masturbating on his bunk at 5 AM.

The fondest goodbye I received thus far today came from

Zack (one of my yoga students): "Piss off back to Wales you bloody Welsh prick."

Saturday 17 Nov 07

... Adam, who has been in prison since the '70s, stopped by. His 70-year-old mum came from Florida to visit him today. The staff denied her entrance citing her low-cut blouse. His quick-thinking mum shuffled to the bathroom, removed her blouse and threw it into a trashcan. She buttoned up her jacket so nothing could be seen cleavage wise that may have excited the prisoners, and she was allowed in.

In the tradition of prisoners stopping by, chatting a while, and then requesting an item of my personal property that I'll no longer need as I'm being released, Adam asked for my belt. How could I refuse when he couched the request in terms of him needing a better belt than the decrepit one he was wearing, for the special visit scheduled with his mum this Tuesday.

I read Tortilla Flat by Steinbeck today and laughed hard. I like how tuned in he was to the music of the ordinary. Almost as good as Winesburg, Ohio by Sherwood Anderson, which I urge you to read. I'm slacking on The Godfather Returns as it doesn't have the potency of The Godfather.

Only three more days ...

Sunday 18 Nov 07

... Spent the morning rereading the Resettlement Handbook issued by Prisoners Abroad. I've often wondered whether England will seem like a foreign country because I've been away for over 16 years. When I see things and people in my hometown that are familiar, what kinds of memories and associations will be triggered? In my mind, I sometimes try and age the faces of people I haven't seen. These faces include those of friends, teachers, school bullies (how would an ex school bully come across after I've been living with and befriended assorted murderers), and girls I had crushes on in my schooldays. I don't imagine the faces of family members as aged so much as I've seen most of them on photos, and you've both aged well in spite of all the worries I've put on you.

I also wonder how my hometown has developed, whether the old shops and pubs still exist or have fallen foul to globalisation. We didn't even have a McDonald's when I left. I remember you driving us seven miles for strawberry milkshakes, but I think you told me you now have two Macs and a KFC.

In the Prisoners Abroad Handbook, Chapter 8 is titled "Welcome Home?" It touches on your pet worry, Mum: adjusting. "You may have been away for so long that you feel totally disorientated and out of touch with life in the UK." Yes, that is true, but at heart I am an adventurer. I see the unfamiliar acting as a stimulus. Look how excited I was coming to America virtually penniless. Challenges galvanise me. In terms of the game of Snakes & Ladders, I was near the end, complacency and over-celebratory wildness set in, and I succumbed to slipping down the massive snake that's taken me back almost to square one. And now I get to play the game all over again but with the new knowledge and maturity I've acquired …

Chapter 8 includes "Change of roles." "Parents of children who are now grown-up may have found that they have resumed a responsibility for their son or daughter's welfare that they have not had for many years." Remember how I mocked Cliff the mailman in the TV series Cheers for being so old and living with his mother? See the karma I created. I know a bonding time is in order and it'll be fun living with you for a while, but I hope to find the means to not be a burden to you and to get my own place at some point, perhaps in the latter half of the first year or in the second depending on how things turn out.

The handbook continues with a list of things that can help: "taking it slowly, allowing time to get reacquainted, not expecting it to be the same as before, some privacy and peace, honesty and openness." They all make sense. If, like Sartre claimed, "hell is other people," (or at least other people you wouldn't choose to live with), then going from being constantly surrounded by people, including some very loud people, to the peacefulness of your garage, will have beneficial effects. Oh, to wake up whenever I want to! But will Mum require I make my bed as tidily as ADOC regulations require during morning cell inspections? Cells must be "in compliance" (including beds made) by 7:30 AM.

"Some returning prisoners have found being in a small room difficult; others find opening and shutting doors strange; many find it hard to get used to everyday life with its bills and worries. Most experience feelings of vulnerability, isolation and feeling like a stranger." Regarding the latter sentence: I've always felt alien and I've learned to live with such thoughts. I like isolation and that's why, unlike most prisoners, I'm perfectly relaxed during lockdowns or periods of solitary confinement. The prisoners joke that I'm the only one on the yard rooting for lockdowns. Regarding the former sentence: I won't know how I really feel about getting used to such things until I'm confronted by them. I imagine it will be strange, but also exhilarating.

... only two more days.

CHAPTER 71

On Monday November 20, 2007, a corpse is found in a cell. The prison is locked-down. I wait in my room, frustrated at being unable to say goodbye to my friends on Yard 1: Shannon, Iron Man and Weird Al. The certainty provided by almost six years of routine is over. Unsure how long my deportation will last, I brace for the unknown. Transiting through stages of immigration detention for weeks or possibly months, I'll have to deal with unfamiliar guards, inmates, rules, regulations …

The door clicks open. My heart beats erratically. I take one long hard last look at my cell as if to say goodbye. I exit, yell a porter over and hand him a property box with instructions to give everything to Iron Man, who I trust to distribute the contents to my friends. I'm escorted by a guard across the yard. Indoors, I sign release papers and exchange my nuclear-orange clothes for "prison blues" – jeans and a T-shirt – in which I feel half human. For hours, I wait in a cell for federal transportation, lost in thought. *Where will they take me? What will it be like?*

Two redneck guards arrive, surprised to be handcuffing an Englishman, a rarity in a state making headlines for deporting so many Mexicans. "Do you know how long it'll take for me to get back to England?"

"You can never be told the day of your deportation for security reasons."

In country twang, they ask questions. Conditioned not to talk to guards, I tell them my charges and shut up. They drive to a detention centre in Florence, a warehouse crammed with Mexicans, men and teenagers, recently rounded up, many having lived peacefully in Arizona for years without committing any crimes, the atmosphere redolent of sweat, discomfort, broken dreams and uncertain futures.

At night, I try to sleep on a hard floor by resting my head on a sandal. For hours, in discomfort, I alternate positions. On my side, I drift into a nightmare of getting chased by Bud and Ken, who are out to kill me. In the morning, unsure where I am, I'm startled awake by something slimy rubbing my cheek. My eyes jolt open to a giant grey spider. In shock, I freeze. As my senses catch up with reality, I realise it's a mop-head. A porter pulls it way, and cleans the area around me. With my body aching, I grab a meagre breakfast sack and try to rest my back against a wall. For half a day, I wait, writhing from the agony of inertia until my name is called.

After a medical examination and a chest X-ray for TB, I'm moved to a cell. *I have no books!* Not knowing how to occupy the space filled by literature, my brain feels like it's going to crash. I don't know what to do with myself. Over several days, I write 100 pages about the ruckus surrounding a Mexican detainee who believes the government is tracking him through a microchip surgically implanted into his body, whom the prisoners have nicknamed La Computadora – The Computer. My withdrawal symptoms from reading last until Claudia's father, Barry, kindly sends three books.

A week later, I'm extracted for a visit. Wondering who it is, I'm ecstatic to find Jade sat waiting in a small room, gazing intensely. We exchange greetings and hug. With only thirty minutes to talk, I get straight down to business: "You've got to come to England!"

"Shaun, no, you're going to get out there, and you're going to meet women, and you're not going to like me as much as you did in prison. You'll fall in love and I'll be easily forgotten."

"Oh, bollox. You're going to come to England and visit me, right? I'm saving my re-virginity for you."

"That's not a maybe. I will. Eventually." She smiles, her eyes glistening with promise.

I feel the warmth of our hearts opening. "Yes!" I yell so loud a guard scowls. "And then what?"

"Who's to say what the future holds. We'll always be good friends."

"Say we become more than that?" I ask, unable to stop grinning.

"Why live in hypothetical worlds?"

"I like the way you said that, but it doesn't have to be hypothetical," I say.

"I knew you'd say that, and that's not quite what I had in mind." Watching her leave, I'm overwhelmed by appreciation for Jade. I return to my cell on a high, and revel in an imaginary world, envisioning her in my hometown, meeting my parents.

After devouring the books mailed by Barry, I focus on yoga and meditation to stay calm. Two weeks of wondering when I'm getting out drag by. When my name is finally called for transportation, my spirit soars. I'm cuffed, leg-shackled, belly-chained and put on a bus full of deportees. Instead of allowing us to occupy the entire vehicle, a guard cramps us into the front seats. In Spanish, I tell my story to fascinated Mexicans: the tale of an Englishman arrested in Arizona for dealing "las tachas" – Ecstasy.

"The Mexicans asked me to ask you where we're going," I say to a guard.

"None of your business!"

Every time my legs spasm, I stand and stretch within the limits the chains allow. The bus parks at a small airport near Phoenix. "The plane isn't here yet," a guard says. "It must have been delayed."

Ignoring our requests to use the toilet and be fed, the guards leave us in the bus for hours with no air conditioning, sweating, suffocating on each other's odours and breath. Dizzy to the point of almost fainting, I tilt my head and raise my mouth, trying to suck in better quality air like a person drowning in a room filling with water.

Eventually, I board a "con-air" plane. Still cuffed, we're ordered to sit in the middle section. Federal marshals stand in rows in front and behind us, forming two walls, monitoring us with cold alert eyes. The plane speeds up for take-off. An alarm sounds. The brakes screech us to a halt. We spend an hour aboard, awaiting repairs. Vans arrive. They squeeze us into them tighter than on the bus earlier. Compressed into a row, I gag and try to ignore the irritation from my sweat-clogged pores. The more the heat rises, the harder it is to breathe.

"If it's not repaired soon, we're gonna take you to Florence prison, and we'll have to reschedule everything all over."

"I have a flight! I've got to get to LA!" I yell.

"You're not gonna make it. You'll have to be rescheduled."

Fretting for hours, I watch a guard ogling porn on his phone. He rants about having to work late to every passing colleague. It's almost 9 PM when we reboard. Some of the Mexicans have never been on a plane. They ask me why they're being flown to California for deportation when they migrated from Mexico by walking over the Arizona border. It's beyond my Spanish to explain that bureaucracies stay in business by creating work for themselves at the taxpayers' expense. The plane zigzags across California picking up and dropping off Mexicans. The guards refuse us access to the toilet. Two of them praise Sheriff Joe Arpaio for doing such a wonderful job rounding up Mexicans who are stealing US jobs, breeding like animals and collecting welfare on behalf of anchor babies. I almost protest, but think better of it. In the small hours, the plane lands near LA. With an Asian-looking Australian, I'm escorted to a van. In a lisp and distressed tone, he says he has no family or help in Australia, and no idea how he's going to survive. I slide around the back of the van, trying to ignore the pain of the cuffs and chains.

There are no bunks to sleep on in a huge holding tank at a detention centre in LA. Sat on an uncomfortable ledge, I chat with Bo Stefan Eriksson, a Swedish Mafioso who crashed a $2 million Ferrari Enzo into a pole in Malibu, splitting the car in half. He mocks the media reports that he was driving at 162mph. He claims a big deal was made because players in the justice system are trying to liquidate the millions he made in Gizmondo Europe, Ltd, a subsidiary of video-game company Tiger Telematics. I'm invited to visit his London residence.

Whether we want to hear it or not, most of us end up listening to the life story of an Argentinian built like a wrestler. "I'm a personal trainer," he says, pacing, his voice filling the room. "My clients pay me hundreds of dollars an hour. They're famous people: actors, supermodels, artists. My girlfriend's a supermodel. She's six foot and has perfect breasts. She paid one of Hollywood's top surgeons for them. She's not fake like most LA women. She's so kind, she always stops to help homeless people, and she makes me stop for them, too. She's great in bed. She wakes me up every day with a blow job. She's the only one who understands me. She's giving up her career and family ties to move to Argentina to be with me, to come and marry me. What does that say about how much she loves me?"

His monologue lasts for hours. When I grow bored, I pace at the far end of the room, trying to tune his voice out, but it bounces off the walls and saturates my ears. When I tire of pacing, I rejoin his audience, my limp body sore from transportation, yearning to rest in deep sleep. When his bloodshot eyes meet mine, I'm compelled to muster enthusiasm. My face animates for a few seconds, before slumping miserably.

Shortly before noon on the second day in the detention centre, when I'm on the verge of madness from insomnia, and my excitement about getting released has dissipated into the stale atmosphere, I'm extracted with the Argentinian. A guard cuffs and escorts us to a bus, resurrecting my energy, hopes, dreams …

"I've waited so long for this. I'm so excited. It's such a long flight to Argentina, but I just don't care. I'm free. I'm gonna see my family. I'm so happy." The Argentinian appears desperate to give me a hug.

The guard parks at the airport, goes inside and returns shaking his head. "Your flights aren't authorised. I'm taking you back to the holding tank. You'll have to reschedule."

I can't believe it!

"What do you mean?" the Argentinian asks, face crinkled.

"For security reasons, I can't give you any more information," the guard responds coldly.

Enraged, the Argentinian says, "What do you mean you can't give any more information? Are you saying I'm not going home? Answer me. Damn it!" He bangs on the divide. The guard ignores him. Their dispute takes my mind off my disappointment. The Argentinian turns to me, his agonised face aging before my eyes. "Do you know how long it takes to reschedule?"

"No," I say, imagining we'll leave tomorrow.

"It takes three weeks to reschedule!"

"No fucking way!" My limp body is seized by a kind of death rattle. I lurch forward, vomit putrid vapour from my empty stomach and recoil from the stench.

"Yes! Three weeks! Can you imagine having to spend three more weeks at these jails? This is one of the worst days of my fucking life! I thought I was out of the system! I thought I was going home! I'm fucked! I can't believe this is happening!"

Three fucking weeks! Is he serious? I know it's true, but don't want to believe it. The shock expands, shaking my core. A crosswind of thoughts – revolving around having to rearrange everything with my parents, who've travelled across England to meet me in London – blows my expectations way off course. Consumed with bad energy, I rock like a patient in a madhouse. "Maybe the guards can tell us more when we get back to the detention centre. The paperwork probably just got messed up somehow, and it'll get fixed," I say, hoping to calm him, but not believing a word of it.

"But my flight is in one hour. It'll be missed. I'm not going home. It's all got to be rescheduled. My girlfriend has flown to Argentina to meet me. Oh, God, how can this be happening?" He prays in a fast voice, like a priest at an exorcism, occasionally making the sign of the cross. As we enter the jail, his tears flow. "I know I can't smoke in this building, and you're not allowed to give me a cigarette, but please, please, give me a cigarette. I really need a cigarette right now."

"This is a federal building. We can't do that."

"I just really need a cigarette," he says, sobbing. "Please, anyone, someone, give me a cigarette. I just wanna cigarette," he says to passers-by. Guards grab and fling him into a plexiglas cubicle. I empathise with him pounding on the glass, lashing out at the system, collapsing mentally.

The driver explains that due to a clerical error he thought I was in the same situation as the Argentinian, but that's not the case. There's still time to make it back to the airport for my flight. The news resurrects my energy and hopes. Galvanised by excitement layered on top of exhaustion, I shuffle back to the van. Every time we get stuck in traffic, I quake at the prospect of being rescheduled. Gazing at cars moving in fits and starts, bumper-to-bumper, I will them to speed up. When we arrive at the airport, I sigh and slump in the seat, satisfied we've made it in time. Trembling as if in the throes of drug withdrawal, I stare longingly at the vessel of my freedom: a United Airlines plane.

"I've really got to pee," I say. "I've been holding it in for hours, but I'm about to pee my pants."

"You've been very well behaved so far. You're not gonna try anything funny, are you?"

"No. I'm not going to jeopardise my flight."

"I'll take you then."

In the restroom, he says, "You pee first, then I'm gonna chain you to the rail in that toilet while I pee, so you can't escape."

He watches me urinate and I'm chained to a cubicle with men coming in and out, overstepping the boundaries of any S&M I've ever contemplated. It's so surreal, I want to laugh aloud. Fearing an outburst might antagonise him, I mute myself.

The flight's delayed. The guard says we can't wait indefinitely. If his shift ends, I'll have to be rescheduled. Too weak to respond verbally, all I can do is widen my eyes in horror and continue to gag on my stale breath. Sitting in the back of the van for hours, bracing for reschedulisation, with sweat leaking from my armpits, releasing a nauseating odour – having no access to showers in days – my fingers and feet tapping and twisting and turning, I drift into a dream state, closeness to freedom pulling me in one direction, the prospect of being rescheduled pushing me in another, ripping my mind in half. Seeing an imaginary cockroach crawl across the ceiling of the van, I fear my peculiar condition is increasing the likelihood of the guard quitting and going home, but I can't stop fidgeting.

It's dark when he says, "It's time. I'm gonna put you on the plane first, so you don't scare the passengers." Smiling, I still worry something may go wrong. "One time, I tried to put this big scary guy on the plane, and the captain said, 'No way am I allowing him on my plane.' He had to be rescheduled."

The word "rescheduled" stings. I jolt back and shake. "Tell the crew I'm a former stockbroker, and perhaps they'll be less frightened, and I won't get rescheduled."

"Let's get your cuffs off then." Minus cuffs and chains, I'm lighter. To ease the pain they've caused, I rotate my hands and wrists.

At the top of the stairs, the crew offer greetings. A man in a white shirt, black trousers and waistcoat shakes my hand. "I'm Jonathan. If you need anything at all, Mr Attwood, just ask for me," he says in a warm London accent.

After being on the receiving end of condescension for almost six years, I'm overwhelmed by being addressed as if I'm a regular person. "Thanks," I say, eager to soak up anything else he cares to say.

"Angela will show you where your seat is. Have a great flight, Mr Attwood." Intoxicated by his courtesy and the trail of perfume Angela's giving off, I find my seat.

The passengers board. A brunette with tribal tattoos on long lithe limbs settles a few seats over. Her scent is such a contrast to the stench of sweaty hairy men that my eyeballs flutter upwards as if I'm on Ecstasy. Conscious of appearing strange, I try not to gawk at people. I raise my hand to get Angela's attention. "Can I use the restroom?" I ask, immediately realising she's not a guard and I don't need permission. Passengers stare in disbelief. I blush.

"It's right there," she says, pointing, her face crinkling with amusement. "There's no need to ask."

In the restroom, I urinate and use soap to give myself a prison "bird bath" in the hope of improving my smell, but it's ingrained in my clothes.

Seatbelts are checked. The engines roar. The plane accelerates. Lifts. *You're free at last, free at last …* The plane banks, providing an aerial view of LA, reduced to a chessboard-shaped grid of light. Even though I'm wary of the plane going down – *To survive prison and die in a crash!* – the flight is smooth. I try to distract myself by watching movies. Spotting the clouds over England, I start to unwind. The plane descends into mist, raising my high. Bumpiness and sharp drops. *Almost home!* Green fields. *Minutes away!* Roads and buildings. *Seconds away!* As the plane touches down, I push my back against the seat. The louder the brakes roar, the broader I smile. *Yes!*

I disembark with a small box containing the remnants of my sixteen-year adventure in America: some books, including Nietzsche, and legal paperwork. Walking through Gatwick Airport, I worry the UK authorities might want a word about my crimes and lifelong ban from America. With the brusque demeanour of a prison guard, an official requests to scan my passport. Automatically, I tense up. I hand it over and gaze nervously. Allowed through customs, I breathe easier.

With blurred vision, I have difficulty locating my parents among the hundred or so people thronging around the gate. Out of nowhere, Mum runs, her jacket flying and landing on the floor, my sister behind, tears streaming. I drop my box, and with an adrenaline surge, I hug Mum off her feet, and hug my sister and Dad. After I reassure them that I'm OK, we make jokes about my Russian dissident appearance due to my lengthy stubble, pale face and dark-ringed eyes.

On what feels like the wrong side of the road, Dad drives away. For the first time, I read Jon's Jail Journal on a computer and post a blog entry myself:

13 Dec 07

I'm free!

This is Jon/Shaun.

I can't thank you enough for all of your comments and support over the years. My prison journey is finally at an end! I'm at my sister's flat in Fulham, London. Tomorrow, I'm heading for my parents' house in Cheshire. Tonight, I'm being treated to Indian food with my family, and I hope to get a good night's sleep after several harrowing days spent in transportation (no food, sleep, showers, etc).

Soon I intend to post the blogs On Shanks and Two Tonys on Jesus Christ.

Much love. Talk to you soon.

Shaun

Comments pour in from around the world, congratulations and well wishes, enhancing my mood. A documentary maker arrives to capture my return to society on film. In the evening, we go for an Indian meal. I order chicken tikka masala, my former favourite, meat in a reddish-orange sauce, but it activates my gag reflex. Flashing-back to red death, the mystery-meat slop in Sheriff Joe Arpaio's jail, I decide to stay vegetarian. I devour chickpea curry and garlic naan twice as fast as the others are eating, unable to stop myself – as if I still only have fifteen minutes to eat – my saliva gushing to the taste of turmeric, coriander and the general spicy atmosphere.

The next day, I do two BBC interviews, glad to expose the human rights violations in Arpaio's jail. We travel home on the motorway, a five-hour drive. We stop at a chip shop. I try to order curry and rice – popular in the north-west – but the young server's thick northern accent is incomprehensible. He brings out a girl who speaks slowly and concisely as if I'm mentally impaired. I smile at the staff with the curiosity of an alien.

We drive through my hometown. Memories surface as if I've entered a dream. At my parents' house, the feeling intensifies.

Checking out each room, I feel as if I've regressed to childhood. I eat, read the latest blog comments and try to sleep. Wearing socks, a beanie, a dressing gown and buried under two fifteen-tog duvets in a room with a radiator on, I can't stop shivering as I'm acclimatised to the Sonoran Desert. My ears turn to ice. I sneeze. My nose runs. I only sleep for a few hours and wake up with my vision still blurred.

The next morning, I go food shopping, loading up on fruit, nuts, cheese, bread and beans. Browsing each aisle, even being able to buy a banana, is the height of ecstasy. At home, I fill a spoon with peanut butter and a cup with milk, eager to consume my main sources of protein in prison. As soon as I put them in my mouth, I feel sick and spit them out.

Claudia calls to wish me good luck. She has a boyfriend now. One of my best friends, Hammy, shows up with champagne and offers to supply a nymphomaniac, so I can make up for lost time. I go clothes shopping with my aunt Mo, still as generous as ever. A friend from high school, Aza, mocks my blue raver pants from America and provides new jeans.

In the day, my mood is mostly up, but exhaustion arrives in waves. The next night, I sleep for thirteen hours. Still traumatised from the experience, I sit down at a desk upstairs in my parents' house and write about my release to the people who understand Arizona prison the most and with whom I feel a lifelong bond: Two Tonys, She-Ra, T-Bone, Shannon, Frankie, Weird Al, Jack, Iron Man ... *We dealt with so much. You helped me survive. But I'll never see most of you again.* Longing for their company, I fill with sadness. Tears pool. I almost want to return to prison just to be with them. An ache expands from my jaw up to my eye sockets and temples. Tears spill onto the paper, moistening it just like my sweat did when I wrote from Sheriff Joe Arpaio's jail. My teeth chatter. My bottom lip quivers. I drop the pen. I miss them so much, I can't stop crying – no matter how hard I try. *I love you guys and I'll never ever forget you and everything we've been through.*

EPILOGUE

July 31, 2012

It's the fifth year since my release and I'm visiting my parents' house for the summer. A few minutes ago, I just finished writing the last paragraph of *Prison Time*. Still overwhelmed by unexpected sadness, I'm sat at the same wooden desk in the small room – my sister's former bedroom – where I composed the release letters to my friends, starting with Two Tonys – who is now dead.

Above the desk, there's a mirror on the wall, framed with wicker. Almost five years ago, I couldn't see myself clearly in the mirror because my vision was so blurred from reading over 1,000 books in five-and-three-quarter years. The optometrist diagnosed permanent eye damage. I had to wear glasses in cinemas and when driving, but my sight recovered after one-and-a-half years, during which I walked and jogged outdoors, staring at long distances.

Looking in the mirror now, with Two Tonys' death from liver cancer weighing on my mind, I see my eyes. Sad. Pink. Watery. Two Tonys was like a second father. He protected my life for no reward – as did the rest of my prison friends. Thinking about the times I shared with them – of which there's only a fraction in this book – hurts because I still miss them so much. Two Tonys said that even if I didn't succeed as an author, I would always be his horse.

Hard Time was published before his death, but the Arizona Department of Corrections classified it as a threat to the security of the institution, and blocked my multiple attempts to get it inside – I even photocopied the whole thing, took the title page out, and had an American friend mail it from Pennsylvania, but it was detected. Two Tonys may be dead, but he lives on in *Prison*

Time, at Jon's Jail Journal, and in the biography he dictated that I aim to publish in the coming years. Here are the last two letters he wrote before he died on September 8, 2010:

Hey! It's me. Guess what? I fell off the john two nights ago. My pals got help for me. Bottom line is I've been moved up to a medical complex, a big building. It seems they have a wing of cells here for blokes such as I. I'm speaking medical talk. They're doing things to me but not too much. I don't know, bro. This could be the end of the road for me. Time will tell. They're talking a lot of making-me-more-comfortable shit, but that's OK with me. I've got my own room, TV, remote, change of diet, change of meds, more nurses on demand. I'm pretty well messed up now as I write. I would and should have wrote to you more, but I was lazy. You're in my thoughts and prayers.

Good news on your speeches and come up in the writing world. Know this, you're a damn good man, and you've enriched my life and soul. Knowing you, I can feel your love and friendship even as I sit here waiting for my number to come up.

Hey, bro. I'm short on stamps till store day, so until then I'll cut this off. I've got a few blogs left as soon as I get a little more energy. My daughter will get in touch if my number comes up, so you can have a pint on my sorry old ass.

L&R,
   Two Tonys

I'm still in the medical complex, but this is all up in the air. What makes me suspicious is they're treating me too nice. (We'll see.) They might send me back to a yard or keep me here. I can't get to the decision maker.

Hey, I'm real proud of you. Not only as a true friend, but also for your achievements. I know you'll keep it up and the sky's the limit. Maybe you'll even make it to Larry King Live. Pond to pond of course. All I ask is as you struggle on, stop and give me a good thought. Now get your bald ass in there and get on with it.

L&R from over the Atlantic!

Two Tonys

The good news is that T-Bone was released at the end of 2011 after serving over twenty years. I've been talking to him weekly, checking on how he's doing, and working on his life story. Some of our conversations are available on my YouTube channel. He said the highlight of his day in prison was receiving printouts I mailed of comments and questions UK students posted to a Facebook page – T-Bone Appreciation Society – that was started at the request of students in Liverpool. T-Bone hopes to get a passport, so he can travel to England and join me speaking to schools about the consequences of drugs and crime. The more T-Bone reveals about himself, the more it's apparent what a big-hearted person he is to have risked his life protecting vulnerable people from rapists, getting stabbed and almost murdered multiple times, but continuing undaunted for no reward. Although he usually sounds level-headed, he suffers from post-traumatic stress disorder, and has broken down on the phone a few times. With a criminal record, no job, and a larger-than-life presence that attracts the wrong kind of people, I worry about him. Publishing his life story will give him the credibility he needs to start doing talks to schools in America, but it takes years to get a book published. In the meantime, I pray he doesn't get in a situation that puts him back in prison.

She-Ra attempted to castrate *herself* and almost bled to death. A helicopter airlifted *her* to a hospital just in time to save *her* life. She-Ra described the operation in a letter:

I removed all of my clothes, and straddling the toilet, I grabbed my scrotum with my left hand and with my right I cut the right side of my scrotum about 1½ inches long. The pain was minimal. Blood began to run down the inside of my thigh. I glanced into the toilet and saw a steady drip, drip, drip from the wound. I placed the razor blade onto my table and reached into my scrotum with my thumb and forefinger. I grabbed my right testicle and pulled it to the surface.

The next step was a little more difficult, cutting the inner layer of tissue surrounding the testicle itself. Remembering what I had read in the Mosby Medical Dictionary, I separated my testes with my left hand using my thumb and forefinger. I placed the razor at the top of the cut and buried the blade about one quarter inch into the testicle itself and began to cut down. The testicle came easily out of the skin. And with great amusement, I realized that there was no pain.

Holding the razor blade between my teeth I grabbed one of the rubber bands from the bowl and tied it around the spermatic cord, below the spermatic bundle of my right testicle. I cinched it tightly, still no pain. Maybe it was adrenaline that was keeping me from feeling anything, or maybe hype with all the thinking that this would be so painful which was just not true. I grabbed the razor from between my teeth. Licking my lips, I could taste the blood on the razor. I placed the blade directly above the cord about one half inch from the tied rubber band. In one swift motion, I severed the testicle from my body. Then holding it like a fisherman would a minnow, I dropped it into the toilet and flushed.

I looked to the ceiling and for the very first real moment I felt pain.

"Oh fuck!" I screamed.

The pain welled up like a hot arrow stabbing my abdomen and pounding as if it were tied to a jackhammer. Coffee is no suitable painkiller. It did not work when I was passing kidney stones five years ago, which at that time was the worst pain I had ever felt. But now the pain which shot into my body was way beyond the mere pain a kidney stone could cause. And coffee was just not doing the trick. The room began to sway and my eyes were losing focus. The pain was so intense I felt that this was all I would be able to do. Of course, I was wrong.

I set the razor blade into the soapy water bowl. Then I began to breathe. Inhaled one deep breath, exhaled, over and over until I regained my focus. I was not going to be defeated by pain. Pain was no match for my mind.

Looking down between my legs, I said, "One down and one left to be cut."

I reached back into my scrotum and found the left testicle residing where it ought to be and brought it forward to the wound in my sack. One small problem, Mosby's Medical Dictionary never mentioned that the testes were wrapped individually from one another, and that there was a divider of thick skin separating the two with a road map of blue and red veins crossing one another throughout this section.

There were only two options. One, let go and go through the other side. Two, cut through the middle and hope for the best. I opted for number two, and grabbing the razor I began to chop. This skin however was a whole lot tougher and hurt a considerable amount more. I don't know whether it was the cup of coffee or the superstitious feelings which were bombarding my mind at that moment. My hands began to shake violently and I had a whole lot of trouble concentrating. I put the razor blade back into the water and let go of what I was doing.

I stared at the ceiling for a long moment. I did not want to believe the events which were accumulating. This operation was not going my way at all. Again I began to breathe. And after a while my hands felt a little more steady.

I reached into my scrotum and began to pull the testicle to the opening when to my total horror the rubber band tied to my right spermatic cord came loose and blood sprayed from inside my scrotum all the way to the bunk, a distance of five feet. Now things went from serious to deadly. I felt for the very first time a panic. It rushed down from my head into my belly and then onward to my extremities. I violently began to shake again, and even though my mind was preoccupied, I still heard the glug-glug-glug of blood in a steady flow from my body. It flowed through the wound of my scrotum and into the toilet. It sounded like water being dumped from a plastic jug into a pool of water.

"Son of a bitch! Son of a bitch!" I kept saying over and over again. I looked down between my legs and thought about just how long it might take for me to bleed out. The blood was a steady stream from my body to the inside of the toilet. I reached back and flushed. I watched the water fill the bowl and realized that the water was already so full of blood that I could not see the bottom of the bowl. I grabbed the wound in my scrotum and squeezed it shut. I was worried that I was not going to be able to complete this job. Too much bleeding, just way too much bleeding.

I stood up and went to the door. I pulled the sheet away from the door and looked out of the window. No one was walking around, and the officer in the tower looked as if he were sleeping. I moved the sheet back and went and flushed the toilet. As I stood there and watched the bowl fill up with fresh water I resolved in my mind that I truly needed to hurry up and cut off the other testicle. After getting it, I pulled it to the surface of the cut and held it there with my left hand. The bleeding was enormous and I began to feel faint for the first time.

I grabbed the razor, and before cutting, I glanced at the clock. It was already 2:30 PM. I had been doing this for forty minutes. At least ten to fifteen minutes of heavy bleeding. No wonder I was feeling faint, and feeling cold chills up and down and throughout my body. Shaking these thoughts out of my head I began to cut again, except now my nerves were shot and I was afraid I was going to die.

I did not want to die. That was not what I was trying to accomplish. All I wanted was to rid my body of that nasty hormone testosterone. All I wanted was to feel like a normal person, one step closer to being a woman. I didn't want to feel what it was like and then die because I bled out.

The testicle slipped from my grasp. I breathed out heavily. I was exhausted and frustrated. I was afraid that if I were not able to finish the job I would never get this chance again. I did not want to accept this scenario. So I reached into my scrotum yet again with my right hand. "Godammit! Where the fuck is it!" I exclaimed, as I shoved three fingers as far as they would go into my scrotum. I was searching around and could not find anything which remotely felt like the left testicle, which must have swam away inside my body somewhere.

Slipping my pinky into the wound I shoved my hand up inside my body, searching frantically for that illusive left testicle. I could hear the news report of this inside my head: This just in ... She-Ra the prison giantess, while trying to feel more feminine, opted to remove her testicles using only a razor blade pulled from a disposable razor. During the attempt, and after the removal of one of the dreaded hormone makers, the other testicle decided enough was enough, packed its bags, and left for a vacation somewhere inside She-Ra's lower abdomen. The medical term for this phenomenon is retraction. However, it is our belief that given the fate of its neighbour to the right, el lefty testosteroni's true desire was to hang around for another thirty-nine-and-a-half years rather than having to swim the septic canal like its dearly departed, el righty testosteroni, is doing now.

I shoved practically my entire hand through the wound in my scrotum looking for the testicle. At one point I could feel my bladder and then something large and squishy, which I believed was part of my intestines. Fed up, I stopped the search and began instead to look for the severed spermatic cord where my right testicle used to be. I searched frantically for almost a minute and then, resolved in my failure, I looked at the clock and it read 2:40.

I removed my hand from inside my body and began to ball up toilet paper and shove it inside the wound of my scrotum. Then I patched up the cut with more toilet paper. I had to name my creation the Bloody Van Gogh Toilet Paper Stucco Nut Sack. I stood up on shaking legs and went to the door. I removed the sheet from the door, and looked out the window, and yelled for help.

Here's what happened with the rest:

Grim – Is being held in a county jail on murder charges, facing the death penalty. Several prisoners including Grim gave a man unable to pay a drug debt poisoned hooch, but he didn't die, so they injected him with a "hot shot," an overdose of heroin, but he didn't die, so they hanged him in his cell from the top bunk and stole his property: TV, clothes, commissary …

Shannon – Continues to blog and expose injustice at Persevering Prison Pages. With ADOC clamping down on prison blogging, he's been moved five times in the last year and has lost his early release. He won a lawsuit against ADOC for them failing to treat his hepatitis C for six years, and bought a house. He's engaged to a Scottish girlfriend, which came about because she read Jon's Jail Journal and emailed me requesting a pen pal. She is going to live with and marry him in Arizona after his release in 2013.

Bud – Is working as a building porter for twenty-five cents an hour. His disciplinary tickets in recent years include tattooing, testing positive for drugs, possession of drugs and tampering with security. He should be out on November 5, 2012.

Ken – Ken has earned more disciplinary tickets than Bud. On his 2009 release date, he was transported to Sheriff Joe Arpaio's Towers jail and then to LA County jail. He served a short sentence in California. His Facebook page shows him riding a motorbike and engaged to a lap dancer.

Magpie – Released, he never got in touch about visiting England.

Frankie – For heroin possession, Frankie's sentence was extended by five years. His latest letter states that after his release in 2013, he's going to get a passport in Mexico, so he can visit my hairy ass to show that "Frankie ain't no joke," and "try out English booty or pussy" as he's "just got to have it."

George – He is a recreation clerk, earning forty cents an hour. He occasionally writes to see how the governor is doing.

Weird Al – Lives in Tucson in retirement. I am the beneficiary of witty emails that he addresses to "Bloody Blokester."

Iron Man – Released in 2010, Iron Man sent this message on Facebook:

Sorry Brother for not getting back to you sooner, working my ass off. Yes, I am the top Sales Tech in the city of Tucson. Things are going great, on my way to Safford AZ today to sign the lease on one of my rental properties. The amazing books I memorized in prison are paying off in spades as I make the most of every moment ... and Live Life in Every Breath ...

L&R Always,

Iron Man

P.S Remember that 40-minute run we did in the 110-degree heat?

Long Island – Doubled his money in gold futures, but reverted to crime. He made headline news for hitting an officer with a car. Released on April 22, 2012, he remains free and is finishing a Bachelor's Degree in Information Technology. He turned 37 and is grateful for every day he spends free – even if the financial empire he planned never happens.

Midnight – Was released to a halfway house in Tucson. He died from cancer.

Slingblade – Unable to sort out a release address, Slingblade is still inside almost a decade after he was eligible to be freed on parole. Senator John McCain – who purports to help Vietnam veterans, but is a recipient of massive political contributions from private prisons – didn't respond to my request to investigate Slingblade's situation. I'm working with Weird Al on trying to get Slingblade released. Weird Al wants to hire an outside expert to evaluate Slingblade's mental health.

Junior Bull – Has settled down into legitimate business interests. With his sister, Karen Gravano, a star of the reality TV show, *Mob Wives*, interest in the Gravano family is at an all-time high. His father, "Sammy the Bull" Gravano, is eligible for release in 2019.

Claudia – On July 31, 2012, Claudia announced her engagement on Facebook. Forever in her debt, I wish her all of the happiness she deserves.

Jade – Flew to England. In London, she led me on a pub crawl. We drank endless pints of cider and walked for miles, with her raining mockery down for my inability to match her alcohol intake and striding stamina. The passion that had simmered over the years erupted, and we ended up in bed. Luckily, my fear of sexual incapacity wasn't realised. I tried to put on the performance of a lifetime – to really impress her with the advantages of dick-lifts – so imagine how I felt the next day when she woke up and declared she'd been so drunk she couldn't remember a thing.

We got along great, but sadly, back in Tucson, Jade fell seriously ill with a form of ulcerative colitis that wouldn't respond to treatment, rendering her unable to do much, including come here. After all of her help, I desperately wanted to see her, but logistics conspired against us. Banned from America, I couldn't move there either. We kept in touch by phone, but months passed that rolled into years, with her wiped out physically and mentally, and under threat of having part of her colon surgically removed. Eventually, our romance petered out. Fortunately, she felt well enough in the past year to return to work. I still feel close to her when we speak on the phone, and we'll always be part of each other's lives.

Me – So much has happened since my release, I don't know where to start. My first year out, I was institutionalised. My mum said I was like a puppy dog following her around the house, awaiting orders. I applied for psychotherapy in my hometown, but was told there was a two-year waiting list. The psychiatrist prescribed medication for the seriously mentally ill, and threatened to double my dosage when I protested. Due to side effects, I stopped taking it. I applied to do a creative writing master's degree at The University of Liverpool, but was rejected for having no college-level English qualifications.

After a year of living with my parents, I moved near to London, hoping to start work and to give the mental-health team the slip as they were insisting on home visits and threatening to section/incarcerate me in a mental hospital for not taking my medication. I started doing talks to schools for Tony McLellan, who heard a BBC Radio interview I did the day after I was released. The first talk was to Year 11 at Bishop's Stortford College. I was so nervous, I couldn't eat my breakfast. At the front of the hall, I paced like a prisoner in a cell for an hour, unable to look at the audience – more afraid of the students than the gangsters and murderers I'd been living with – sweat soaking my black shirt, raw nervous energy crackling off my skull, my thoughts and pulse on overdrive, my mind overwhelmed by a rush like when I first tried crystal meth. Afterwards, I called my mum: "I'm not cut out for public speaking. They must have thought I was a lunatic." With limited job prospects due to my criminal record, I became depressed. A few months after the talk, the school emailed:

Dear Shaun,

You may remember coming to speak at Bishop's Stortford College earlier this year.

Our pupils rated your talk as the best one they had received all year!!

I would very much like to invite you to give the same talk again next year.

Would you be able to manage Thursday Jan 28 or Thursday Jan 21 at 2.15?

Many thanks

Chris Woodhouse

The email raised my confidence. Since then and with feedback from helpful teachers, my talks have gone from strength to strength. I've been doing over 100 talks per year – sharing my story with tens of thousands of students. The furthest I've been so far is Germany at a military school, Prince Rupert in Rinteln.

But I'm still unable to speak to schools in the US – unless I get a presidential pardon. Having a passion for writing and speaking, I feel blessed to be doing this work. The constant feedback from students, teachers and even students' parents motivates me to keep sharing my story, and I realise I was meant to go through everything to get on this path. The talks feel like a better way of repaying my debt to society than the sentence. Almost daily, I get emails from students. This one put a big smile on my face one morning:

Dear Shaun,

You came to speak at my school a while ago now and I have been meaning to thank you ever since.

People come into schools and speak about drugs, sex and danger on a regular basis, yet the most these presentations amount to are jokes dotted throughout the week about how people do all of the above anyway before the talk is completely forgotten. Your account of your time in prison was the first that I'd seen to really and truly touch every person in that room. You didn't tell us to never look at drugs, to report anyone who had the slightest knowledge of narcotics or to stick to every guideline we've ever been given. As a teenager I can well and truly say that this wouldn't have and continues not to have any effect whatsoever on the well-being or common sense of my classmates.

The way you delivered your speech inspired me. The facts were clear but the humour was prominent, keeping us all on the edge of our seats. You taught me that after a high there often comes a low, and however hard and rock-bottom that low may feel, determination and perseverance can always amend things in the end. I learnt about the hardships in jail, and what happens if you come head-to-head with the law; but on top of that there are so many more things that will always stay with me from your talk: The importance of family, the dissolution of dreams that may well result in something better, and yes, how to get my priorities straight. I'm sure you receive countless emails daily remarking on what an awe-inspiring man you are and what a change you make – but I felt that it would only be fair to give back even the tiniest bit of what you have given to me in a talk over a year ago.

Thank you so much,
  Keep inspiring,
  Grace Beverley, Francis Holland School, London

After moving to London, I met my literary agent, Robert Kirby, whose help and mentorship resulted in the publication of all three books from the English Shaun Trilogy. Without his help, Two Tonys' horse never would have come in.

Although I'm still a workaholic, Dr Owen's advice is never far from my mind. I often think about how lucky I was to have met him. I wish I knew how to get in touch with him to thank him for the profound effect he's had on my life. *Dr Owen, if you ever read this book, please email me.* He was right about incarceration creating skills to deal with awkward situations. Being forced to live with the Buds and Kens of the world strengthened my mind and crushed out my anxiety. From time to time, I still hear the wolves howling to come out and party. When I hear a rave tune, I get a jolt of excitement that runs up my spine. But the howl of the wolves is nowhere near as strong. I have mental discipline thanks to incarceration and Dr Owen. Now I channel my energy into positive addictions.

I live with my friend, DJ Mike Hotwheelz, one of my former Ecstasy suppliers who served federal time and was deported. Three times a week we jump around to thumping dance music in a mirrored room with sixty sweaty women – but not at a rave – at an aerobics class called BodyCombat taught by my friends TJ,

Tony Coker and Steve Hope. We've both realised the error of our ways and become fitness fanatics. I don't even drink alcohol. Our friends at the sports centre find it hard to believe Hotwheelz' stories about us, such as the time he played at one of my raves, and afterwards in his Scottsdale villa, he opened the refrigerator and found an Uzi sub-machine gun. Iron Man insisted I continue martial arts, so I joined the Guildford Seiki-Juku Karate Club run by Sensei Brian Shrubb, and I'm training for a black belt.

I consider myself lucky to have emerged from incarceration relatively unscathed. Although I often have nightmares, I mostly wake up with a smile on my face – I'm free and in the West where we have it so good – unlike the people of Chad and Somalia as mentioned in Two Tonys' Positive Mental Attitude. When I see someone on the verge of a heart attack for being stuck in traffic, I automatically think, *That wouldn't even register if they'd survived a life and death environment.*

Jon's Jail Journal is going strong, and my prison friends' voices are still being heard. If you want to read the latest from them, just Google Jon's Jail Journal and their stories will come up.

Concentrating on finishing this epilogue has taken my mind off how sad I felt when I began it and memories of Two Tonys were flooding my brain. Looking at the wicker-framed mirror now, I don't see any tears in my eyes at all. In fact, they're sparkling. Above the mirror is a tiny picture on the wall that I failed to notice five years ago that lifts my spirits even further – an orange sunset, a dark-blue ocean, the silhouette of a bird gliding carefully over massive waves.

AFTERWORD

September 23, 2012

I just found out that Raw TV in association with National Geographic Channel are going to televise my story worldwide as an episode of *Locked Up Abroad/Banged Up Abroad* called "Raving Arizona." It was a guard at the maximum-security Madison Street jail who motivated my blogging when he told me, "The world has no idea what really goes on in here."

To him, I'd like to say, "That's about to change."

April 27, 2013

Excerpt from a letter I wrote:

The Locked Up Abroad episode premiered three days ago in the US to almost 10 million viewers at 2 AM UK time. I awoke to 500 emails/messages from American's outraged at Arpaio, the jail conditions and human rights violations. People showed strong support for my family and activism. Since then, the emails/messages have risen to over 1,000, and Jon's Jail Journal's hits have surged by 20,000. All of my social media pages have been flooded. On Thursday, I couldn't blink without an email coming in. Many people expressed their own pain and suffering, detailing horrific things that happened at the hands of the US justice system. Here are three examples:

Shaun, thank you for all you have done! My brother, Lawrence Edward McCarty, was in the same jail years ago ...

mainly for little things like DUI [drunk driving]. Each time, he was beaten up, robbed of his things ... when he was released, he was found dead a few days later in Arizona on his way home to California to be with his family. It's too late for my brother but you are helping so many other families and prisoners ... Joe Arpaio needs to be recalled!!

Good luck to you and again, thank you for all of your selfless efforts to bring about change.

Much love and light,

Stacie

Dear Shaun, I just watched your story on 4/23/13, great story and love to read the rest of the books you wrote. love to hear back from you, you are special kind of man to have love like that, your friend Peggy Larkin-Patton, hope one day we meet, a little about me, I have four brothers that did time, My older brothers name is James T Larkin, the cops killed him, they said he hung himself with a pair of blue jeans that was brand new, it happen at the 26th police district in Philadelphia PA, a friend of his was in the jail when they brought him in he was lifeless, nothing was done to the cop that killed him, that was in 1976, my other brother Michael Kevin Larkin, hung himself in great ford prison in Penn, feeling a little down, talk later

Shaun, I don't know if you can help me but I just saw your show, and it's weird cause Friday morning I'm going to a mistrial hearing for my son in Detroit, he was shot by police after trying to commit suicide and jumping out his window, I was on the phone with him and walking towards where he was when a policeman came around the corner and shot him, two months after getting off at the hospital, he was arrested and put in jail for two months, he's been on a tether ever since. It's been a year and a half, he was charged with arson and six counts of resisting arrest resulting in injury because the police bullet casings headed each other in the face, they had fired 18 shots at my son close range, I'm living in the nightmare, there was no evidence yet he was found guilty about charges which goes up to twenty years in prison, I would greatly appreciate if you could contact me and we could talk, I will give you my phone number if you like, let me know, you're the only person I've reached out to, I am scared to contact the local media for fear of retribution, I am begging you to hear my plea, I apologize for some of the messed up language, Patty

I realise that everything I've been doing around Jon's Jail Journal for the past ten years has led up to this moment. It's as if the trauma on US society caused by injustice, corruption and state-sanctioned violence opened up to me. I'm responding to every message, trying to give back some of my own positive energy. Adrenaline keeps me going through the nights. At some points, I was typing so fast and focussed, I went hours before I noticed my shoulders had frozen. I had to stop to stretch for a few minutes to shake the numbness off. Thanks to social media, I was able to alert thousands of people to a petition to recall Arpaio. Even some Arpaio supporters emailed that the episode had changed their minds about him. I've only received four death threats from Arpaio loyalists, which isn't bad out of over 1,000 messages, almost universal support. I had no idea which parts of the episode the director, Harry Hewland, had selected. I'm thankful to him for including the activism. His decision to flash Jon's Jail Journal on the screen contributed to the deluge of correspondence. When Hard Time was published in America at the same time Osama bin Laden was killed, I lost my news coverage, the book didn't sell, and I felt the realisation of the dream of exposing Arpaio slipping away. None of that matters now.

The activism doesn't stop here. Arpaio is still in power, and there's work to be done. The episode has planted a seed in the

US conscience that evil things are going on in his jail system. The episode posted a statistic on the screen: 62 inmates died in Arpaio's jails from 2003-2007. Arpaio is motivated by power and money. Look where he gets his political contributions: the prison industries. His jail is a conveyor belt feeding the prison system human beings reduced to commodities. Most of them are non-violent drug offenders. Many are mentally ill. Vulnerable people who get no education or rehabilitation because the prison wants them to come right back to keep the money rolling in. As shown in the emails, this corrupt system is traumatising American society to its core. With 1 in 100 adults in prison, every family in America has or knows someone in prison, unless of course they're politically connected or wealthy enough to bribe the system. The mission to expose Arpaio continues. Over the next six months, the episode is being televised to over 50 million viewers in 36 countries, ranging from India to all of Europe. I've finally realised the dream I set 10 years ago when I first picked up that golf pencil in the maximum-security Madison Street jail, hoping to show the world what really goes on in there.

Oct 1, 2018

It's been five years since the publication of this book by Random House, which I'm now republishing with Gadfly Press, my own publishing company. I'll start with the good news: Shannon and his wife had a baby. Despite suffering continued health problems and undergoing major surgery, Jade got married and had a baby. Also now married, Claudia has two children. Sherriff Joe Arpaio got kicked out at the last election. He was found guilty in federal court for contempt of court for racial profiling, and was facing six months in his own jail, until President Trump pardoned him.

In 2014, Weird Al died from advanced hepatitis C, which had progressed during his incarceration due to the Arizona Department of Corrections refusing to treat it. In 2017, Slingblade died in prison from natural causes. Frankie was released long enough to get a lady pregnant, but is now back in prison, scheduled to be released in late October 2018. After being put on suicide watch, She-Ra waited for over a year and cut off *her* other testicle. After getting released, Bud was arrested in New Mexico in 2017 for aggravated burglary and larceny of stolen property.

Rearrested on bogus charges and facing a 200 year maximum sentence, T-Bone had a trial for three offences: two of robbery and one of kidnapping. There was a security camera at the location of one alleged robbery. During the trial, T-Bone's lawyer asked the policeman for footage of him doing the robbery. The policeman responded that he didn't have the time to obtain the video. On kidnapping and one robbery, he was found innocent. On one robbery he was found guilty of taking $20 off a counter top in a shop and sentenced to 13 years, with 5 left to serve. The circumstances of the robbery are in question. It seems like the prosecutor set him up. T-Bone wrote from prison:

"Being an American and a Marine means that I love this country and I've never had anything bad to say about it, but after dealing with the racist court system here in Arizona, I know now that my country has let me down.

When the cops first stopped me in August 2012, she said to me that there was no evidence or any reason for her to arrest me, and "it was her word against mine" and that she had no probable cause to arrest, but they still came after me!

Now they denied my appeal! Why? They didn't give me a reason. I didn't rob anybody, and these people know it. I need to find a way with God's help to attack the case in my next stage of appeals. I am doing a Rule 32, as I write this letter, and God willing I'll get a different judge, not that trial judge who allowed this case to go to the jury without any evidence."

As for me, I continue to apply the slow and steady progress prescribed by Dr Owen, including taking time out for yoga, meditation, swimming, jogging and fitness classes. I'm still doing over 100 speaking engagements per year, mostly to schoolkids, and occasional tours across England for adults. With almost 10 books published, I became a bestseller on Amazon when I wrote about Pablo Escobar. In 2018, I finally published Two Tonys' life story: *The Mafia Philosopher*. I'm still posting the prisoners' stories at my blog and now at my YouTube channel, which has taken off in the last year since I appeared on the True Geordie podcast. I've done two TED talks: one on happiness and one on overcoming fear and building resilience. I became the patron of a mental health charity in Guildford called Oakleaf. I started a long-form podcast, interviewing people with unusual and inspirational stories – available on my YouTube channel and iTunes. I continue to campaign for human rights, including participating in a demonstration outside of the US embassy in London at the injustice exposed by *Making a Murderer* on Netflix. Occasionally, I go out and dance all night to rave music – but sober and without the wolves!

If you want to help prisoners, please contact these organisations:

Koestler Trust – Help UK prisoners rehabilitate through art

Prisoners Abroad – Support UK citizens incarcerated overseas

Howard League for Penal Reform – Help UK prisoners and hold government agencies to account

Arizona Prison Watch – Campaigns against the prison-industrial complex in Arizona

Middle Ground Prison Reform – Help prisoners in Arizona and hold government agencies to account

Prison Legal News – Provide a newsletter to prisoners in America to help enforce human rights

American Civil Liberties Union – A guardian of human rights, including prisoners

Get A Free Book:

Join Shaun's Newsletter

www.shaunattwood.com/
newsletter-subscribe/

SHAUN'S BOOKS

English Shaun Trilogy
Party Time
Hard Time
Prison Time

War on Drugs Series
Pablo Escobar: Beyond Narcos
American Made: Who Killed Barry Seal?
Pablo Escobar or George HW Bush
The Cali Cartel: Beyond Narcos
We Are Being Lied To: The War on Drugs (Expected 2019)
The War Against Weed (Expected 2019)

Un-Making a Murderer:
The Framing of Steven Avery and Brendan Dassey
The Mafia Philosopher: Two Tonys
Life Lessons

Pablo Escobar's Story (4-Book Series)
T-Bone (Expected 2022)

SOCIAL-MEDIA LINKS

Email: attwood.shaun@hotmail.co.uk
YouTube: Shaun Attwood

Blog: Jon's Jail Journal
Website: shaunattwood.com
Instagram: @shaunattwood

Twitter: @shaunattwood
LinkedIn: Shaun Attwood
Goodreads: Shaun Attwood
Facebook: Shaun Attwood, Jon's Jail Journal,
T-Bone Appreciation Society

Shaun welcomes feedback on any of his books.
Thank you for the Amazon and Goodreads reviews!

SHAUN'S JAIL JOURNEY STARTS IN HARD TIME NEW EDITION

Chapter 1

Sleep deprived and scanning for danger, I enter a dark cell on the second floor of the maximum-security Madison Street jail in Phoenix, Arizona, where guards and gang members are murdering prisoners. Behind me, the metal door slams heavily. Light slants into the cell through oblong gaps in the door, illuminating a prisoner cocooned in a white sheet, snoring lightly on the top bunk about two thirds of the way up the back wall. Relieved there is no immediate threat, I place my mattress on the grimy floor. Desperate to rest, I notice movement on the cement-block walls. *Am I hallucinating?* I blink several times. The walls appear to ripple. Stepping closer, I see the walls are alive with insects. I flinch. So many are swarming, I wonder if they're a colony of ants on the move. To get a better look, I put my eyes right up to them. They are mostly the size of almonds and have antennae. American cockroaches. I've seen them in the holding cells downstairs in smaller numbers, but nothing like this. A chill spread over my body. I back away.

Something alive falls from the ceiling and bounces off the base of my neck. I jump. With my night vision improving, I spot cockroaches weaving in and out of the base of the fluorescent strip light. Every so often one drops onto the concrete and resumes crawling. Examining the bottom bunk, I realise why my cellmate is sleeping at a higher elevation: cockroaches are pouring from

367

gaps in the decrepit wall at the level of my bunk. The area is thick with them. Placing my mattress on the bottom bunk scatters them. I walk towards the toilet, crunching a few under my shower sandals. I urinate and grab the toilet roll. A cockroach darts from the centre of the roll onto my hand, tickling my fingers. My arm jerks as if it has a mind of its own, losing the cockroach and the toilet roll. Using a towel, I wipe the bulk of them off the bottom bunk, stopping only to shake the odd one off my hand. I unroll my mattress. They begin to regroup and inhabit my mattress. My adrenaline is pumping so much, I lose my fatigue.

Nauseated, I sit on a tiny metal stool bolted to the wall. *How will I sleep? How's my cellmate sleeping through the infestation and my arrival?* Copying his technique, I cocoon myself in a sheet and lie down, crushing more cockroaches. The only way they can access me now is through the breathing hole I've left in the sheet by the lower half of my face. Inhaling their strange musty odour, I close my eyes. I can't sleep. I feel them crawling on the sheet around my feet. *Am I imagining things?* Frightened of them infiltrating my breathing hole, I keep opening my eyes. Cramps cause me to rotate onto my other side. Facing the wall, I'm repulsed by so many of them just inches away. I return to my original side.

The sheet traps the heat of the Sonoran Desert to my body, soaking me in sweat. Sweat tickles my body, tricking my mind into thinking the cockroaches are infiltrating and crawling on me. The trapped heat aggravates my bleeding skin infections and bedsores. I want to scratch myself, but I know better. The outer layers of my skin have turned soggy from sweating constantly in this concrete oven. Squirming on the bunk fails to stop the relentless itchiness of my skin. Eventually, I scratch myself. Clumps of moist skin detach under my nails. Every now and then I become so uncomfortable, I must open my cocoon to waft the heat out, which allows the cockroaches in. It takes hours to drift to sleep. I only manage a few hours. I awake stuck to the soaked sheet, disgusted by the cockroach carcasses compressed against the mattress.

The cockroaches plague my new home until dawn appears at the dots in the metal grid over a begrimed strip of four-inch-thick bullet-proof glass at the top of the back wall – the cell's only source of outdoor light. They disappear into the cracks in the walls, like vampire mist retreating from sunlight. But not all of them. There were so many on the night shift that even their vastly reduced number is too many to dispose of. And they act like they know it. They roam around my feet with attitude, as if to make it clear that I'm trespassing on their turf.

My next set of challenges will arise not from the insect world, but from my neighbours. I'm the new arrival, subject to scrutiny about my charges just like when I'd run into the Aryan Brotherhood prison gang on my first day at the medium-security Towers jail a year ago. I wish my cellmate would wake up, brief me on the mood of the locals and introduce me to the head of the white gang. No such luck. Chow is announced over a speaker system in a crackly robotic voice, but he doesn't stir.

I emerge into the day room for breakfast. Prisoners in black-and-white bee-striped uniforms gather under the metal-grid stairs and tip dead cockroaches into a trash bin from plastic peanut-butter containers they'd set as traps during the night. All eyes are on me in the chow line. Watching who sits where, I hold my head up, put on a solid stare and pretend to be as at home in this environment as the cockroaches. It's all an act. I'm lonely and afraid. I loathe having to explain myself to the head of the white race, who I assume is the toughest murderer. I've been in jail long enough to know that taking my breakfast to my cell will imply that I have something to hide.

The gang punishes criminals with certain charges. The most serious are sex offenders, who are KOS: Kill On Sight. Other charges are punishable by SOS – Smash On Sight – such as drive-by shootings because women and kids sometimes get killed. It's called convict justice. Gang members are constantly looking for people to beat up because that's how they earn their reputations and tattoos. The most serious acts of violence earn the highest-ranking tattoos. To be a full gang member requires murder. I've observed the body language and techniques inmates trying to integrate employ. An inmate with a spring in his step and an air of confidence is likely to be accepted. A person who avoids eye contact and fails to introduce himself to the gang is likely to be preyed on. Some of the failed attempts I saw ended up with heads getting cracked against toilets, a sound I've grown familiar with. I've seen prisoners being extracted on stretchers who looked dead – one had yellow fluid leaking from his head. The constant violence gives me nightmares, but the reality is that I put myself in here, so I force myself to accept it as a part of my punishment.

It's time to apply my knowledge. With a self-assured stride, I take my breakfast bag to the table of white inmates covered in neo-Nazi tattoos, allowing them to question me.

"Mind if I sit with you guys?" I ask, glad exhaustion has deepened my voice.

"These seats are taken. But you can stand at the corner of the table."

The man who answered is probably the head of the gang. I size him up. Cropped brown hair. A dangerous glint in Nordic-blue eyes. Tiny pupils that suggest he's on heroin. Weightlifter-type veins bulging from a sturdy neck. Political ink on arms crisscrossed with scars. About the same age as me, thirty-three.

"Thanks. I'm Shaun from England." I volunteer my origin to show I'm different from them but not in a way that might get me smashed.

"I'm Bullet, the head of the whites." He offers me his fist to bump. "Where you roll in from, wood?"

Addressing me as wood is a good sign. It's what white gang members on a friendly basis call each other.

"Towers jail. They increased my bond and re-classified me to maximum security."

"What's your bond at?"

"I've got two $750,000 bonds," I say in a monotone. This is no place to brag about bonds.

"How many people you kill, brother?" His eyes drill into mine, checking whether my body language supports my story. My body language so far is spot on.

"None. I threw rave parties. They got us talking about drugs on wiretaps." Discussing drugs on the phone does not warrant a $1.5 million bond. I know and beat him to his next question. "Here's my charges." I show him my charge sheet, which includes conspiracy and leading a crime syndicate – both from running an Ecstasy ring.

Bullet snatches the paper and scrutinises it. Attempting to pre-empt his verdict, the other whites study his face. On edge, I wait for him to respond. Whatever he says next will determine whether I'll be accepted or victimised.

"Are you some kind of jailhouse attorney?" Bullet asks. "I want someone to read through my case paperwork." During our few minutes of conversation, Bullet has seen through my act and concluded that I'm educated – a possible resource to him.

I appreciate that he'll accept me if I take the time to read his case. "I'm no jailhouse attorney, but I'll look through it and help you however I can."

"Good. I'll stop by your cell later on, wood."

After breakfast, I seal as many of the cracks in the walls as I can with toothpaste. The cell smells minty, but the cockroaches still find their way in. Their day shift appears to be collecting information on the brown paper bags under my bunk, containing a few items of food that I purchased from the commissary; bags that I tied off with rubber bands in the hope of keeping the cockroaches out. Relentlessly, the cockroaches explore the bags for entry points, pausing over and probing the most worn and vulnerable regions. *Will the nightly swarm eat right through the paper?* I read all morning, wondering whether my cellmate has died in his cocoon, his occasional breathing sounds reassuring me.

Bullet stops by late afternoon and drops his case paperwork off. He's been charged with Class 3 felonies and less, not serious crimes, but is facing a double-digit sentence because of his prior convictions and Security Threat Group status in the prison system. The proposed sentencing range seems disproportionate. I'll advise him to reject the plea bargain – on the assumption he already knows to do so, but is just seeking the comfort of a second opinion, like many un-sentenced inmates. When he returns for his paperwork, our conversation disturbs my cellmate – the cocoon shuffles – so we go upstairs to his cell. I tell Bullet what I think. He is excitable, a different man from earlier, his pupils almost non-existent.

"This case ain't shit. But my prosecutor knows I done other shit, all kinds of heavy shit, but can't prove it. I'd do anything to get that sorry bitch off my fucking ass. She's asking for something bad to happen to her. Man, if I ever get bonded out, I'm gonna chop that bitch into pieces. Kill her slowly though. Like to work her over with a blowtorch."

Such talk can get us both charged with conspiring to murder a prosecutor, so I try to steer him elsewhere. "It's crazy how they can catch you doing one thing, yet try to sentence you for all of the things they think you've ever done."

"Done plenty. Shot some dude in the stomach once. Rolled him up in a blanket and threw him in a dumpster."

Discussing past murders is as unsettling as future ones. "So, what's all your tattoos mean, Bullet? Like that eagle on your chest?"

"Why you wanna know?" Bullet's eyes probe mine.

My eyes hold their ground. "Just curious."

"It's a war bird. The AB patch."

"AB patch?"

"What the Aryan Brotherhood gives you when you've put enough work in."

"How long does it take to earn a patch?"

"Depends how quickly you put your work in. You have to earn your lightning bolts first."

"Why you got red and black lightning bolts?"

"You get SS bolts for beating someone down or for being an

enforcer for the family. Red lightning bolts for killing someone. I was sent down as a youngster. They gave me steel and told me who to handle and I handled it. You don't ask questions. You just get blood on your steel. Dudes who get these tats without putting work in are told to cover them up or leave the yard."

"What if they refuse?"

"They're held down and we carve the ink off them."

Imagining them carving a chunk of flesh to remove a tattoo, I cringe. He's really enjoying telling me this now. His volatile nature is clear and frightening. *He's accepted me too much. He's trying to impress me before making demands.*

At night, I'm unable to sleep. Cocooned in heat, surrounded by cockroaches, I hear the swamp-cooler vent – a metal grid at the top of a wall – hissing out tepid air. Giving up on sleep, I put my earphones on and tune into National Public Radio. Listening to a Vivaldi violin concerto, I close my eyes and press my tailbone down to straighten my back as if I'm doing a yogic relaxation. The playful allegro thrills me, lifting my spirits, but the wistful adagio provokes sad emotions and tears. I open my eyes and gaze into the gloom. Due to lack of sleep, I start hallucinating and hearing voices over the music whispering threats. I'm at breaking point. Although I have accepted that I committed crimes and deserve to be punished, no one should have to live like this. I'm furious at myself for making the series of reckless decisions that put me in here and for losing absolutely everything. As violins crescendo in my ears, I remember what my life used to be like.

OTHER BOOKS BY SHAUN ATTWOOD

The Mafia Philosopher: Two Tonys

"A fast-paced true-crime memoir with all of the action of *Goodfellas*" – UNILAD

"*Sopranos* v *Sons of Anarchy* with an Alaskan-snow backdrop" – True Geordie Podcast

Breaking bones, burying bodies and planting bombs became second nature to Two Tonys while working for the Bonanno Crime Family, whose exploits inspired *The Godfather*.

After a dispute with an outlaw motorcycle club, Two Tonys left a trail of corpses from Arizona to Alaska. On the run, he was pursued by bikers and a neo-Nazi gang blood-thirsty for revenge, while a homicide detective launched a nationwide manhunt.

As the mist from his smoking gun fades, readers are left with an unexpected portrait of a stoic philosopher with a wealth of charm, a glorious turn of phrase and a fanatical devotion to his daughter.

Party Time: Raving Arizona

Shaun Attwood arrived in Phoenix, Arizona, a penniless business graduate from a small industrial town in England. Within a decade, he became a stock-market millionaire. But he was leading a double life.

After taking his first Ecstasy pill at a rave in Manchester as a shy student, Shaun became intoxicated by the party lifestyle that would change his fortune. Years later, in the Arizona desert, Shaun became submerged in a criminal underworld, throwing parties for thousands of ravers and running an Ecstasy ring in competition with the Mafia mass murderer Sammy 'The Bull' Gravano.

As greed and excess tore through his life, Shaun had eye-watering encounters with Mafia hit men and crystal-meth addicts, enjoyed extravagant debauchery with superstar DJs and glitter girls, and ingested enough drugs to kill a herd of elephants. This is his story.

Hard Time New Edition

"Makes the *Shawshank Redemption* look like a holiday camp"
– NOTW

After a SWAT team smashed down stock-market millionaire Shaun Attwood's door, he found himself inside of Arizona's deadliest jail and locked into a brutal struggle for survival.

Shaun's hope of living the American Dream turned into a nightmare of violence and chaos, when he had a run-in with Sammy the Bull Gravano, an Italian Mafia mass murderer.

In jail, Shaun was forced to endure cockroaches crawling in his ears at night, dead rats in the food and the sound of skulls getting cracked against toilets. He meticulously documented the conditions and smuggled out his message.

Join Shaun on a harrowing voyage into the darkest recesses of human existence.

Hard Time provides a revealing glimpse into the tragedy, brutality, dark comedy and eccentricity of prison life.

Featured worldwide on Nat Geo Channel's Locked-Up/ Banged-Up Abroad Raving Arizona.

Un-Making a Murderer:
The Framing of Steven Avery and Brendan Dassey

Innocent people do go to jail. Sometimes mistakes are made. But even more terrifying is when the authorities conspire to frame them. That's what happened to Steven Avery and Brendan Dassey, who were convicted of murder and are serving life sentences.

Un-Making a Murderer is an explosive book which uncovers the illegal, devious and covert tactics used by Wisconsin officials, including:

– **Concealing Other Suspects**

– **Paying Expert Witnesses to Lie**

– **Planting Evidence**

– **Jury Tampering**

The art of framing innocent people has been in practice for centuries and will continue until the perpetrators are held accountable. Turning conventional assumptions and beliefs in the justice system upside down, *Un-Making a Murderer* takes you on that journey.

The profits from this book are going to Steven and Brendan and to donate free books to schools and prisons. In the last three years, Shaun Attwood has donated 20,000 books.

Pablo Escobar's Story 1: The Rise

*"Finally, the definitive book about Escobar,
original and up-to-date" - UNILAD*

Pablo Escobar was a mama's boy who cherished his family and sang in the shower, yet he bombed a passenger plane and formed a death squad that used genital electrocution. Most Escobar biographies only provide a few pieces of the puzzle, but this action-packed 1000-page book reveals everything about the king of cocaine.

Mostly translated from Spanish, Part 1 contains stories untold in the English-speaking world, including:

The tragic death of his youngest brother Fernando.

The fate of his pregnant mistress.

The shocking details of his affair with a TV celebrity.

The presidential candidate who encouraged him to eliminate their rivals.

Pablo Escobar: Beyond Narcos

War on Drugs Series Book 1

The mind-blowing true story of Pablo Escobar and the Medellín Cartel beyond their portrayal on Netflix.
Colombian drug lord Pablo Escobar was a devoted family man and a psychopathic killer; a terrible enemy, yet a wonderful friend. While donating millions to the poor, he bombed and tortured his enemies – some had their eyeballs removed with hot spoons. Through ruthless cunning and America's insatiable appetite for cocaine, he became a multi-billionaire, who lived in a $100-million house with its own zoo.

Pablo Escobar: Beyond Narcos demolishes the standard good versus evil telling of his story. The authorities were not hunting Pablo down to stop his cocaine business. They were taking over it.

American Made: Who Killed Barry Seal? Pablo Escobar or George HW Bush

War on Drugs Series Book 2

Set in a world where crime and government coexist, *American Made* is the jaw-dropping true story of CIA pilot Barry Seal that the Hollywood movie starring Tom Cruise is afraid to tell.

Barry Seal flew cocaine and weapons worth billions of dollars into and out of America in the 1980s. After he became a government informant, Pablo Escobar's Medellin Cartel offered a million for him alive and half a million dead. But his real trouble began after he threatened to expose the dirty dealings of George HW Bush. *American Made* rips the roof off Bush and Clinton's complicity in cocaine trafficking in Mena, Arkansas.

"A conspiracy of the grandest magnitude." Congressman Bill Alexander on the Mena affair.

We Are Being Lied To: The War on Drugs

War on Drugs Series Book 3

A collection of harrowing, action-packed and interlinked true stories that demonstrate the devastating consequences of drug prohibition.

The Cali Cartel: Beyond Narcos

War on Drugs Series Book 4

An electrifying account of the Cali Cartel beyond its portrayal on Netflix.

From the ashes of Pablo Escobar's empire rose an even bigger and more malevolent cartel. A new breed of sophisticated mobsters became the kings of cocaine. Their leader was Gilberto Rodríguez Orejuela – known as the Chess Player due to his foresight and calculated cunning.

Gilberto and his terrifying brother, Miguel, ran a multi-billion-dollar drug empire like a corporation. They employed a politically astute brand of thuggery and spent $10 million to put a president in power. Although the godfathers from Cali preferred bribery over violence, their many loyal torturers and hit men were never idle.

ABOUT SHAUN ATTWOOD

Shaun Attwood is a former stock-market millionaire and Ecstasy supplier tu rned public speaker, author and activist, who is banned from America for life. His story was featured worldwide on National Geographic Channel as an episode of Locked Up/ Banged Up Abroad called Raving Arizona.

Shaun's writing – smuggled out of the jail with the highest death rate in America run by Sheriff Joe Arpaio – attracted international media attention to the human rights violations: murders by guards and gang members, dead rats in the food, cockroach infestations...

While incarcerated, Shaun was forced to reappraise his life. He read over 1,000 books in just under six years. By studying original texts in psychology and philosophy, he sought to better understand himself and his past behaviour. He credits books as being the lifeblood of his rehabilitation.

Shaun tells his story to schools to dissuade young people from drugs and crime. He campaigns against injustice via his books and blog, Jon's Jail Journal. He has appeared on the BBC, Sky News and TV worldwide to talk about issues affecting prisoners' rights.

As a best-selling true-crime author, Shaun is presently writing a series of action-packed books exposing the War on Drugs, which feature Pablo Escobar and the cocaine Mafia.

CPSIA information can be obtained
at www.ICGtesting.com
Printed in the USA
BVHW080729251021
619802BV00016B/698